THE HEINEMAN[N]
ACCOUNTANCY AND ADMINIST[RATION]

General Editor:
J. BATTY, D.Com.(S.A.), M.Com.(Du[rham]),
M.Inst.A.M., M.B.I.M.

AN
INTRODUCTION TO
FINANCIAL ECONOMICS

AN INTRODUCTION TO FINANCIAL ECONOMICS

E. L. FURNESS, M.SC.(ECON.)
*Professor of Economics at
Haile Sellassie I University, Addis Ababa
(seconded from the Department of Economics,
University of Strathclyde)*

HEINEMANN : LONDON

William Heinemann Ltd
15 Queen Street, Mayfair, London W1X 8BE

LONDON MELBOURNE TORONTO
JOHANNESBURG AUCKLAND

© E. L. Furness 1972
First published 1972
Reprinted 1974

434 90595 X (hardback)
434 90596 8 (limp)

Printed Offset Litho and bound in Great Britain
by Cox & Wyman Ltd
London, Fakenham and Reading

Editor's Foreword

The Heinemann Accountancy and Administration Series is intended to fill a gap in the literature that caters for accountants, company secretaries, and similar professional people who are engaged in giving a vital information service to management. As far as possible, due recognition is given to the fact that there are two distinct bodies of readers: those who aspire to professional status – the students – and others who are already managing and/or serving management.

An understanding of Financial Economics is essential whether concerned with the banking world, accountancy, company financing, or other area where money and credit play a vital role. Indeed, an *appreciation* of this vital subject is necessary for the businessman who is concerned with liquidity problems and the provision of permanent and working capital.

In planning and drafting this book Mr Eric Furness has paid special attention to the needs of students. All too often, other works in this field either present a very superficial over-simplified view of the subject *or* show a particular facility for making the subject complex and uninteresting. I believe that in this book a happy compromise has been achieved and, therefore, a much more acceptable presentation is made available.

I am very glad indeed to welcome this book and Mr Furness into the Series. It should certainly meet a need for an up-to-date book on this vitally important subject.

J. BATTY

Preface

This book is concerned primarily with the role of money and credit in the economic system. The intention has not been to describe in detail the organization and operation of particular financial institutions but rather to provide an analytical study of the functioning of the financial system. At the same time an effort has been made to keep analysis realistic by relating discussion, where possible, to the British economy and to the British institutional framework.

The book falls fairly naturally into four parts. Chapters 1 and 2 are essentially surveys. The former is a survey of the functions and problems of money and finance, and stress is given throughout to the real impact of finance on productivity and living standards. The latter chapter provides a sketch of British financial institutions which, it is hoped, will provide an up-to-date source of reference and a useful revision of previous elementary study. Chapters 3 to 6 deal with the supply of money and credit. Chapter 3 discusses at some length the manner in which bank deposits are created and the principles and practice of bankers' choice of assets. Chapter 4 contains a long theoretical discussion on the determination of the volume of bank deposits, covering the principles of open market operations, the liquidity ratio controversy, and the theory of the deposit multiplier. In Chapter 5 the reader is introduced to the determination of the money supply in practice, to money supply statistics, and to the concept of *domestic credit expansion*; and this section of the book is rounded off, in Chapter 6, with a discussion of the role of financial intermediaries.

The third part of the book deals with what is more conventionally termed monetary theory. In a sense, however, just as Chapters 3 to 6 can be regarded as dealing with the supply of money and credit, so Chapters 7, 8, and 9 can be thought of as being concerned essentially with the demand for money and credit. Chapter 7 discusses the concept of the *velocity of circulation* and earlier versions of the *quantity theory*, while Chapters 8 and 9 are devoted respectively to the Keynesian and Monetarist views of the economic significance of money. The remaining two chapters of the book are concerned mainly with monetary and financial policy – within a country in Chapter 10, and internationally in Chapter 11.

In writing this book I have sought to meet the needs of students interested in specializing in the general field of money and banking, either as undergraduates or in pursuit of professional qualifications. I have assumed that most readers will have had at least one year of economics and will be familiar with the terminology of the subject. In particular I have had in mind the second or third year undergraduate or a student preparing for, say, the Monetary Theory and Practice examination of the Institute of Bankers. At the same time I have tried to consider the more general reader by avoiding the use of rigorous or mathematical analysis.

I have drawn ideas and information liberally from numerous published books and articles, and I am certainly indebted in varying degrees to the authors of all the publications listed at the end of each chapter, and to many others besides. I am also indebted to my former colleagues in the Department of Economics at the University of Strathclyde for many fruitful discussions, and to Mrs Moira MacInnes who gave me so much help with the typing and preparation of the manuscript.

E. L. FURNESS

Contents

EDITOR'S FOREWORD — *Page* v

PREFACE — vii

1 THE NATURE AND FUNCTIONS OF MONEY AND FINANCE — 1

Introduction – The role of money – The forms of money – The role of finance – The relationship between money and non-money assets – Some weaknesses of the financial system

2 AN OUTLINE OF BRITISH FINANCIAL INSTITUTIONS — 22

Introduction – The banking sector – Non-bank financial intermediaries – Financial markets – The Bank of England

3 CURRENCY AND BANK DEPOSITS — 43

The supply of currency in the United Kingdom – Bank deposits as money – How bank deposits are created – Factors influencing the distribution of bank assets – The asset structure of British deposit banks in recent years

4 THE THEORY OF THE VOLUME OF BANK DEPOSITS — 70

Factors limiting the creation of deposits – Introduction to the theory of control of deposits – The theory of control via the cash base – The theory of control via total liquid assets – The Radcliffe view of the controversy – The theory of the bank deposit multiplier – The limitations of the multiplier process – Some conclusions

5 MONEY SUPPLY STATISTICS AND DOMESTIC CREDIT
  EXPANSION   105

   The change in money supply equations – The analytical
   value of the equations – Domestic Credit Expansion –
   The purpose of the D.C.E. equations – Definitions of
   money supply – Money supply equations and D.C.E.
   equations in practice

6 FINANCIAL INTERMEDIARIES   132

   The nature of financial intermediation – The economic
   significance of financial intermediation – The multiple
   creation of financial claims – Comparative growth rates
   of deposit banks and other financial intermediaries –
   Non-bank financial intermediaries, monetary policy, and
   velocity

7 MONEY AND ECONOMIC ACTIVITY: AN INTRODUCTION   152

   Introductory survey – The velocity of circulation of
   money – Some classical versions of the quantity theory

8 THE ROLE OF MONEY IN THE ECONOMICS OF KEYNES   169

   An introduction to the economics of Keynes – The effect
   of changes in the quantity of money

9 THE MONETARIST VIEW   186

   The demand for money – The causative role of money –
   The monetarist view of monetary policy – The transmission mechanism – Are changes in money supply
   exogeneous or endogeneous? – The nominal rate and the
   real rate of interest – Conclusions

10 MONETARY POLICY   203

   The nature of monetary policy techniques – Bank rate
   policy – Debt policy – Special deposits – Controls on
   lending – The new credit control arrangements – Statutory control of terms of consumer credit – The effectiveness of monetary policy – The availability of credit

11 INTERNATIONAL PAYMENTS	229

Introduction – The balance of payments – Balance of payment problems – Balance of payment policies – The International Monetary Fund system – International liquidity and payments adjustment

QUESTIONS	259
INDEX	267

1 The Nature and Functions of Money and Finance

1.1 INTRODUCTION

Much of the growth in the productivity and in the living standards of the modern industrial state has been attributable to two developments. An intricate system of exchange has made it possible to break down production into numerous processes, and thus to employ a high degree of specialization in the uses of labour, equipment, and natural resources. Productivity has also been raised by the development of extremely roundabout methods of production and distribution, involving the construction of means of communication, buildings, and machinery, and the evolution of education and research.

The development of exchange has been dependent on a parallel development in the efficiency of settling exchange, and it is here that the monetary system has played a vital role. Roundabout methods of production and distribution involve waiting periods, sometimes extremely long, before such processes bear fruit fully in the satisfaction of human wants. In the meantime provision must be made for the wants of all those engaged in these processes. Some members of the community must consume less of current output than they are entitled to, and the surplus must be made available to those engaged in the lengthy production processes. The development of roundabout methods is therefore dependent on a parallel development in methods of transferring claims to output. This is the basic function of finance or credit. Money and finance have played a contributory role of enormous importance, in the growth of productivity and living standards.

1.2 THE ROLE OF MONEY

In a modern community a great deal of output is produced and organized on a communal basis. For this to be efficient, or indeed to develop at all, three pre-conditions are vital. It must be possible to make rational decisions in the use of resources and output; there must be an effective means of co-ordinating the decisions and preferences of a great number of producers, consumers, and owners of resources; and there must be a means whereby innumerable exchanges can be settled efficiently. The role of money can be viewed as facilitating these requirements. Traditionally, this role has been analysed under the headings of Unit of Account, Medium of Exchange, and Store of Value.

1.21 *Money as a Unit of Account*

One function of money is to provide, within a community, a common unit in which values can be measured, compared, and expressed. Just as lengths can be measured in yards or metres so values can be measured in pounds or francs. Values expressed in terms of money are of course known as prices.

To make any rational decision about the use of different resources or of different outputs one must be able to make comparisons. A common unit in which to make such comparisons is clearly a vital requirement. But rational decision-making requires more than simple comparisons of value; it necessitates abstract calculations about values, and it requires the maintenance of records or accounts. Again, such activities would clearly be impossible in the absence of a common unit of account. Much economic activity can only be completed in the future. But activity for the future necessitates contracts, and these would be impossible on any scale or intricacy were they not expressible in a unit of account. In brief, money prices make possible the attempt to optimize the allocation of resources.

Money prices also transmit information; to consumers about the relative availability of commodities; to producers about the relative wants of consumers and about the relative scarcity of resources; and to resource owners (of labour and capital) about the relative needs for resources. Prices, therefore, provide the basic information which makes possible the co-ordination of innumerable decisions and preferences. Moreover movements of money prices tend to provide at least some incentive for consumers, producers, and resource owners to adjust their plans and preferences so that they become mutually consistent.

Money, as a unit of account, makes possible the price mechanism. This in turn makes feasible the optimum use of resources and the continuous adjustment of the productive process in accordance with the collective wishes of the community. The price mechanism has many defects, as will be shown later, but it is hard to imagine a system which combines freedom of individual decision as to consumption, occupation, and production, with efficiency in the meeting of collective wants, in the absence of a price mechanism.

1.22 *Money as a Medium of Exchange*

Everyone is familiar with the defects of barter. Simple barter requires a double coincidence of wants, not only as regards the nature of the commodities bartered, but also as regards the quantities traded. Thus a farmer who wishes to exchange sheep for a suite of furniture must find not only a furniture maker who happens to want sheep, but also one who happens to want just that number of sheep which would make the barter satisfactory to both parties. Since such a coincidence of wants is likely to be very rare, barter trading will usually necessitate a series of transactions. For example our furniture maker may not wish to retain all, or indeed any, of the number of sheep which are exchanged for a suite of furniture. A satisfactory exchange will therefore be conditional on the furniture maker finding other people who are prepared to take sheep in exchange for what he really wants. Moreover, because of the indivisibility of many of the items traded, it will often be extremely difficult to conclude a bargain which properly satisfies both parties. Barter trading is clearly a complex, costly, and inefficient system, and it is unlikely that the communal organization of production would have developed beyond a primitive stage on such a basis.

Society overcame this constraint by the development of a commonly acceptable medium of exchange. This broke each exchange into two separate transactions – a sale and a purchase, each in exchange for the commonly acceptable medium. The problem of the need for a double coincidence of wants was then overcome. Our sheep farmer who wants a suite of furniture is faced with two comparatively simple tasks. He has to find enough people who are prepared to buy his sheep, and then he has to find a furniture maker with a suite for sale. Moreover, provided that the medium of exchange is reasonably divisible, it should always be possible to conclude bargains satisfactory to both parties.

Whatever is used generally by a community as a medium of exchange can be regarded as money. The actual form or substance employed can affect the efficiency of exchange, but it is not the substance which makes the medium money. There is only one essential element for any medium of exchange and that is the general confidence that everyone in the community is prepared to accept it in exchange without quibble.

Money, as a medium of exchange, enormously facilitates exchange, partly because money makes possible the separation of sale from purchase decisions, and partly because, by virtue of its divisibility, money enables each transaction to be made in preferred quantities. And, by facilitating exchange, money has permitted the great developments in the division of labour which have contributed so much to the growth of productivity.

1.23 *Money as a Liquid Store of Value*

The use of a medium of exchange not only splits exchange into separate sale and purchase transactions, it also facilitates their separation in time. In the absence of money a transactor can delay acquisition of what he really wants by obtaining, through barter, some tangible asset which he holds until such time as he is ready to barter it for what he wants to consume. But, as stores of wealth for this purpose, tangible assets can have serious disadvantages. Tangible assets may be costly to store; they may deteriorate; the terms of barter on which they will be exchanged ultimately may be very uncertain; there may be considerable delay in effecting the barter. Where, however, there is a medium of exchange, some part of each transactor's wealth can be stored in this form. Since, by definition, a medium of exchange is generally acceptable, it can be exchanged for anything, at any time, without delay, and without much uncertainty of the terms on which it can be exchanged for other things in general. These advantages are known as *liquidity*. A store of money is a store of liquid claims to real wealth or output.

In a sophisticated exchange economy there is a great need for a liquid store of value. The separation of sale and purchase decisions means that receipts and payments rarely synchronize precisely. Transactors accumulate wealth while sales are exceeding purchases, but they need to deplete such wealth whenever purchases are exceeding sales. Moreover the timing and the amount of expected receipts and payments may be irregular or uncertain. There is, therefore, a need for a buffer store of wealth in a *liquid* form to meet fluctuating requirements with the minimum of delay, inconvenience, risk, and cost. Generally speaking, the larger the gap in time between recurring receipts and payments, the greater the uncertainty of requirements in the near future; and the greater the volume of exchange transactions

NATURE AND FUNCTIONS OF MONEY AND FINANCE

per period of time, the greater will be the advantage of holding wealth in a liquid form.

As will be seen presently, in more detail, wealth can be stored also in the form of other financial assets, such as bonds or shares. These avoid some of the disadvantages of tangible assets and have an advantage over money in that they earn interest or dividends. They are less liquid, however, than money. Before they can be exchanged for other things they must first be sold or converted into money. This may involve inconvenience, cost, delay, or uncertainty as to the price obtainable. The degree of such liquidity disadvantages will differ from one type of financial asset to another. At one extreme, some financial assets, such as building society shares or deposits, are only slightly less liquid than money. Liquidity is a matter of degree. There is no clear-cut division between liquid and illiquid assets. As a store of value, money is only distinct in being the *most liquid* of assets. The choice between holding wealth in money or in other assets of varying degrees of illiquidity is largely a matter of balancing the advantages of liquidity against the advantages of yield obtainable, in the light of the prevailing need for liquidity and of the current and prospective rates of interest or dividend distributions.

The store of value function of money has been given considerable attention by modern economists. This is because it is widely believed that changes in the aggregate demand to hold liquid assets, in relation to the supply of such assets, will have important effects on economic activity, employment, and the price level. Money, as the most liquid of assets, and the asset the supply of which is most easily controlled, has naturally received most attention in this respect.

1.24 *Conclusions on the Role of Money*

The full extent of the usefulness of money to society is not easy to appraise. Indeed it is only by trying to imagine how effectively the world could function without the services of money that one can attempt to gauge its utility. It is rather like trying to measure the value of language to humanity. There are in fact features in common between language and money. Both permit, and provide a means of, intricate communication, and both facilitate rational appraisal.

A unit of account and a medium of exchange have been a necessary condition for the great forward strides in economic efficiency. Money has, therefore, played an immense, if immeasurable, part in helping to raise living standards. Nevertheless the functioning of money is far from perfect, and mal-functioning, at times, has been the cause of grave social distress.

1.3 THE FORMS OF MONEY

It is easier to describe what money does than to define what money is, partly because forms of money and methods of debt settlement change in the course of time and, in modern times, are changing rapidly. Money as a medium of exchange and store of value can be anything that is generally acceptable in payment or in settlement of debt. Before the invention of coins, commodities such as cattle, cowrie shells, salt, etc., commonly served as money. Metals such as gold and silver were used for this purpose from very early times. The widely appreciated commodity value of these things helped to make them generally acceptable. But as the volume and complexity of exchange grew, these forms of money became increasingly inconvenient. In varying degrees they were deficient in transportability, divisibility, uniformity, and stability of value. So commodities in use gave way to full-weight coins, and these in turn gave way to forms of debt such as token coins, bank notes, and bank deposits. The acceptability of the newer forms of money was made possible largely by the growth of confidence in governmental and banking institutions. But along the way, acceptability was helped by devices such as conferment of legal tender status on certain coins or notes. The legal convertibility of certain bank notes into gold or into legal tender was another device. Even belief in convertibility has been sufficient to establish acceptability of bank deposits as money. But legal tender status or convertibility into gold, etc. are not essential features of money. Acceptability is the only essential element.

Money as a unit of account is abstract. Even when commodities such as cattle were the medium of exchange, the unit of account was presumably an abstract concept of a standard quality cow or sheep, etc. Some early units of account described a standard weight and quality of metal. 'Librum', for example described a pound troy of silver. National units of account did not describe weights of metal but were linked to weights of gold or silver, either because the unit was expressed in terms of full-weight coins, or in terms of token money which was convertible into weights of gold or silver at fixed prices. After the First World War full-weight coins were generally withdrawn from circulation; and since then the linkage between units of account and weights of gold or silver has weakened or has changed frequently.

NATURE AND FUNCTIONS OF MONEY AND FINANCE 7

The unit of account in which values are expressed can differ from the unit in which the medium of exchange is expressed. For example, some values used to be expressed in guineas, while the medium of exchange was expressed in pounds, shillings, and pence. Or again, values may be expressed in marks, and the medium of exchange may be dollars. There must, of course, be some rate of exchange between the two units. Within a national frontier convenience usually demands that values and the medium of exchange should be expressed in the same unit.

The main forms of money in use in the United Kingdom are token coins, Bank of England notes, deposits with commercial banks, and deposits in the National Giro. These are all debts of institutions and, from the holder's point of view, claims on institutions. So money, as a medium of exchange and store of value, which is itself a liquid claim to output, takes the form of claims on specific institutions.

As soon as society abandons simultaneous bartering it introduces debts and claims. Whenever a transactor acquires a commodity or service, without simultaneously giving a commodity or service in exchange, that transactor becomes indebted to other units in the community. Whenever any transactor sells a commodity without simultaneously receiving a commodity or service in exchange, that transactor acquires a claim on other units in the community. Thus transactors are continuously creating debts or acquiring claims.

Debts and claims must be expressible in money as a unit of account, but settlement of debts and claims does not necessarily require the use of such concrete forms of money as coins or bank notes, or even something as intangible as a bank deposit. In principle, debts and claims could be settled by means of a clearing mechanism. Indeed, some debts and claims are settled in this way, for example, among stock exchange brokers and among banks. One can imagine a kind of communal ledger in which all transactions are recorded. Some transactors would experience periodic net debt and net claim positions, though on the average over time debts and claims would cancel out. For some transactors there would be a growing net debt position, with a counterpart growing net claim position for others.

There are fairly obvious difficulties in operating such a system. There are so many transactions, involving so many transactors, that comprehensive recording would be a very costly and cumbersome business. There would be difficulties in reconciling growing net debt positions of some transactors with willingly held net claim positions of others. And closely allied to this problem would be the whole problem of control and stability. How would the extent to which any individual could incur debt be limited? Indeed it would seem that the aggregate purchasing power of the community would have no anchor at all.

On grounds both of simplicity and stability, society has found it necessary to use a stock of instruments, limited in supply, which are generally acceptable for settlement of debt. Such instruments constitute the concrete forms of money. When a debt is settled by payment of money, what really happens is that the recipient exchanges a claim against individual transactors for a liquid claim against the community at large, and adds to his stock of such liquid claims. The advantage, from the recipient's point of view, is that he exchanges a claim on output which he cannot exercise, except by barter with the debtor, for one which he can exercise whenever and for whatever he wishes. The payer, on the other hand, reduces his debts to individual transactors by reducing his stock of liquid claims against the community.

Settlement of debt between transactors may be made simultaneously with the incurrence of debt, as when buyers pay 'on the nail'. But many debts cannot be settled simultaneously with their incurrence because this would be impossibly inconvenient. This is true of any more-or-less continuous service. One cannot envisage debts to employees being settled second by second. Employers settle their debts to employees periodically, for example once a week or once a month. House occupiers settle accumulating debt to landlords periodically. Those who borrow capital pay for its service periodically. Thus income, which is the return for the more-or-less continuous service of persons or of property, consists of a series of periodic and usually regular debt settlements. It is also often convenient to settle for the purchase of commodities periodically, so that sales receipts may also take the form of periodic debt settlement.

In the economy as a whole there is a continuous process of extending and extinguishing debt. Some debts are extinguished immediately by the depletion of a stock of money, usually in anticipation that the stock will be replenished when accumulating debts due are settled. Other debts may be allowed to accumulate (subject to the acquiescence of the creditors) in anticipation that settlement will coincide with the settlement of debts due. Over any period of time, the settlement of debts incurred by a transactor can only exceed the settlement of debts due to him to the extent that he can run down his stock of money, sell claims on others that he holds, or sell tangible assets.

1.4 THE ROLE OF FINANCE

Over any period of time some transactors will find it necessary, convenient, or profitable to acquire more worth of goods and services than they currently produce and give in exchange. Similarly other transactors will create more worth of goods and services than they consume. In more common parlance, some individuals, corporate bodies, etc. will wish to spend more over a period than their receipts for that period, while others will wish to spend less.

There are many reasons for these differences in the time patterns of the flows of receipts and payments. We have already seen that it is not possible for payment for a continuous service to be made continuously; convenience requires that settlement be periodic. Some commodities are indivisible and also costly in relation to the income that can be earned over a short period of time. To acquire such commodities transactors must either accumulate wealth gradually, by spending less than income, until there is sufficient to exchange for the commodity, or else they must arrange to pay for the commodity out of future income. Over the life span of the individual, needs will differ in relation to productive capacity. The individual may feel it wise to create more output than he consumes during his vigorous years so as to build up a stock of wealth which he can consume when he is old or sick. One very basic reason for differences in the patterns of receipts and payments arises from differences between the time interval necessary for the completion of production and the time interval of producers' needs. In farm output, for example, there may be a period of many months between sowing and reaping, but the farmer will have daily needs which must be met. A much more important example in modern society is that of roundabout methods of production. Such methods, though usually highly productive, involve periods of gestation which may be extremely long, and the purchase of equipment etc. which may be extremely costly in relation to the earnings that can be derived over a short period of time. The needs of all those involved in the project must be met from long before until long after the project has begun to earn a return, since it may take months or years of earnings to pay for a costly construction.

In the simplest type of economy, a transactor can only acquire more output than he is able to create to give in exchange, over some period of time, either if he has previously accumulated a stock of tangible wealth which he can deplete in exchange, or if he can persuade the seller to wait for settlement. In the latter case debt is created. Debt can therefore be regarded as delayed settlement. The counterpart to this is of course a claim, and the creditor is involved in a period of waiting for settlement, during which time he will be forced to run down his stock of tangible assets or reduce his rate of consumption in relation to his current output. Thus the basic function of finance or credit is to facilitate the transfer of either existing wealth or of current saving to transactors seeking to spend in excess of current receipts.

1.41 *The Variety of Financial Assets*

In an economy the only financial asset of which is money, the finance of spending in excess of current receipts (deficit spending) is limited to one of three methods. The transactor can run down his stock of money; he can sell part of his accumulated tangible assets in exchange for some other transactor's stocks of money; or he can delay payment. The commonest example of the latter is trade credit. The effect of delaying payment is exactly as though the creditor had lent a money balance to the debtor. The creditor is deprived of an addition to his stock of money which he would otherwise have received, and since he himself will continue to deplete his own stock of money in making his own payments, his money balance will be reduced by the amount of the extension of credit. Of course some creditors may avoid this by delaying their own payments, but somewhere along the line some creditor will suffer this depletion.

If the finance of spending in excess of current receipts were limited to these three methods, it is clear that deficit spending would be very restricted indeed. Such spending on any scale would be limited to the rich. The ordinary transactor would not have much in the way of a money balance or of tangible assets that he could deplete. Delaying payment merely forces the depletion of wealth on to creditors, so that here again only the rich trader could afford to acquiesce on any scale.

Clearly most ordinary households would be denied the great convenience of being able to spend in anticipation of income on any scale. But from society's point of view, probably the greatest disadvantage would be that those with enterprise, know-how, and ability, but without wealth, would be largely precluded from establishing roundabout methods of production or of acquiring productive tangible assets. The accumulation of tangible wealth would tend to remain in the hands of those who do the saving. And since the majority of savers are likely to be anxious to minimize risk and are likely to lack technical know-how, saving would tend to be invested in assets such as mansions or jewellery, which, though perhaps of cultural value to posterity, are of low value to economic growth. Moreover it is likely that the incentive to save would be weak where saving can accumulate only in either money balances which offer no yield or in tangible assets which are illiquid and possibly risky.

The deadlock was broken by the invention of interest-bearing debt instruments and of dividend-earning shares in ownership. The sale of such instruments provides a mechanism whereby deficit spenders can tap the spare money balances of the relatively wealthy and the current saving of the many. Those relatively few with enterprise, know-how, and ability can invest in roundabout methods of production and acquire tangible assets far in excess of their net wealth. In consequence accumulating real wealth tends to move into their control and to take a form of greater productive value. At the same time aggregate current saving is likely to be stimulated since savers can accumulate wealth in the form of financial assets which are more rewarding than money and more liquid and often less risky than tangible assets. Moreover large-scale organization is encouraged. The possibility of issuing equities or shares means that business ownership need not be confined to partnerships or sole traders. Large limited liability companies can emerge which, by virtue of their size, often suffer less risk, enjoy greater ease of raising finance, and can often make more effective use of resources. Thus the introduction of non-money financial assets has encouraged a greater rate of wealth accumulation and at the same time has helped to direct such accumulation into a far more productive form. Such financial assets have therefore played an important role in accelerating the rate of economic growth. But beyond this, debt instruments have enormously facilitated the anticipation of income by ordinary households, making possible the early acquisition of such things as houses and comparatively costly durable consumer goods.

Debt instruments and shares are claims which are exercisable only in the future. Indeed in the case of undated bonds and shares the date of the maturity of the claim is indefinite. Sales of such claims would be very restricted, and the compensation for holding them would have to be very considerable, had the buyers no option but to hold such claims until maturity. This difficulty was substantially overcome by the development of markets in which ownership of claims can be exchanged. Examples are of course the stock exchange and bill markets. The provider of finance can recover his money either by waiting until maturity or by selling his claim in the market. He has to accept, therefore, either the burden of waiting or the uncertainty of the market price he may obtain. There may also be some risk of default. To accept these burdens the buyer requires a compensation in the form of interest or yield on his investment. The user of finance, on the other hand, is willing to pay interest, either because he anticipates that he can employ the finance to produce a return that will more than cover the interest, or because he values, at more than the interest cost, the convenience of spending in anticipation of income or sales receipts.

1.42 *Financial Intermediaries*

The marketable claims issued by ultimate users of finance (generally against the security of the tangible assets acquired) are known as *primary securities*. Although primary securities enormously ease the flow of finance, their use does not remove all impediments to the flow of funds. Direct transactions between owners of spare money balances and savers on the one hand and the ultimate users of finance on the other hand, are limited by lack of knowledge about available opportunities, by the fact that primary securities are often too risky and too long-term for the tastes of many savers, and by the high costs of direct communication between numerous small borrowers and lenders.

These difficulties have been overcome by the establishment of financial intermediaries. An intermediary splits the borrowing–lending transaction into two separate transactions. The intermediary offers its own debt to ultimate lenders in exchange for money, and separately lends the money to ultimate borrowers in exchange for their primary securities. The debt issued by intermediaries (usually against the security of the primary securities they acquire) is known as *secondary securities*. There are many types of intermediary, each tending to specialize either in its form of lending, or in the form of secondary security it offers. Banks offer deposits and specialize in short-term advances. Building societies offer deposits and shares and lend to house buyers against mortgage. Finance companies offer deposits and finance the purchase of durable consumer or producer goods. Life assurance companies offer policies and acquire primary securities. Savings banks offer deposits and lend to the government. Unit trusts offer their units and acquire primary securities; and so on.

The secondary securities offered by intermediaries are generally safer, more convenient, of shorter maturity, and more readily convertible into money, or more exchangeable than primary securities. Since secondary securities are relatively liquid, savers and lenders are willing to acquire them on terms which are comparatively favourable to the intermediary. At the same time intermediaries are often able to lend in more convenient ways and on cheaper terms to ultimate borrowers than the latter could manage by direct borrowing. Intermediaries therefore cheapen the provision of finance.

Intermediaries are able to reduce the costs of finance largely because of the economies of scale that they enjoy. By operating on a large scale they can reduce the unit costs of transactions. The average risk on the primary securities they acquire is reduced by diversification. Their secondary securities can be made highly liquid to holders because, where there are a large number of depositors, claims for repayment at any one time become predictable, and the maturity of the primary securities acquired can be scheduled to synchronize with the anticipated claims for repayment.

By providing comparatively liquid secondary securities, intermediaries give a further impetus to saving, facilitate further the flow of saving into real investment, and, by cheapening the terms on which finance is provided, encourage a greater rate of real investment. They also facilitate other mechanisms of finance. Traders become more willing to extend credit if they themselves can borrow easily from intermediaries. New issues of primary securities become easier if intermediaries are among the buyers and are willing to underwrite issues. Markets for the exchange of securities are widened where intermediaries are among the traders.

1.43 *Conclusions on the Role of Finance*

The financial system is vitally dependent on confidence – confidence that borrowers and intermediaries will not default on their debt, and confidence that the prices and real values of debt will not fall so far as to involve holders in significant losses. Hence measures to protect confidence have been a most important element in the development of finance. Such measures include legal regulations and redress in connection with debt and transactions in securities, the establishment of reserve requirements for intermediaries, disclosure of accounts, and the development of central bank supervision of the financial system.

The modern financial system has made possible a divorce between the ownership of capital and the control of its use, thereby enormously raising the productivity of the accumulating real wealth of society. It has greatly encouraged the willingness to save by providing safe yet profitable outlets for saving. It has made possible the tapping of the host of small savings which otherwise would largely run to waste. Market competition for funds, and the mediation of experts, have helped to ensure that the flow of funds is directed to the most productive uses and into the hands of those most capable of using such funds. In short, the financial system has played a vital role in the achievement of our standard of living.

1.5 THE RELATIONSHIP BETWEEN MONEY AND NON-MONEY ASSETS

Money, in its concrete sense, consists of those instruments the transfer of which provides the generally acceptable way of settling debts. Such instruments have changed considerably in the course of history and are still changing. But in present-day Britain debts are almost entirely settled by the transfer of coin, bank notes, current account bank deposits, or deposits with the National Giro. Is there any justification, from the point of view either of economic analysis or of economic policy, in distinguishing this particular group of instruments from other financial claims?

The analytical difference between money instruments and other financial assets is that money can settle debt directly, whereas the use of other financial assets for this purpose requires, generally speaking, prior conversions into money. W. T. Newlyn, in his book *The Theory of Money* (O.U.P., Second edition, 1971), has argued that such prior conversion not only involves some degree of delay, inconvenience, cost, or uncertainty, but will also have secondary repercussions on economic activity.

The sale of a bond, for example, involves cost, inconvenience, and uncertainty of the price obtainable; and the sale itself will tend to depress bond prices, thus provoking some further disturbance to economic activity. The withdrawal of money from the National Savings Bank will deprive the government of funds and, since the government must replace these funds by borrowing in some other way, there will be some disturbance to asset markets, with further repercussions similar to those following bond sales. Withdrawal of money from a building society will put some pressure on the society either to curtail its lending or to dispose of other assets.

In contrast to the use of such assets for the settlement of debt, the transfer of coin or bank notes clearly involves no cost, delay, inconvenience, or uncertainty. And, it is argued, since the transfer only affects the state of indebtedness between the payer and the payee, there can be no secondary repercussions on economic activity. This would be equally true of the transfer of current account bank deposits, though, one should note, the withdrawal of notes or coin from a bank would involve secondary repercussions. Time deposits in a British bank are a rather special case. The use of such deposits to settle debt requires prior conversion into normal forms of money. On the other hand, since such conversion can usually be made easily and immediately, and since British banks do not distinguish between current and time deposits in their liquidity conventions, the use of time deposits to settle debt will have no secondary repercussions. Hence there is a case for including time deposits in the stock of money. Overdraft facilities are another special case. Their use does not require any prior conversion. On the other hand the use of an overdraft facility has the effect of increasing the total advances of a bank. Either the bank will have to dispose of other assets to make room for the additional advance, or there will be an increase in the total volume of bank deposits. In either case there will be secondary repercussions on economic activity, so, it is argued, outstanding overdraft facilities should not be included in the stock of money.

On this approach money can be defined as constituting all those instruments, the use of which in settling debt involves no delay, inconvenience, cost, or uncertainty, and no secondary repercussions on economic activity. But this definition is open to challenge on two grounds. First, it can be argued that the use of normal money instruments to settle debt can have secondary repercussions. Second, there are many other financial assets the use of which in settling debt will have secondary repercussions so slight as to make these assets scarcely distinguishable from money. If both grounds of criticism are acceptable then, from an analytical point of view, the difference between money and other financial assets is simply one of degree.

It is clear that if a bond has to be sold in order to settle debt there will be secondary repercussions, but one cannot be equally clear that settlement of debt by simple transfer of money will have no secondary repercussions. In whatever way debt is settled the balance sheet positions of payee and payer will be disturbed. The payee will in any event find his assets changed from a debt due to a larger money balance. He is more liquid than before. The payer, in any event, will experience an equal reduction in his liabilities and assets. His liabilities to creditors are reduced and, in the case of simple transfer of money, his assets in the form of money are reduced. He is less liquid than before. One cannot rule out the possibility that the changed liquidity position of each party will affect their respective asset preferences and attitudes to saving. Nor can one assume that the repercussions of each party's reactions will be mutually offsetting. Some secondary repercussions on markets and economic activity are possible, and the differences between such repercussions and those accompanying debt settlement, other than by simple transfer of money, may be merely a matter of degree.

Turning to the second criticism of the 'Newlyn' definition of money, some economists argue that the development of financial markets and of financial intermediation has reached the stage at which many non-money claims have a degree of liquidity scarcely distinguishable from that of money instruments. Experience has shown that some claims on intermediaries can be exchanged for money with little or no delay, inconvenience, cost, or uncertainty. To this extent transactors will scarcely be conscious of much difference in their liquidity position whether they hold money or claims on such non-bank intermediaries. This means that it would be easy to persuade owners of stocks of money to deplete such stocks in exchange for claims on intermediaries. This in turn implies that the conversion of such claims into money for the purpose of settling debt would have the minimum of secondary repercussions because other holders of these claims could be readily found. Moreover, even where marketable debt such as bonds or bills is sold to settle debt, the secondary repercussions would be modified if intermediaries can easily persuade wealth-owners to shift their wealth out of money and into claims on intermediaries, so providing the latter with the funds to absorb the sales of marketable debt.

If the secondary repercussions of disposing of claims on non-bank intermediaries are so slight, and the repercussions of selling some classes of marketable debt only very moderate, what remains of the analytical justification for drawing a sharp line between those assets which are money and those which are not? Perhaps a stronger case can be made for distinguishing money assets from the point of view of economic policy. Experience suggests that the supply of coin, bank notes, and bank deposits is more subject to the control and influence of the central bank than is the supply of other financial assets. Monetary policy may justify the defining of money.

Nevertheless, the very notion of monetary policy seems to imply that there is some peculiar significance in the size of the stock of those instruments which constitute money. The quantity theory of money, for example, holds that the rate of expenditure will vary more-or-less

NATURE AND FUNCTIONS OF MONEY AND FINANCE 17

in proportion with the stock of money. An increase in the money supply, in this theory, will lead to an increase in the level of prices and/or output. But economists who stress the close similarity of money with many other financial assets, including claims on intermediaries, often argue that the quantity of money is of little significance. The link between the rate of expenditure and the stock of money is weak. It is argued that, if it is easy to persuade wealth-owners to shift from holding money to holding *near-money* assets, then it is also easy for would-be spenders to borrow from intermediaries. The latter can supply the funds so long as it remains easy to borrow the money from wealth-owners. If this is so, then what matters is not so much the quantity of money as the proportion of that stock which is drawn into active circulation, particularly via the operations of intermediaries. Proponents of this view maintain that one should think not just in terms of the money supply, but of the general liquidity of the economy. This includes the money supply, but also the ease with which that supply can be increased, the volume of highly liquid non-money claims, and the general ease of borrowing. Monetary policy should seek to influence this entire liquidity situation.

Other economists, however, retain the more traditional view that it is the money supply that is of crucial importance. They also maintain that the precise definition of money is of secondary significance. These views must be examined in detail later in this book, and it is sufficient here to discuss the matter in very general terms.

One can exaggerate the similarities between money and other liquid assets such as claims on non-bank intermediaries. There is one major difference and that is convenience to a transactor who requires to settle debts immediately or in the near future. Because of this there will be for every transactor some average money balance which he will regard as a minimum. The size of such minimum balances for each transactor, and for the community as a whole, will be influenced by many factors which must be examined later in this book. But one factor is paramount, and that is the value of the prospective transactions per period of time which will have to be financed. Thus the willingness with which transactors will be prepared to deplete their money balances, either to finance their own deficit spending, or to extend credit to others, or to transfer funds to intermediaries, or to buy marketable securities, will be influenced by the ratio of the stock of money to the current value of transactions per period of time. It can be argued, therefore, that a contraction of the money supply in relation to the value of transactions will, if carried far enough, cause a contraction in all methods of financing, thereby exerting a powerful restraint on expenditure.

Conversely, if the money supply is made excessive in relation to the current value of the flow of transactions, all methods of financing expenditure will become extremely easy. But more than that, since many transactors will find themselves far more liquid than they feel the need for, they will have an incentive to substitute other forms of wealth for money. Transactors will tend to deposit surplus funds with intermediaries, to buy marketable debt or shares, and to acquire tangible assets. The prices of financial and real assets will rise, and the ease and terms of borrowing will improve. This, as will be shown later, will encourage a greater rate of expenditure on output.

Undoubtedly the money supply does have an influence on the rate of expenditure. How important this influence is, and in what circumstances, is still a matter of considerable controversy.

1.6 SOME WEAKNESSES OF THE FINANCIAL SYSTEM

Although money and credit facilities have played a contributory role of enormous importance in the growth of economic prosperity, the financial system has some inherent weaknesses which can permit and can even provoke disturbances in economic activity. At times such disturbances have proved catastrophic.

One weakness lies in the variability of the money supply. Some variability is desirable since, in a growing economy, there is a growing volume of exchange transactions, and therefore in the work that money has to do. A fixed quantity of money would act as a drag on economic activity. In a modern economy the government is in a position to control, or at least influence, the money supply. But this can mean that a government which is weak, foolish, in difficulties, or extravagant, may be tempted to finance its requirements, directly or indirectly, by increasing the quantity of money. The rate of increase may exceed what is required for stable growth or it may be more than is consistent with stability in the value of money. Extreme action of this sort has led, on occasion, to hyper-inflation. This is a state of affairs when prices are rising so fast that confidence in the monetary system becomes completely lost, and production and exchange become paralysed. Since the Second World War and its immediate aftermath many countries have experienced a growth in the money supply which, though very moderate compared with conditions of hyper-inflation, has nevertheless been very much more rapid than generally prevailed in pre-war days. This has been associated with more-or-less continuous price inflation which has had some damaging social and economic consequences. But this weakness in the system is not incurable; and indeed the famous American economist, Milton Friedman, has advocated that governments should control the money supply in such a way that there is a steady but moderate rate of growth in the supply, say 4 per cent per annum.

More fundamental and intractable than the dangers of inflation are the inherent defects of the price mechanism. The mechanism is sometimes blamed for the inequality in the distribution of income. The services of property earn an income, and where property is privately owned and concentrated in the hands of the few there will be great inequalities in incomes received. But this is a problem which, presumably, can be mitigated by fiscal measures.

The inherent weakness in the price mechanism lies in the transmission of information. A perfect price mechanism would disseminate all the information necessary for the co-ordination of the activities, plans, and decisions of the host of independent transactors. Price movements would provide sufficient incentive for transactors to adjust their plans so that they become consistent in the aggregate. When changes occur in the plans in one sector, prices should change instantaneously and sufficiently to ensure that other plans are adjusted appropriately and immediately. Prices should move so that markets clear continuously and so that resources are always fully employed. Perhaps in the very long run the response to any single disturbance might approximate to this if, in the meantime, no other disturbance were to occur. But in the short run prices do not adjust instantaneously, nor do they provide the incentive for a sufficient or immediate adjustment of plans. When demand for some commodity falls away no one knows what the new set of prices should be which would ensure the right redistribution of resources and the right adjustments to the entire pattern of demand. Nor is there any market mechanism which would produce this result automatically. What we find in practice is uncertainty. Price adjustments in commodity and labour markets are delayed while sellers seek around for further information. In the meantime output remains unsold and labour is unemployed. This is not to argue that the price mechanism is useless. Prices do tend to move in the right direction in time. Plans tend to be adjusted in the right direction, in time. But the mechanism is not perfect and in a world of change there will be frictional unemployment.

Again, many economic plans and activities are concerned with markets in the future, perhaps the very distant future. And here the price mechanism may be almost totally defective in providing satisfactory information. An entrepreneur planning an investment project finds no market which will indicate the prices which will prevail for his product when he is in a position to sell in the future. All he has to guide him is expectations. Saving is essentially postponement of consumption. But the saver does not place an order for future consumption. There is therefore no price mechanism to ensure that saving will stimulate the right type of production for future use.

It is sometimes claimed that the financial market should at least ensure equality between the values of investment and saving plans in aggregate. An increase in real investment is an increase in the demand for output; an increase in saving is a decrease in the demand for output. If, therefore, the financial market were to ensure a continuous equality between investment and saving plans in the aggregate, aggregate demand for output would at least remain stable. But the financial market does not ensure such equality. The financial system permits a divorce between the saving decision and the decision to accumulate tangible assets. Saving not directly used to accumulate tangible goods is used to accumulate claims. Such claims can be either money or claims on the future. But when saving is accumulated in the form of money balances it gives no signal to the economic system to encourage greater expenditure on real investment. An increase in planned saving in these circumstances may merely result in part of total output remaining unbought, so that resources are left idle. Similarly an increase in real investment does not require a concurrent increase in planned saving. Nor does greater investment expenditure necessarily give a signal to the economic system to encourage greater planned saving, if it is financed by the creation of new money or by the depletion of the spender's money balance. An increase in investment expenditure, unaccompanied by an equal increase in planned saving, will raise the aggregate expenditure of the community. Even where saving takes the form of additional lending, and where investment is financed by additional borrowing, the response of interest rates is unlikely to be great enough to keep investment and saving plans in balance. This is because speculative activity in financial markets is normally so predominant as to swamp the influences of changes in either saving or investment plans, at least in the short run.

Earlier in this chapter it was argued that a great advantage of the financial system is that it permits a divorce between those who decide to save and those who decide to make real investments. Unfortunately this advantage also carries with it an inherent defect since the financial market cannot ensure a continuous equality between the two sets of decision in aggregate. The danger is not merely that an excess of planned investment over planned saving causes a rise in aggregate demand, or that an excess of planned saving over planned investment causes a fall in aggregate demand. The real danger is that such disturbances can feed on themselves, resulting in a multiple expansion or contraction in aggregate expenditure, with perhaps distressing consequences to the levels of income, employment, and prices.

This potential instability can be aggravated by the behaviour of confidence. The state of confidence among lenders, borrowers, and intermediaries is strongly influenced by the prevailing business outlook. When the outlook is good, lenders in general have greater confidence in borrowers in general, and businessmen are more eager to borrow. The sale of claims will be encouraged and intermediaries will have a strong incentive to mobilize surplus stocks of money. The finance of deficit spending will be easy and cheap. These are the circumstances to encourage greater expenditure; and the consequential rise in output and prices will, for a time, give a further fillip to confidence, and thus a further stimulus to expansion. The exact opposite will operate when the prevailing business outlook is gloomy. Such swings in confidence can therefore accentuate inflationary or deflationary tendencies and contribute to the intensity of the business cycle.

SUGGESTED READING

R. S. Sayers, *Modern Banking*, 7th ed. (Oxford, 1967), ch. i.

A. T. K. Grant, *The Machinery of Finance and the Management of Sterling* (Macmillan, 1967), chs. i, ii.

T. Scitovsky, *Money and the Balance of Payments* (Unwin, 1969), chs. i–iii.

W. T. Newlyn, *Theory of Money*, 2nd ed. (Oxford, 1971), chs. i, ii.

R. S. Sayers, 'Monetary Thought and Monetary Policy in England', *Economic Journal* (Dec. 1960).

R. C. Rowan, *Output, Inflation and Growth* (Macmillan, 1968), ch. xiv.

B. J. Moore, *An Introduction to the Theory of Finance* (Collier-Macmillan, 1968), ch. i.

2 An Outline of British Financial Institutions

2.1 INTRODUCTION

It is not the purpose of this book to describe in any detail the organization and function of the host of financial institutions, since there are many excellent sources of such information, a few of which are listed at the end of this chapter. The reader, however, may appreciate a sketch outline of the major institutions in the British financial system.

At the risk of over-simplification one can list the basic functions of a financial system as:

(*a*) to provide an efficient mechanism of debt settlement;
(*b*) to facilitate the transfer of finance from current savers or from holders of money balances to those who wish to spend in excess of current income or of current receipts;
(*c*) to provide adequate liquidity to this transfer process;
(*d*) to incorporate a satisfactory method of control and supervision.

Unfortunately financial institutions cannot be classified neatly in this fashion, nevertheless the institutions as grouped in this chapter: the banking sector, non-bank financial intermediaries, financial markets, and the Bank of England, correspond in some measure at least to the four functions listed.

We live in a world in which change appears to be occurring ever more rapidly, not least in the field of finance. There was a time when one would be justified in describing the 'City' as a closely knit community of highly specialized institutions. But this is becoming less and less true. As individual institutions adapt to the changing nature and scale of financial needs and as they exploit the economies of computer technology, they take on new activities, they amalgamate, and their functions increasingly overlap those of other institutions. Moreover this trend may well become more pronounced if the measures introduced by the authorities in 1971 to

AN OUTLINE OF BRITISH FINANCIAL INSTITUTIONS 23

promote competition and innovation in banking and finance are fully implemented.

2.2 THE BANKING SECTOR

The banking sector of the United Kingdom is defined as comprising the United Kingdom offices of four groups of financial institutions: the deposit banks (including the Banking Department of the Bank of England), accepting houses and overseas banks, the discount houses, and the National Giro. This grouping is followed below, except that the Bank of England is dealt with separately.

2.21 *Deposit Banks*

Deposit banks (other than the Bank of England) consist of the London clearing banks, the Scottish and Northern Ireland banks, and a few others, such as Hoare & Co., the Isle of Man Bank, Lewis's Bank, the Yorkshire Bank, and the Co-operative Bank. For many years there were eleven London clearing banks including the 'big five', but the economies to be derived from data processing, the growing scale of financial requirements, and some encouragement from the government led to considerable amalgamation. Today the London clearing banks consist only of six banks – Barclays Bank Ltd., Coutts & Co., Lloyds Bank Ltd., Midland Bank Ltd., National Westminster Bank Ltd., and Williams and Glyn's Bank Ltd. Similar amalgamations occurred in Scotland leaving only the Bank of Scotland, the Clydesdale Bank Ltd., and the Royal Bank of Scotland Ltd. Seven Northern Ireland banks however still remain. Measured in terms of total deposits the London clearing banks far and away predominate, as can be seen from Table 2.1.

TABLE 2.1
GROSS DEPOSITS OF DEPOSIT BANKS

April 1971	(£ million)
London clearing banks	10,988
Scottish banks	1,119
Northern Ireland banks	288

The distinguishing feature of deposit banks is the predominant role which they play in the community's system of debt settlement through the transfer of deposits by cheque, standing order, etc. But deposit banks are also extremely important financial intermediaries, receiving savings in the form of deposits and lending such savings to the private sector via advances, credit cards, and the discount of commercial bills, and to the public sector through purchase of government securities. Although their lending is predominantly short-term, the deposit banks have shown an increasing readiness to lend at medium-term both directly and through their finance company subsidiaries. Many other services are also provided including safe custody, investment advice, foreign exchange, tax returns, executor and trustee, and general financial guidance.

2.22 *Accepting Houses and Overseas Banks*

There are seventeen accepting houses which include many famous names such as Baring Brothers, Hambros, Lazard Brothers, Morgan Grenfell, and Rothschilds. The term 'accepting house' is derived from their traditional business of acceptance credit (bills drawn on an accepting house instead of on an ultimate debtor can be discounted much more readily and on better terms). Capital issues for overseas borrowers have also been a traditional business, though nowadays these merchant banks are also much concerned with domestic new issues, investment managing, raising funds for finance companies, and advice on take-overs and amalgamations. An important recent development is participation in the international short-term capital market including the market for euro-currencies. Accepting houses also conduct normal banking business and their customers include many foreign banks.

The Central Statistical Office classifies the overseas and other banks with offices in the United Kingdom as follows (figures in brackets refer to the number of existing banks):

> British overseas and Commonwealth banks (37)
> American banks (32)
> Foreign banks and affiliates (25)
> Other overseas banks (39)
> Other banks (including deposit bank subsidiaries) (49).

These banks are concerned with the financing of trade between the United Kingdom and other countries in which they operate, the financing of capital movements between London and abroad, investment of overseas funds in Treasury bills and other securities, foreign exchange dealings, and euro-currency operations.

There has been an enormous increase in the total deposits of accepting houses and overseas banks from under £5,000 million in 1964 to over £28,000 million in 1971. Deposits in sterling increased very substantially from approximately £2,000 million to £6,500 million, but deposits in foreign currencies increased enormously, from £2,000 million to £21,000 million, of which £14,000 million are owned by overseas residents (largely Western European banks and international oil companies). This mainly reflects the astonishing growth of the euro-currency market.

2.23 *The Discount Houses*

The eleven discount houses belonging to the London Discount Market Association are not banks in the ordinary sense, but they are a unique feature of the British banking system, providing a link and buffer between the deposit banks and the Bank of England, and a means by which temporary flows of funds between the banks can be adjusted.

TABLE 2.2

THE LONDON DISCOUNT HOUSES

December 1970 (£ million)

Sources of Borrowed Funds		Assets	
Deposit banks	1,544	British government stocks	160
Accepting houses and overseas banks	510	British government Treasury bills	876
Other sources	204	Other sterling bills	697
		Local authority securities	189
		Negotiable certificates of deposit	307
		Other	123

It can be seen from Table 2.2 that deposit banks are the main source of funds. The funds are lent 'at call'. This enables the banks to keep cash holdings to a minimum since they can replenish cash at very short notice by calling in such loans. Frequently when one bank is short of cash others will have a temporary surplus which they are eager to lend, so that it is easy for the banks to adjust their day-to-day cash position. When there is a general cash shortage the discount houses have recourse to the Bank of England as lender of last resort, and can borrow against the security of Treasury bills, short-dated government stock, or certain 'eligible' commercial bills. Bills can also be re-discounted though this is rarely done. The Bank of England reserves the right to charge the 'penal' Bank rate for such indirect provision of cash to the banking system.

The original function of the discount houses was to deal in trade bills and these still constitute an important part of their assets. But as can be seen from the table, holdings of Treasury bills are rather more substantial. Dealing in short-dated government bonds (with not more than five years to run) is another function, though since 1968 holdings of such stock are much reduced. Recently they have helped to establish a secondary market in certificates of deposit. Discount houses also provide a valuable service by selling to the banks parcels of bills of the maturity that the banks require; and they act as underwriters for the weekly issue of Treasury bills, by tendering for the whole issue.

2.24 *The National Giro*

The National Giro is operated by the Post Office. It was founded in 1968 to modernize the remittance service of the Post Office and to provide a cheap and efficient system of debt settlement available to the community generally. Payments between account holders are made by sending a transfer instruction to the National Giro Centre; payments to someone without a giro account can be made by a giro cheque; and cash deposits and withdrawals can be made at any post office. There is a small service charge, and no interest is paid on giro balances. There are no overdraft facilities but personal loans are available to deposit holders through the Mercantile Credit Company, a finance house.

Deposits in the National Giro are still very modest compared with those of the banks. Average monthly deposits were approximately £20 million in 1969, and £40 million in 1970, and may reach £60 million in 1971. Between 30 and 40 per cent of deposits are held in liquid assets, mostly money at call and short notice, though also including till money, balance at the Bank of England, and bills discounted. The remaining assets consist of British Government and local authority securities, generally short-dated, and advances to local authorities repayable within one year.

2.3 NON-BANK FINANCIAL INTERMEDIARIES

Table 2.3 shows the value of the holdings of the non-bank financial institutions listed in *Financial Statistics*. Though not strictly comparable these holdings give some impression of the relative importance of these intermediaries. Nearly 80 per cent of the total is controlled by insurance companies, superannuation funds, and building societies.

TABLE 2.3

NON-BANK FINANCIAL INTERMEDIARIES

INVESTMENTS AND ASSETS

End 1969	(£ million)
Insurance companies (investments)	14,201
Superannuation funds (investments)	7,247
Building societies (assets)	9,336
Investment trusts (assets)	4,902
Unit trusts (investments)	1,344
Property unit trusts (investments)	119
Trustee savings banks special investment departments (investments)	1,296
National Savings Bank investment account (investments)	226
Finance houses (certain assets)	1,141

The inflow of funds to non-bank intermediaries has recently been about £3,000 million a year of which 50 to 55 per cent has been absorbed by life assurance and pension funds, and 30 to 40 per cent by building societies.

2.31 *Insurance Companies and Superannuation Funds*

In return for premium payments insurance companies give cover for many types of risks. These can be conveniently classified as *general* (fire, accident, motor, marine, etc.) and *life*. In terms of premiums received the former is the larger, but funds received in general insurance are typically held only for short periods before being paid out in claims, whereas life assurance premiums are a form of long-term contractual saving, and annual receipts vastly exceed payments. Accumulated life funds (£12,741 million at end 1969) are therefore much greater than general funds (£1,460 million at end 1969). Pension fund contributions are another form of long-term contractual saving. The statistics of accumulated superannuation funds shown in Table 2.3 include the funded schemes of the public sector and of the private sector, but they do not include the main state scheme which is unfunded, nor funds operating through insurance companies which are included in life fund statistics.

Table 2.4 shows that life fund investments in 1969 were in the ratio of fixed interest to equity of about two to one. An article in the Bank of England Quarterly Bulletin of December 1970 points out that this high ratio of fixed interest investment has been maintained fairly

TABLE 2.4

INSURANCE COMPANIES AND SUPERANNUATION FUNDS

DISTRIBUTION OF ASSETS

End 1969	Life funds %	General funds %	Pension funds %
Cash and short-term assets	1	9	2
Fixed interest investment	65	58	39
British government	23	14	12
Local authorities	3	3	7
Other	39	41	20
Equity investment	33	33	59
Ordinary shares	22	27	51
Property	11	6	8

consistently over a number of years, presumably on the grounds of matching the redemption dates of assets with those of liabilities. Nevertheless there have been large switches between fixed interest and equity investment from time to time according to market prospects. General fund investment shows a much higher liquidity ratio; and in contrast to the relatively consistent investment pattern of life funds, general fund investment has shown a clear movement from gilt-edged to ordinary shares in recent years. The asset distribution of pension funds is different again, with nearly 60 per cent of assets in equities in 1969. The movement of pension fund investment from fixed interest to equities was indeed quite marked in the period 1963 to 1969. The Bank of England Quarterly Bulletin article, referred to above, suggests that this may have been a process of catching up following the Trustee Investment Act of 1961 which permitted some funds to buy ordinary shares. The development of property unit trusts also gave a boost to property investment. Many pensions too are related to final salary so it is important that investment should provide a hedge against inflation.

Investments by the major institutions described in this section are nearly always made in very large amounts, e.g. £50,000 or more, and only after intensive investigation of market prospects.

2.32 *Building Societies*

Building societies are fairly specialized intermediaries. Their main function is to channel small, generally short-term, personal savings into long-term finance of house purchase. The societies obtain funds by offering shares and deposits. Their shares are unlike those of a public company in that they are not marketable and are repayable at short notice; indeed they differ from deposits only in that the latter have priority of repayment in the event of liquidation. Shares and deposits earn a fixed rate of interest on which no income tax has to be paid (the societies pay a special composite rate of tax), and withdrawal is very simple and, in practice, often immediate.

TABLE 2.5
BUILDING SOCIETIES

End 1969 (£ million)

Liabilities		Assets	
Shares and deposits	8,652	Cash and bank balances	146
Other liabilities	684	Other short-term	325
		Investments	1,035
		Mortgages	7,722
		Other	108

As can be seen from Table 2.5, over 80 per cent of building society assets are concentrated in mortgages, and indeed the societies provide three-quarters of the total finance of private house purchase. Most of the residue of assets are liquid, consisting of currency, balances with banks, and British government and local authority securities both short-term and long-term. Investment of liquid assets is restricted to forms prescribed by the Registrar of Building Societies, and there are rules governing the maturity of securities in accordance with the size of the liquidity ratio (the ratio of liquid to total assets). In practice the liquidity ratio, though maintained at a high level, has fluctuated considerably, and in recent years has varied from under 15 per cent to over 18 per cent.

Building society business has expanded rapidly since the First World War, the number of share accounts rising from less than a million in 1918 to over nine million in 1969. At the same time there has been a growing concentration in a diminishing number of societies, though there were still more than five hundred societies on the register in 1969. Among non-bank intermediaries the societies now rank second to the insurance companies in terms of total funds.

Growth has been encouraged by the demand for house loans, in turn stimulated by the tax relief on such borrowing, by housing shortage, and by inflation. To meet the demand for loans the societies have to attract funds in competition with bank deposit accounts, unit trusts, national savings, and the stock market. But the societies are slow to adjust rates offered because of their reluctance to alter mortgage rates for existing borrowers, so that they tend to lose funds when market rates of interest are rising and to gain when rates are falling. Over recent years the annual net acquisition of shares and deposits has averaged about £800 million, but has been as low as £500 million and as high as £1,100 million. Fortunately the flexibility of the liquidity ratio has permitted less fluctuation in lending, though modified movements of mortgages follow those of net receipts with a time lag of a month or so. The development of the 'save as you earn' scheme may help to reduce the volatility of building society funds.

2.33 *Investment and Unit Trusts*

Investment and unit trusts both re-invest capital raised from the public in a variety of assets so enabling the small investor to obtain advantages of a wide spread of investment under skilled management.

Investment trusts are public companies which derive funds mainly by public issue of their own ordinary shares, preference shares, and debentures. Until there is a further issue of capital, new holdings in these trusts can be obtained only by purchasing existing holdings at the current market price. At the end of 1969 there were 264 major trusts with total assets of about £4,900 million. Nearly 90 per cent of assets are invested in ordinary shares, about $3\frac{1}{2}$ per cent in short-term assets including cash and bank balance, and only around 1 per cent in government stock, though there is a certain amount of switching between government stock and equities as market prospects change from time to time.

The unit trust is rather different. It is a trust in the strict sense, investment and management being subject to a trust deed and investments held by a trustee. The public subscribe to the trust by purchasing a unit or fractional interest in the block of securities in which the fund is invested. Income consists of the dividends from the investments, and it is paid to unit holders in proportion to size of holdings. The manager of the trust is responsible for the establishment of a market in the units, selling to new subscribers, or buying back at a price reflecting the prices of the securities held, in accordance with a formula established by the Department of Trade and Industry. The total capital of a unit trust is therefore variable. The funds of each trust are invested in a wide range of securities to spread risk, though some specialize in securities with high dividend expectation, or with high growth prospects, or of a certain class of industry. Of the £1,344 million total of investments at end 1969, 91 per cent was in ordinary shares, (largely United Kingdom), 3½ per cent in short-term assets (mostly cash and bank balances), about 1½ per cent in British government stock, and about 3½ per cent in other fixed interest securities. Unit trusts were first established in the United Kingdom in 1931 but the really remarkable expansion occurred in the 1960s. The rate of growth is of course much influenced by the prospects of ordinary shares.

Property unit trusts developed as a consequence of the 1965 Finance Act which made it advantageous for tax-exempt superannuation funds and charities to invest directly in property rather than in the shares of property companies. They differ from ordinary unit trusts in being permitted to invest directly in property but can raise funds only from approved superannuation funds and charities. By end 1969 there were 13 property unit trusts with total assets of £119 million of which about 83 per cent was invested in property and most of the remainder (15 per cent) in cash and bank balances.

2.34 Savings Banks

Trustee savings banks are local banks, managed by boards of honorary trustees under close government supervision, and are designed to channel small savings primarily to the government. There are 77 of these banks, with some 1,500 branches and over 10 million depositors. Most trustee savings banks maintain an ordinary department and a special investment department. The former provide savings accounts and current accounts, and almost all the funds received are passed to the National Debt Commissioners for investment in government securities. Accumulated funds at the end of 1969 amounted to £1,033 million. Special investment departments are required to invest only part of their funds in British government stock. Deposits of one month, three months, and six months are received with interest rates varying accordingly. At the end of 1969 total funds of these departments amounted to £1,296 million of which approximately 75 per cent was in United Kingdom local authority long-term debt, 22 per cent in British government stock, 3 per cent in local authority temporary debt, and 1 per cent in cash and bank balances. At least 20 per cent of funds has to be in liquid assets but these can include government and local authority securities with less than five years to run.

The National Savings Bank, formerly the Post Office Savings Bank, also has ordinary accounts and investment accounts. There are over 20 million depositors and, of course, an enormous number of offices. As in the case of the trustee savings banks, funds received on ordinary accounts pass to the National Debt Commissioners. Balances in these accounts amounted to £1,493 million at the end of 1969. Investment accounts earn higher rates of interest and are subject to notice. These funds, amounting £226 million at end 1969, are managed centrally by the National Debt Commissioners. More than half is invested in British government stock and the balance in local authority debt.

The Post Office and the trustee savings banks also provide facilities for the purchase of national savings certificates, British Savings Bonds, and Premium Savings Bonds. The amounts outstanding of these at end 1969 amounted to £1,942 million (plus accrued interest of £559 million), £825 million, and £749 million respectively. They also provide facilities for the 'Save As You Earn' scheme which started in 1969.

2.35 *Finance Houses*

Finance houses are concerned essentially with hire purchase and instalment credit for consumer durables such as cars, television sets, washing machines, etc., and also for industrial plant and machinery. Although there are perhaps more than one thousand firms engaged in instalment credit, the bulk of the business is conducted by the 41 members of the Finance Houses Association. The increasing competition between banks and finance houses for deposits and loans has led to a number of the largest houses being absorbed as subsidiaries of the deposit banks.

Apart from issued capital and reserves, the houses rely nowadays on deposits to the extent of nearly 80 per cent of their funds, the remainder being obtained by bank advances, and discounting of bills. Of the £1,141 million of assets at the end of 1969 about 70 per cent consisted of hire purchase and instalment credit, 9 per cent of advances and loans, and 11 per cent of leasing. An article in the *Bank of England Quarterly Bulletin* of March 1971 points out that although finance of car purchase remains the major business, the finance houses have been increasingly concerned with finance of home improvement and of industrial and commercial equipment. More than half their total lending may now be for industrial purposes. Personal loans and other banking activities have been developing recently. An interesting point made by this March 1971 article is that, unlike many other financial intermediaries, the finance houses are able to adjust their lending and borrowing rates very quickly because their assets are largely short-term and their borrowers rather insensitive to interest charges. The houses tend to plan their lending first, relying on attracting sufficient deposits subsequently or on being able to fall back on their bank overdraft facilities.

2.36 *Special Finance Agencies*

A number of financial institutions have been established under official auspices to meet needs which, it was thought, could not be satisfied adequately from normal sources. In general, these institutions have been designed to fill the gap to which the Macmillan Committee Report of 1931 drew attention, i.e. to provide medium-term capital where the period required is too short for normal new issues and too long for banks, and to provide long-term capital for undertakings which are either too small or whose business is too risky for normal financing. The sources of funds for special finance agencies vary considerably but the deposit banks and other major financial institutions have supplied much of the capital of the big agencies. Capital has also been raised by debenture issues. The most important of the agencies are as follows.

> *The Agricultural Mortgage Corporation Ltd:* established 1928, to provide finance for farmers by means of long-term loans against mortgages; loans outstanding in 1969 were around £150 million.
> *The Industrial and Commercial Finance Corporation Ltd:* established 1945, to finance the expansion of small- and medium-sized concerns with good growth prospects by means of either straight loans, subscriptions to equity capital, convertible loans, or leasing. Total investments were in the region of £130 million in 1969. The Corporation has a large number of specialized subsidiaries.
> *The Finance Corporation for Industry Ltd:* established 1945, to

supplement the normal provision of finance for industries of national importance (e.g. the steel industry) and for projects of national interest where the scale of finance required is beyond the capacity of normal sources. Investments in 1969 amounted to around £30 million.

The Commonwealth Development Finance Company Ltd: established 1953, to provide share capital and loans for business concerns mainly, but not exclusively, in the Commonwealth. Investments in 1969 totalled around £30 million. The company has a number of subsidiaries.

Special finance agencies also include the *Commonwealth Development Corporation* designed to assist development in former dependent countries; and the *National Film Finance Corporation* which has the function of making loans to film producers and distributors. The *Industrial Reorganisation Corporation* which was founded in 1966 to assist productivity, and promote rationalization with the aid of government funds, is now being wound up.

2.37 *Other Credit Granting Institutions*

Local Authorities are major providers of credit for house purchase and home improvement; indeed outstanding loans of local authorities at the end of 1969 are estimated to have been as high as £1,176 million. An interesting recent development has been the establishment by merchant banks, export houses, and some of the deposit banks of *factoring organizations* which provide facilities for firms to liquidate working capital tied up in invoiced debts. The factor buys the debt from the firm at full value less a factoring charge and becomes responsible for the debt collection. Alternatively a firm can sell its goods to the factor for cash, and the factor then appoints the firm as agent to resell the goods to the public and collect payment for the factor in due course. In this way a firm gets cash payment for goods and yet appears to be granting credit to normal customers, while the existence of the factor remains undisclosed.

The Crowther Report on Consumer Credit provides a very comprehensive study of consumer credit granting institutions in Britain. In addition to the institutions already discussed in this chapter there remain a host of sources of consumer credit ranging from sellers of goods and services, such as retailers, mail order houses, merchants, and door-step sellers, to a variety of lenders of money. The latter include check-traders, pawnbrokers, money-lenders, and mortgage-lenders. An impression of the scale of such credit can be gained from Table 2.6 which is based on statistics in the Crowther Report.

TABLE 2.6
MISCELLANEOUS SOURCES OF CONSUMER CREDIT

Outstanding credit 1969	(£ million)
Sellers of goods and services	
Retailers and itinerant credit traders	605
Mail order houses	170
Other	229
Miscellaneous sources of loans	
Check traders	93
Pawnbrokers and money-lenders	31
Private lenders and small loan societies	11
Mortgage-lenders	455
Overdue debts	54

2.4 FINANCIAL MARKETS

The prime function of most financial markets is to provide liquidity for existing debt by enabling holders to dispose of debt to other investors; but many markets also have an intermediary function of raising new capital either short-term or longer-term. This is true, for example, of the money market, the local authority market, and the new issue market. The foreign exchange market also facilitates debt settlement. In this section the various short-term capital markets are discussed first, then the longer-term new issue market and stock exchange, and finally the foreign exchange and gold markets.

2.41 *Discount Market or Money Market*

The main operators in the money market are the discount houses, the deposit banks, the accepting houses, and the Bank of England. The market deals in short-term securities including Treasury bills, commercial bills, and short bonds, and its function is to bring together the major banking institutions with money to lend for very short periods and those which need to borrow for short periods. The Bank of England, acting on behalf of the Treasury, offers Treasury bills for tender in the market each week to provide short-term finance for the government. The Bank also gives assistance to, or eases conditions in, the market, either by lending to the discount houses at or above Bank rate, or else by purchasing bills (mainly Treasury bills) in the market. It may also mop up surplus money by sales of Treasury bills.

2.42 Parallel Money Markets

During and since the 1950s parallel short-term money markets have developed in deposits of foreign currency and sterling owned by non-residents, and in the sterling funds of banks. The main operators in these markets are accepting houses, British overseas and foreign banks, and the discount houses.

2.421 *Euro-Dollar and other Euro-Currency Markets.* Euro-dollars are dollar deposits in United States banks owned by non-United States residents abroad (usually banks). Dollar balances come into the hands of non-United States residents from sales of commodities to the United States, or from sales of American securities. Foreign central banks also acquire dollars from exchange rate stabilization operations. The dollar balances could of course be left idle in the United States but the interest earnable is low and a higher return can be gained by lending the deposit (i.e. lending the ownership of the dollar balance) in the euro-dollar market to another bank, business organization, government, etc. Indeed the balance may be on-lent many times, creating multiple liabilities. This is a highly competitive unregulated market, in which unsecured generally short-term loans, in very large sums, are made between well established institutions.

The enormous expansion of this market, which is mainly centred in London, has been attributable partly to the dollar deficit and the relatively low interest that can be earned on bank deposits in America, partly to the efficiency of the market which makes euro-dollar rates often lower than rates of interest in domestic markets, and partly because of domestic credit restriction particularly for overseas purposes. The most important borrowers have been United States corporations and European public authorities. There has been a similar development of other euro-currency markets with the on-lending of guilders, Swiss francs, pounds sterling, etc. by non-resident owners of the respective currencies.

2.422 *Certificate of Deposit Markets.* Dollar certificates of deposit were first introduced in London in 1966 and sterling certificates of deposit in 1968. Instead of making a straightforward deposit of dollars or sterling in a bank, customers (generally institutions with temporary surplus funds) can purchase certificates of deposit from authorized banks, principally American and other overseas banks, merchant banks, and subsidiaries of deposit banks. A secondary market has been established, in which the discount houses play a part, for the purchase and sale of these certificates, so that these negotiable instruments have become highly liquid.

2.423 *The Inter-Bank Market.* The inter-bank market is one in which the non-clearing banks borrow and lend to each other on a very short-term basis. The banks concerned, which include American and other foreign banks, are very active in the euro-currency market, and deal in deposits and loans of very large individual amounts. The inter-bank market makes it possible for a bank to accept a large deposit even if it has no immediate use for the funds or to lend without prior receipt of a deposit since surplus funds are readily lent in, or deficiencies made good from, this market.

2.43 *The Market in Local Authority Short-Term Debt*

Local authorities have been encouraged by the central government to finance their capital needs in the market, and the high level of interest rates has persuaded many authorities to borrow on a short-term basis. Methods of raising finance include the issue of negotiable short-term bonds either through the stock exchange or direct to large institutions, and by the issue of bills. Temporary borrowing is by the issue of deposit receipts, mostly repayable at two or seven days notice. Lenders include merchant banks, foreign banks, other financial institutions, companies, and persons. There is indeed a lively market in local authority debt and considerable amounts are invested from abroad. At the end of 1969 local authority temporary debt amounted to approximately £1,900 million of which £1,400 million was repayable at up to seven days notice, £200 million between seven days and three months, and £300 million between three and twelve months.

2.44 *New Issue Market*

Longer-term finance is mainly obtained by the sale of new issues of bonds and shares, etc. The raising of new capital for the private sector is largely in the hands of *issuing houses* which include merchant banks, investment trust managers, and, recently, deposit banks; but, in all, there are some 60 members of the Issuing Houses Association.

An issuing house advises a client as to the method and terms of raising capital, organizes the actual issue, and arranges for the underwriting (insurance companies play an important part in underwriting). Methods of raising capital include the *issue by prospectus*, where the issue is offered direct to the public on behalf of the borrowing company; the *offer for sale*, where the issuing house buys the securities from the company and then offers them to the public; and *placing* the issue with a limited number of investors. Issues and redemptions of government debt are conducted by the Bank of England.

TABLE 2.7

CAPITAL ISSUES AND REDEMPTIONS IN THE UNITED KINGDOM

1969 (£ million)

	Gross issues	Redemptions	Net
Excluding British government securities	1,040	355	684
British government and government guaranteed securities	766	1,130	−364

Table 2.7 gives some idea of the volume of new issues. As far as non-government issues are concerned 1969 was a fairly typical year. Approximately two-thirds of the net provision was loan capital and one-third equities. The year 1969 was less typical of government issues. Over the period 1965 to 1970 government issues averaged £1,220 million, redemptions £1,000 million, and average net purchases £220 million.

2.45 *The Stock Exchange*

The stock exchange, by offering a market in existing long-term securities, provides a vital element of liquidity to past issues. Securities are bought and sold at market prices and these are a gauge of market opinion as to the performance and prospects of individual companies and of economic prospects in general.

The public buy and sell through brokers who act as agents on a commission basis. In the London stock exchange there are also jobbers who buy from and sell to brokers or to each other as principals, and who tend to specialize in particular classes of securities.

AN OUTLINE OF BRITISH FINANCIAL INSTITUTIONS 39

The London stock exchange, which can claim to be the largest in the world, is governed by a Council elected by the members of the exchange. It publishes quotations for about 9,000 securities. There are also a Scottish stock exchange and a number of provincial exchanges. Table 2.8 gives some idea of the volume of business in the London stock market.

TABLE 2.8
THE LONDON STOCK EXCHANGE

1969	Turnover (£ million)	Transactions (thousands)
Total	30,391	5,788
British government	19,549	440
Local authorities	839	98
Overseas governments etc.	141	35
Debenture and preference shares	1,238	675
Ordinary shares	8,713	4,539

2.46 *The Foreign Exchange Market*

Since each country has its own currency, transactions between residents of different countries normally involve exchange of currencies. Where this exchange is conducted in a free market, demand for and supply of currencies are equated by movements of the price of one currency in terms of another, i.e. by movements of exchange rates. Although some elements of exchange control still exist in Britain, the London foreign exchange market is essentially free, but, as in most other countries, exchange rate fluctuations have been constrained by official intervention.

The operators in the London market consist of the banks authorized by the Bank of England for this purpose, approximately 180 in all, together with 9 foreign exchange brokers, Banks buy and sell foreign currencies in exchange for sterling on behalf of their customers and to some extent on their own account, either via the brokers or directly with other banks. They also buy and sell one foreign currency against another (arbitrage), where exchange rate differentials between international centres make this profitable. Generally speaking the exchange of currencies in the London market reflects the flow of payments and receipts between Britain and the rest of the world arising from foreign trade and international investment, including the movements of short-term capital in response to interest rate changes. Rates of exchange can be quoted 'spot', i.e. for immediate delivery of the currency, or 'forward', where the rate is agreed now for currency to be delivered at a future date. A forward contract protects a transactor during the period of the contract against the risk of a significant change in the exchange rate.

2.47 *The London Gold Market*

The market in gold is in one sense a commodity market but it is included among the financial markets because of the important connection between gold and foreign exchange. The London market was closed at the beginning of the Second World War and was not reopened until 1954. It has rapidly recovered its former pre-eminence, handling more than 80 per cent of the total world dealings.

The market consists of five firms – N. M. Rothschild, Samuel Montague, Mocatta and Goldsmid, Sharps Pixley, and Johnson Matthey. Representatives of these five meet twice a day to fix the price of gold so as to match sales with amounts on offer from new production and other sources, though much business is also done outside of these 'fixings'. The Bank of England keeps in close contact with the market through Rothschilds. Prior to March 1968 the Bank acted as agent for the South African Reserve Bank and for the 'gold pool' central banks of the United Kingdom, Belgium, France (until 1967), West Germany, Italy, Netherlands, Switzerland, and the United States.

The policy of the gold pool had been to keep the price of gold close to the official United States price of $35 per ounce by buying or selling sufficient gold in the market to offset whatever surplus or deficiency arose from the interaction of new production, industrial demand, hoarding, and dishoarding. Speculation against the dollar after the sterling devaluation of 1967 put such a strain on the gold price support system that in March 1968 the gold pool central banks and other central banks agreed to cease all official dealings in the gold market. Direct gold transactions between monetary authorities continued at the price of $35 per ounce, while the price of gold in the market was left to be determined by market forces. This is the 'two-tier' gold price system. The free market price has fluctuated considerably in accordance with prevailing expectations about the likelihood of official revaluation of gold. By April 1969 the market price had risen as high as $43·60, threatening the insulation of the official price, though by the end of the year it had fallen back to $35. Later in 1970 speculative pressures again began to develop and the price had once more reached $43 in August 1971 when President Nixon declared the dollar to be no longer convertible into gold at a fixed price.

2.5 THE BANK OF ENGLAND

The Bank of England is the central bank of the United Kingdom and, as such, it has primary responsibility for supervision and control of the financial system of the country. It is able to exercise authority and influence partly through its various roles as banker to other banks, banker to the government, controller of foreign exchange transactions, and controller of the note issue; and partly in consequence of powers vested by the Bank of England Act 1946. Under this Act the Bank is managed by a board of directors, called the Court, consisting of a Governor, Deputy Governor, and 16 directors, all appointed by the Crown. Although the Act empowered the Treasury to give directions to the Bank (after consultation with the Governor) it also empowered the Bank to 'request information from and make recommendations to bankers, and may, if so authorized by the Treasury, issue directions to any banker for the purpose of securing that effect is given to any such request or recommendation'. The only limitations on this authority are that requests and recommendations shall not relate to any particular bank customer and that bankers shall have an opportunity of making representations to the Treasury before directions are put into effect.

The Bank is banker to the deposit banks and, via the discount houses, acts as lender of last resort to the banking system; it also holds accounts and working balances for many overseas central banks as well as for the International Monetary Fund and the International Bank for Reconstruction and Development. As banker to the government it keeps the accounts of government departments; it manages the short-term borrowing requirements of the government through the Treasury bill issue and by 'Ways and Means Advances'. It manages the longer-term debt of the public sector, maintaining the register of stock, paying dividends, and conducting new issues, redemptions, and conversions; and it is responsible for financial advice to the government. Through its control of the fiduciary note issue and through daily operations in the money market and gilt-edged market, the Bank exerts a powerful influence on the money supply and on the structure of interest rates. Finally, as agent for the Treasury the Bank operates the Exchange Equalization Account and negotiates finance with other central banks and international institutions with the object of restricting the fluctuations in the exchange rate, of conserving international reserves, and of preserving equilibrium in international payments.

SUGGESTED READING

British Financial Institutions (H.M.S.O., 1969).

A. R. Prest, (Ed.), *The UK Economy A Manual of Applied Economics*, 3rd ed (Weidenfeld and Nicolson, 1970), ch. ii.

N. J. Gibson, 'Financial Intermediaries and Monetary Policy', *Hobart Paper* (No. 39, 1967).

Radcliffe Report (H.M.S.O., 1959), chs. iv, v.

Crowther Report (H.M.S.O., 1971), part ii.

Bank of England Quarterly Bulletin, Jun. 1965, Dec. 1970, Mar. 1971, Jun. 1971, Jun. 1969, Jun. 1967, Jun. 1968, Mar. 1969, Sep. 1969, Mar. 1970, Sep. 1970.

'Recent Developments in London's Money Markets', *Midland Bank Review*, Aug. 1969, Nov. 1969.

R. S. Sayers, *Modern Banking*, 7th ed. (Oxford, 1967), chs. ii–v, vii.

3 Currency and Bank Deposits

3.1 THE SUPPLY OF CURRENCY IN THE UNITED KINGDOM

Currency consists of coin and bank notes. Coin is manufactured by the Royal Mint, which is a government department, and the cost of manufacture is financed by cheques drawn on the government's account at the Bank of England (the account is known as *Public Deposits*). The coin is sold to the Bank of England at face value and the Bank of England pays by crediting Public Deposits.

The supply of coins is determined simply by the demand of the general public for small change. Coin comes into circulation when bank customers draw coin from their banks. A net withdrawal of coin from the deposit banks causes an equal reduction in bank deposits and bank cash reserves. The banks will probably wish to replace their till holdings and do so by drawing coins from the Bank of England, paying by running down their *Bankers Balances* at the Bank of England. Since Bankers Balances are part of the banks' cash reserves, the replenishment of till money does not restore the cash reserves. However the Bank of England reserves of coins have also been reduced and the Bank orders new coins from the Royal Mint, paying for them by crediting Public Deposits. In the meantime the Royal Mint has to purchase materials and services from the private sector to manufacture additional coins. The Royal Mint must therefore draw cheques for this purpose on Public Deposits and these are paid into the deposit banks. Bank deposits rise by the cost of manufacturing the new coins, and, when the cheques are cleared, Bankers Balances at the Bank of England rise by the same amount. Thus at the end of the cycle bank deposits and bank cash reserves have been reduced by an amount equal to the face value of the extra coins in circulation and both have been increased by the cost of manufacturing such coins. The banking system is therefore unaffected by the increase in the coin issue except to the extent of the difference between the face value of the coins and their cost of production.

Notes in circulation consist of Bank of England, Northern Ireland, and Scottish bank notes. The Scottish and Northern Ireland bank notes in circulation must be backed by Bank of England notes, except for a small fixed amount, so that they merely circulate in lieu of Bank of England notes.

Regulations governing the note issue have changed considerably in the course of history and readers interested in these developments are recommended to refer to the concise and authoritative article entitled 'The Note Issue' which appeared in the Bank of England Quarterly Bulletin of March 1965. As far as the current situation is concerned it is sufficient to note that the link with gold was severed in 1939 when virtually the whole gold reserve was transferred from the Bank of England's Issue Department to the Exchange Equalization Account of the Treasury. The note issue then became in August 1970 entirely fiduciary. At present the issue is governed by the Currency and Bank Notes Act of 1954. The Act provided for a fiduciary issue of £1,575 million but allowed the Treasury to vary this at the instance of the Bank of England. Treasury Orders permitting a continuous increase above £1,575 million must be laid before Parliament every second year; and Parliament could, if it chose, veto increases on these occasions. No such control has been exercised, and thus, in effect, the note issue is determined by the Bank of England, with the permission of the Treasury. The fiduciary issue reached £3,700 million in December 1970.

An increase in the fiduciary issue is really initiated by the general public. When the public make net withdrawals of notes from the banks on any scale the latter require to replenish their till money by drawing new notes from the Bank of England in exchange for a reduction in Bankers Balances. This reduces the reserve of notes in the Banking Department of the Bank of England, and, when the reduction is more than can be reasonably sustained, an increase in the fiduciary issue is called for, usually in amounts of £50 million at a time. The opposite happens when the general public pays in notes to the banks on any scale.

To trace the effects of such events it is convenient to suppose that the public make a net withdrawal of £50 million in notes from the banks over some period, and that this leads to an increase in the fiduciary issue of this amount. In Stage 1 we suppose that the public have withdrawn £50 million from the banks, so that bank deposits and bank cash reserves in the form of till money are each reduced by this amount. In Stage 2 we suppose that the banks replenish their till money by drawing £50 million of new notes from the Bank of England. Bankers Balances at the Bank of England and the Bank of England reserve of notes are each reduced by £50 million. The total cash reserves of the deposit banks (Bankers Balances plus till money) remain reduced by £50 million. In Stage 3 the fiduciary issue is increased. £50 million of notes are printed by the Issue Department of the Bank of England and sold to the Banking Department in exchange for Treasury bills. The Banking Department of the Bank of England has now restored its reserve of notes but its holdings of Treasury bills are reduced by £50 million. Finally, in Stage 4, we may suppose that the Bank of England replenishes its holdings of Treasury bills by buying these in the market, in effect from the deposit banks, paying for them by crediting Bankers Balances.

The net effect of all these stages is that notes in circulation have increased by £50 million and bank deposits are reduced by the same amount, i.e. the public has changed the form in which it chooses to hold money. The cash reserves of the deposit banks have been restored but their holdings of Treasury bills (or call loans to the Discount Houses) are down by £50 million. The government has also changed the form of its borrowing from the private sector. It has been able to substitute notes for Treasury bills, and is thus borrowing in a

TABLE 3.1

EFFECT OF INCREASE OF NOTES IN CIRCULATION AND INCREASE IN FIDUCIARY ISSUE

(£ millions)

	Stage I	Stage II	Stage III	Stage IV	Net change
Notes in circulation	+50				+50
Banks					
Deposits	−50				−50
Cash (*a*) till money	−50	+50			0
(*b*) balances at Bank of England		−50		+50	0
Money market assets					
(Treasury bills or money at call)				−50	−50
Bank of England					
Deposits (*a*) Public deposits					
(*b*) Bankers' deposits		−50		+50	0
Reserve of notes		−50	+50		0
Government securities					
(Treasury bills)			−50	+50	0

Note: The table assumes that £50 million of notes are withdrawn from banks and that this leads to an increase in the fiduciary issue of £50 million.

cheaper way. This is not really the end of the story because the liquidity position of the banks has been disturbed. The banks hold the same amount of cash as they did originally but their deposit liabilities and their money market assets are each reduced by £50 million. They are holding more cash and less money market assets than they probably wish, and the Bank of England may need to take steps to correct this situation. But the nature of such action must be investigated later. The steps in this analysis are summarized in Table 3.1.

The public demand for currency has marked fluctuations of a fairly regular nature, both weekly and seasonally, but the longer-term trend in the demand appears to be strongly influenced by the general level of expenditure. Table 3.2 compares the annual average currency in circulation from 1955 to 1968 with the value of the Gross Domestic Product at factor cost, and also with the value of Consumer's

TABLE 3.2

ESTIMATED CURRENCY IN CIRCULATION, CONSUMERS' EXPENDITURE, AND GROSS DOMESTIC PRODUCT AT FACTOR COST

	Currency in circulation £ million	Consumers' expenditure £ million	Gross domestic product £ million	Currency per cent of consumers' expenditure %	Currency per cent of G.D.P. %	Increase in currency per cent of increase in C.E. %	G.D.P. %
1955	1,657	13,100	16,800	12·6	9·9		
1956	1,765	13,821	18,186	12·8	9·7	15·2	7·8
1957	1,842	14,582	19,284	12·6	9·5	10·1	7·0
1958	1,905	15,296	20,115	12·4	9·5	8·8	7·6
1959	1,969	16,106	21,151	12·2	9·3	7·9	6·2
1960	2,062	16,909	22,563	12·2	9·1	11·6	6·6
1961	2,151	17,810	24,139	12·1	8·9	9·9	5·6
1962	2,161	18,906	24,230	11·4	8·6	0·9	0·9
1963	2,210	20,125	26,826	11·0	8·2	4·0	3·0
1964	2,332	21,493	28,966	10·8	8·1	8·9	5·7
1965	2,483	22,865	30,895	10·9	8·0	11·0	7·8
1966	2,637	24,236	32,590	10·9	8·1	11·2	9·0
1967	2,700	25,339	34,386	10·7	7·9	5·7	3·5
1968	2,827	27,065	36,267	10·4	7·8	7·4	6·8

Expenditure. The table also compares the annual increase in currency in circulation with the annual increases in the other two expenditure totals. Although currency as a percentage of either of the two expenditure totals has shown a steady decline, the increases in currency in circulation as a percentage of increases in gross domestic product has averaged about 7 per cent, and as a percentage of increases in consumer expenditure about 9 per cent. In both cases there has been a good deal of fluctuation around these averages.

Another factor influencing currency in circulation is likely to be the volume of bank deposits. Indeed this may be the more important influence. Table 3.3 shows that currency in circulation as a percentage

TABLE 3.3

ESTIMATED CURRENCY IN CIRCULATION AND NET DEPOSITS OF THE LONDON CLEARING BANKS

	Currency in circulation £ million	Net deposits £ million	Currency as per cent of net deposits
1955	1,657	6,184	27
1956	1,765	6,012	29
1957	1,842	6,138	30
1958	1,905	6,330	30
1959	1,969	6,617	30
1960	2,062	6,867	30
1961	2,151	7,035	31
1962	2,161	7,228	30
1963	2,210	7,556	29
1964	2,332	8,069	29
1965	2,483	8,498	29
1966	2,637	8,864	30
1967	2,700	9,024	30
1968	2,827	9,645	29

of the aggregate net deposits of the clearing banks has remained consistently at 29 or 30 per cent each year from 1956 to 1968. This seems to indicate that the public like to keep a steady proportion between the two main forms of money that they hold. Bank deposits have risen less fast than gross domestic product, and this probably explains why the proportion of currency in circulation to national expenditure has fallen steadily.

The tentative conclusion appears to be that changes in the volume of bank deposits are the most important determinant of changes in currency in circulation. It is necessary, therefore, to examine bank deposits as a form of money.

3.2 BANK DEPOSITS AS MONEY

The transfer of bank deposits by cheque, standing order, or credit transfer, etc. is one of the most important methods of debt settlement. Current account bank deposits must therefore be regarded as part of the total stock of money.

Bank deposits have become money because sufficient people and institutions have become prepared to accept settlement of debt by their transfer. It is because transactors are confident that others will accept debt settlement by transfer of deposits that transactors are prepared to accept an addition to their own bank deposits. If it were not for this confidence, bank deposits when transferred would not stay in existence, since recipients would tend to exchange them for currency.

Why has this general confidence developed? Partly it is because for many types of debt settlement the transfer of a deposit is more convenient and efficient than the use of currency. Partly it is because bank deposits are a safer and more conveneint form of holding large stocks of money. But perhaps the basic reason why so many have come to accept and hold bank deposits is that there is complete confidence that the deposits can be turned into legal tender at any time. Paradoxically, the main reason why most transactors do not cash additions to deposits as they receive them is their confidence that they could cash such deposits if they so wished. It is vital to the existence of the banking system that this confidence should remain absolute.

Bank deposits are of two main types. Current accounts or demand deposits are those that are chequeable, and normally earn no interest. They are drawable on demand. Deposit accounts or time deposits require notice of withdrawal, but they earn interest. They are not chequeable. Deposit accounts or time deposits are not really media of exchange. But in the case of ordinary time deposits the banks seldom insist on the period of notice so that such deposits can readily be transferred to current account for the purpose of making payments. For this reason ordinary time deposits are often included in the stock of money. Fixed-term deposits may be developed by commercial banks in the future.

3.3 HOW BANK DEPOSITS ARE CREATED

A bank deposit is simply a credit balance in favour of a customer. It is the debt the banker owes to his customer. The creation of, or the addition to, bank deposits is the consequence of an exchange of claims. The banker gives his debt to a customer, i.e. credits the customer's account, in exchange for claims received from the customer. But the normal banker deals generally only in a limited number of types of claims. The banker will credit a customer's account in exchange for currency, for another bank deposit, for certain types of securities (government bonds, Treasury bills, and bills of exchange), and, finally, in exchange for a claim on the customer himself. Thus, since bank deposits are created by the exchange of claims, an increase in the banker's deposit liabilities is always matched by an increase in his assets in the form of the claims he has received in exchange.

Currency paid in by one customer will often have been withdrawn from some other bank account. The bulk of currency withdrawals and payments in will therefore leave the total of bank deposits unaffected except for temporary fluctuations. Such fluctuations tend to be fairly regular. For example, on a Friday withdrawals of currency to pay wages etc. will usually exceed payments in of currency. Whereas on a Monday, payments in of currency by shops and places of entertainment, etc. may well exceed withdrawals. Peak holiday periods are also times when the public find it convenient to hold a larger proportion of their stock of money in currency. At such times withdrawals of currency from banks will generally exceed payments in.

Any net withdrawal of currency from banks will of course reduce bank deposits below what they would otherwise have been. Table 3.3 shows that the trend of currency in circulation has been rising continuously. One might suppose, therefore, that there would be a counterpart falling trend in the total of bank deposits. But of course Table 3.3 shows this to be the opposite of the truth. The reason for this state of affairs is that it is the rise in the volume of bank deposits which is the cause of the rise in currency in circulation. The causal relationship may be direct in so far as the public likes to keep a steady proportion between money held in bank deposits and money held in currency, or it may be indirect, in that a rising trend of bank deposits is associated with rising expenditure, and the latter causes a rising trend in the demand for currency. Generally speaking, the rising trend of currency in circulation merely moderates the rise in the volume of bank deposits. Of course currency in circulation could be the cause of a more permanent change in the volume of bank deposits, or in their trend of increase, were the public to make long-term changes in their preference as to the proportions in which they choose to hold money as between bank deposits and currency.

The second way in which a bank deposit is created or increased is when a banker gives his debt in exchange for another bank deposit. That is to say, a bank deposit is credited when another deposit is transferred via the payment in of a cheque, or by a direct transfer within a bank or between banks by a credit transfer or a standing order. Of course it is obvious that a transfer from one deposit to another within a particular banking system will make no difference to the total deposits of that banking system. Individual banks may be affected. For example, if, over some period of time, there are net transfers from deposits in Bank A to deposits in Bank B, then the total of deposits in the former will fall, and those in the latter will rise. Moreover Bank A will have to settle with Bank B for this net transfer by a payment of cash. In the British setting this settlement is achieved via the clearing house, and the end result is that Bank A's balance at the Bank of England is reduced by the net transfer, and that of Bank B is increased by that amount. However, we are more interested in transfers of bank deposits which affect the total of bank deposits in a banking system. And, clearly, this can only occur when there are transfers of deposits from or to another banking system.

In Chapter 2 it was shown that there are several groups of banking institutions in Britain, including merchant banks and foreign banks as well as the deposit banks. For the purpose of the present exposition it is useful to concentrate mainly on two groups – the Bank of England, which is the central bank, and the ordinary deposit banks. One can then distinguish two important separate banking systems. The first is the public sector banking system which consists of the Bank of England and its chief customer the government together with other public sector bodies. The second is the private sector banking system, consisting mainly of the ordinary deposit banks and their customers, i.e. persons, business houses, etc. resident within the United Kingdom. Transfers of deposits between these two banking systems are a major factor determining the volume of deposits in the private banking system.

It is useful to classify the transfers between the public and private banking systems into those resulting from internal transactions and those resulting from external transactions. The internal transactions can also be divided into three groups. First, there are all the normal payments being made between the public and private sectors. The public sector makes vast payments for the services of administrators, teachers, doctors, police, servicemen, etc., and for the purchase of commodities; and it also makes what are termed transfer payments, including grants, pensions, benefits, and interest on national debt. All such payments cause a transfer of money to the private sector, and this is held in the form of additional bank deposits or additional currency. At the same time the private sector is making payments to the public sector in various forms of taxation and for the purchase of public sector produced commodities or services. These payments, of course, transfer money from the private sector to the public sector. A net excess of public sector payments will be causing bank deposits and currency in the private sector to rise, and conversely.

The second group consists of debt transactions. When the public sector repays debt it transfers money to the private sector. When the public sector adds to its borrowing there is a transfer of money the other way. But debt operations can be conducted with the deposit banks as well as with bank customers. It is only net borrowing from bank customers (i.e. sales of government debt to bank customers) that will directly reduce bank deposits, or net repayment of debt to bank customers that will directly raise bank deposits. When the public sector sells debt directly to banks payment is settled by a reduction of Bankers Balances at the Bank of England. In effect, the banks simply substitute government bonds or Treasury bills for cash among their assets. There may be indirect effects upon deposit creation as a result of the change in the banks' cash holdings, but if the banks buy the additional government debt simply because they are holding more cash than they wish, there need not necessarily be further repercussions on deposit creation.

The third group of internal transactions is really a special variation of the second. The Bank of England can engage in debt operations on its own account, that is to say, independently of whether the government is borrowing or repaying debt. The Bank of England, through its broker, can buy government securities in the market, paying by cheques on itself. Such open market purchases, as they are called, will transfer money to the private sector. Alternatively the Bank of England can sell government securities in the open market causing a transfer of money away from the private sector. But here again it is only when the transactions are conducted with bank customers that bank deposits are directly affected. Purchases of securities from the banks will only directly affect the composition of bank assets, i.e. they will hold more cash and less government securities. Similarly sales of securities to the banks* will result in their holding less cash and more securities. Bank deposit creation may be affected indirectly as a consequence of the change in the distribution of bank assets. But that is a matter which must be investigated later.

It must be emphasized that all transfers between the public sector and the private sector will affect the cash holdings of the banks, whether the transfers are between bank customers and the public sector, or whether they are direct transactions between the banks and the public sector. We have just seen how direct government debt transactions between the public sector and the banks, and also direct Bank of England open market operations with the banks, both affect bank holdings of cash. But this is equally true of all transactions between the public sector and bank customers. Suppose there is some net payment by the public sector to bank customers, amounting to, say, £X. This could be the result of a purchase by the public sector from the private sector of services or commodities; it could be repayment of government debt; or it could be an open market purchase of securities by the Bank of England. Whatever the cause, the payment will be made by cheques on the Bank of England. The bank customers who receive these cheques pay them into their accounts, so bank deposits rise by £X in total. The banks now present these cheques to the Bank of England, and the latter will credit the respective Bankers Balances at the Bank of England. It will be remembered that bank cash holdings consist partly of currency in the tills and partly of Bankers Balances at the Bank of England. The rise in Bankers Balances of £X means, therefore, a rise in bank cash holdings by that amount. Similarly any net payment by bank customers to the public sector will cause an equal fall in bank deposits and bank cash holdings.

One point that follows from all this is that the Bank of England has the power to influence the cash holdings of the banks by means of open market operations. It may use this power to neutralize disturbances to bank cash holdings arising from other transfers between the public sector and the private sector, or arising from changes in currency in circulation. On the other hand, it may attempt to use this power to cause a change in bank cash holdings as a matter of deliberate monetary policy. One should note, however, a distinction

---

* In the past it has been the practice of the clearing banks not to tender directly for Treasury bills on their own account but to buy them indirectly from the discount houses. In the interests of simplicity this complication is ignored in this chapter since it makes no difference in principle to bank deposit creation.

of some importance between open market purchases or sales of securities involving bank customers, and those made directly with the banks. In the former case the change in bank cash holdings occurs involuntarily, i.e. not by the volition of the banks. On the other hand, banks themselves will only buy securities from the Bank of England if they are holding more cash than they wish to hold, and will only sell securities to the Bank of England if they choose to add to their cash holdings. This distinction is equally true of other transfers between the public sector and the private sector. It is only the transactions between bank customers and the public sector which cause involuntary changes in bank cash holdings.

It is time to examine the effects of external transactions. Here we are concerned with payments between private sector residents of the United Kingdom and residents of other countries. These payments arise from international trade, and also from international investment, including loans, repayments of loans, and transfers of funds from or to abroad. The finance of international payments is a complex matter, but the effects of such payments, in principle, can be sketched quite simply.

First it must be said that the vast bulk of payments abroad made by United Kingdom residents will be neutralized by payments from abroad as far as the effect on the level of bank deposits is concerned. It is only a net excess of payments abroad over some period, or a net excess of payments from abroad, which is relevant. But to keep the analysis as simple as possible let us represent a net excess of payments abroad by an isolated payment made by a United Kingdom resident to a resident abroad, and assume that the payment is of a significant sum.

Such a payment can be made either in foreign currency or in sterling. If the payment is to be made in foreign exchange, then, in effect, the customer instructs his bank to buy the foreign currency from the Exchange Equalization Account and to debit the customer's account. Now the E.E.A. (as it is usually called) is a department of the Treasury – the department which holds the nation's reserves of foreign exchange or of gold which can be converted into foreign exchange. This payment therefore causes a transfer of a bank deposit from the private sector to the public sector, an equal fall in the cash reserves of the bank, and also, of course, a fall in the foreign exchange reserves of the E.E.A. Had this payment been the other way – a payment by a resident abroad to a resident in the United Kingdom – the consequences would have been the opposite. The customer would have sold the foreign exchange to his bank. The bank would credit the customer with the proceeds, and would in turn sell the foreign exchange to the E.E.A., being paid by a rise in Bankers Balances at the Bank of England.

If the payment is made in sterling, the overseas recipient will normally sell the sterling to his own bank in exchange for a deposit in his own country. The foreign bank now owns the sterling bank deposit. If the foreign bank were a customer of a British bank there would simply have been a transfer in the ownership of bank deposits in the British bank. If this foreign bank subsequently wishes to turn the additional deposit into foreign exchange, the effects will be the same as if the original payment had been made in foreign exchange. The foreign bank, however, may keep its sterling cash reserves, not with an ordinary British bank, but with the Bank of England. In this case the payment will cause a fall in the bank deposits of the British bank and an equal fall in its holdings of cash (i.e. a fall in its Bankers Balance at the Bank of England). The opposite of these results will occur where a payment is made to a resident of the United Kingdom in sterling.

As a generalization one can say that any net excess of payments abroad by United Kingdom private sector residents over receipts from abroad will cause a fall in private sector bank deposits and in the cash holdings of British banks, except to the extent that there is an increase in the ownership of commercial bank deposits by foreign banks (or other foreign residents). And the opposite will occur if there is a net excess of receipts from abroad over payments abroad. Of course, as was indicated earlier, the Bank of England may choose to neutralize the effects of such net payments on bank cash holdings by means of open market operations.* Or, indeed, the effects of external transactions may be wholly or partly offset by other transfers between the private and public sectors arising from internal transactions.

After this rather lengthy description of the effects of transfers of deposits between the private and public sectors we must not lose sight of the fact that there remain two other ways in which bank deposits can be changed. Fortunately these can be examined more briefly. It may be recalled that the third type of claim for which a banker will give his debt in exchange (i.e. credit a customer's account) consists of certain types of securities, including government bonds, Treasury bills, and bills of exchange. That is to say, when a banker

---

* This neutralization tends to occur automatically because the E.E.A. matches sales of foreign exchange with purchases of Treasury bills and purchases of foreign exchange with sales of Treasury bills.

buys such securities from his customers he pays by crediting their account. Or, if he buys securities from customers of other banks he pays by cheques drawn on himself. These are paid into other banks and when the cheques are presented to the banker on whom the cheques are drawn there will be a transfer of the ownership of Bankers Balances at the Bank of England. But from the point of view of the private sector banking system as a whole, net purchases of securities from bank customers will cause a rise in the total of bank deposits, and net sales of securities to bank customers will cause a fall in the total of bank deposits.

The final way in which bank deposits can change is where bankers exchange their debt for the debt of their customers. Bank deposits will rise when bankers increase advances to customers, and fall when advances are repaid. Advances can be made by loan or by overdraft. The loan is a straightforward exchange of debts. Suppose a bank makes a loan of, say, £1,000. The banker credits his customer's account with this sum, thus recording his indebtedness to his customer. At the same time the customer's indebtedness to the bank for £1,000 is also recorded in the books of the bank. The customer will normally proceed to transfer this deposit to other bank accounts as he makes additional payments, but the larger amount of bank deposits stays in existence so long as it is not permanently withdrawn in currency or transferred to the public sector. When the loan is repaid bank deposits fall because repayment is effected by the customer's account being debited. There is, of course, an equal fall in bank assets since the customer's debt to the bank will be cancelled. More commonly an advance is made by way of overdraft. A customer given an overdraft limit of, say, £1,000, is allowed to draw on his account beyond his credit balance to the extent of £1,000. He can go 'into the red' up to this amount. Bank deposits, in total, are not affected until the overdraft facility is utilized. But when the customer does overdraw he does so by paying cheques to other bank customers, and, as these cheques are paid in, bank deposits in total will rise. Bank deposits remain at a higher level until the overdraft is paid off.

We have seen that the bank deposits of the private sector banking system as a whole can increase for four different reasons. The first can be because the general public decide to hold more of their money in the form of bank deposits and less in the form of currency, that is to say, bank deposits rise when there are net payments in of currency. The second reason can be the transfer of money from the public sector to the private sector, in consequence either of internal or external transactions. The third reason can be that banks make net purchases of securities from customers, and the fourth, that the banks make net additional advances to customers. For the opposite of any of these reasons bank deposits in aggregate will fall. In practice various combinations of these changes will be occurring all the time, and some changes may offset each other. For example, banks may be selling securities to customers and increasing advances to customers at the same time, so that the effects on total bank deposits will be offsetting.

Although each of these four types of exchange of claims can be a cause of a change in the total of bank deposits, there is an important distinction as between the first two types of exchange and the second two types. Payments in or withdrawals of currency by bank customers and transfers of deposits between the public and private sectors occur quite independently of the volition of the banks. The banks are entirely passive actors in such changes in deposits. Moreover both causes of change in deposits also cause an equal change in the cash holdings of the banks. On the other hand, over the second two types of exchange bankers have some degree of control, and these exchanges do not directly cause a change in bank cash holdings. In the case of advances the banker is free to grant or refuse an advance. He does not, of course, have complete control over this way of changing deposits, because he cannot make additional advances if there is no demand for advances. Nor can he easily force customers to repay advances at will. In the case of purchases and sales of securities, the banker is entirely a free agent. He can choose to buy or sell at the current market price as he wishes. But it must be remembered that it is only security transactions with bank customers that will directly cause changes in the total of bank deposits.

But even if there were a continuously unsatisfied demand for bank advances it does not follow that banks could raise the level of deposits indefinitely by expansion of their advances and of their purchases of securities from customers. There are important limitations on the ability of banks to expand deposits of their own volition. These limitations must be examined later.

3.4 FACTORS INFLUENCING THE DISTRIBUTION OF BANK ASSETS

We have seen that bank deposits are created by the exchange of claims. Thus for every increase in bank deposits there is always a counterpart increase in bank assets. For the private sector banking system as a whole, for an increase in deposit liabilities resulting from the net payment in of currency or from a net transfer from the public sector, there will be a counterpart increase in bank cash holdings. For an increase in deposits due to bank purchases of securities from bank customers, there will, of course, be a counterpart increase in securities held. Similarly an increase in deposits resulting from additional loans or overdrafts will be accompanied by a rise in bank advances. But the proportionate distribution of bank assets is not simply the chance result of the manner in which deposits have been created. If bankers find themselves holding a larger proportion of assets in cash than they wish they can substitute securities for the unwanted cash by buying additional securities from the public sector, while leaving deposits and assets in aggregate unaffected. Alternatively bankers can reduce the proportion of cash by increasing the proportion of other assets held. This can be done by buying additional securities from bank customers or by making additional advances. But in either event the total of deposit liabilities and the total of assets would increase. It is necessary now to examine two questions: why do banks restrict the types of assets they acquire; and what considerations influence the distribution of assets they seek to maintain?

A bank is a business concern and at least one aim of a bank must be to earn a satisfactory profit. This means that a bank must aim at achieving a satisfactory excess of earnings over running costs. Most of a bank's earnings are derived from the assets it holds, but, leaving aside shareholders' capital and reserves, a bank can only acquire assets to the extent that it succeeds in persuading customers to keep deposits with the bank. The banker competes for current account deposits by the range and efficiency of services he offers, by providing attractive premises, and by advertising; and he attracts time deposits by the interest offered. Probably the most important service offered is that of debt settlement, but the banker also provides facilities for borrowing and for safe custody, investment advice, and many other services. These services are costly to provide and bank charges cover only a small part. In addition there are costs of maintaining premises, advertising, and paying interest on time deposits, so that the total costs of a bank are very considerable. Hence it is vital that the bank should hold assets which yield a good return. But, as we have seen earlier, the willingness of customers to keep deposits with a bank is also conditional on complete confidence in the bank. Partly this is the confidence that current account deposits can always be cashed on demand, and time deposits after short notice. Partly it is confidence in the soundness of the bank, i.e. that the bank's assets are good. Since maintenance of this confidence is paramount, a banker cannot afford to choose his assets solely with regard to their yield. He is forced to compromise in his choice of assets between profitability, on the one hand, and liquidity and safety on the other hand.

Cash is the only asset which is perfectly liquid and risk-free, but cash is an asset which earns no return. It is important, therefore, to a banker, to keep his cash holding to the minimum compatible with maintaining confidence. The banker must hold a reserve of cash, either in the form of currency or as a balance with the central bank, so as to be able to meet immediately any probable net encashment by customers, net clearing payments to other banks, or net transfers to the public sector, liable to occur on any one day. The size of this reserve depends on the size of the potential cash loss that is liable to occur at any one time. Clearly the amount of the potential cash loss will vary with the size of the bank's total deposit liabilities. The cash reserve must therefore bear some proportionate relationship* to the total deposit liabilities.

A bank can minimize its cash holdings if it holds an adequate proportion of other assets which it can turn into cash immediately, or with a very short delay, without the risk of significant loss. These assets are known as money market assets. They include bills of exchange and Treasury bills, and, in the British banking system, short-term loans to the discount market. Bills can be sold easily in the bill market and, since they have only a short period to maturity, the market price obtainable is unlikely to fall far short of the maturity value. When one bank suffers cash losses, other banks will frequently be the gainers, and, with surplus cash, they will be eager buyers of bills. The bank losing cash could therefore easily sell bills with little adverse effect on bill prices. In any case, provided a fair proportion of the bills held are very close to maturity, a bank can quickly add to its cash holdings by failing to renew bill holdings as existing holdings mature. Short-term loans to the discount market can be over-night, day-to-day, week-to-week, etc., and such loans are in some ways even more liquid than bills. An individual bank, losing cash to other banks, would find it easy to call in such loans, since other banks, with surplus cash, would be eager to increase loans to the discount market.

The position would be very different, however, if the banks as a group were losing cash, in consequence, for example, of net transfers of deposits to the public sector. In these circumstances banks might find it difficult to sell bills without heavy loss, since there would be

---

* British banking practice with respect to liquidity ratios is discussed in Section 3.5.

few buyers among the banks. Discount houses would find it difficult to repay loans with few banks able to provide an alternative source of funds. Money market assets would no longer be highly liquid. To preserve the liquidity of these assets the Bank of England undertakes to lend cash to the discount houses against the security of Treasury bills, short-term government bonds, and first-class trade bills, or to re-discount Treasury bills and first-class trade bills. While the Bank of England may provide this cash at current rates of interest, it reserves the right to charge Bank rate for such loans or re-discounts; and borrowing at this rate, as will be seen in detail later, involves the discount houses in losses. The point to note, however, is that the high liquidity of money market assets rests ultimately, not so much on the fact that they are short-term assets, but on the fact that the Bank of England has chosen to make these assets eligible as the basis for central bank loans of cash.

The other main 'banking' assets are investments (mostly government or government guaranteed bonds) and advances. They are sometimes referred to as 'earning' assets, since they are not held primarily for liquidity reasons, and, certainly in the case of advances, their yield is normally greater than that on money market assets. Nevertheless considerations of liquidity and safety continue to exert an influence.

Investments have a liquidity advantage in that they are highly marketable, but a liquidity disadvantage in that the market price obtainable is unpredictable. Indeed long-term bonds can involve investors in heavy losses in the event of a sharp decline in bond prices. British banks attempt to minimize this liquidity disadvantage by keeping a high proportion of investments in fairly short-term bonds, for example of less than five years' maturity. Generally speaking, the shorter the maturity of a bond the narrower is the range of fluctuation in its market price. Safety is preserved by restricting investments largely to government or government guaranteed bonds. Investments can be regarded as a kind of second line liquidity defence; indeed prior to the First World War they were commonly included among liquid assets. Provided some minimum proportion of assets is held in the form of investments, the banker can afford to hold most of the remainder of his assets in the more profitable form of advances.

Though advances are the most profitable of the bank assets they have a very serious liquidity disadvantage. They cannot be sold on a market, nor can a banker rely on forcing borrowers to repay at short notice, since the attempt to do so would often put customers in very grave difficulties. British banks have tended to restrict advances to those which are short-term (e.g. six months or a year) and to prefer those which are self-liquidating, that is where the completion of some project automatically provides the funds for repayment. It is sometimes suggested that the reason for this restriction is to minimize the illiquidity of advances. But R. S. Sayers, in his book *Modern Banking*, argues that the safety factor may be important, in that the degree of riskiness of a short-term self-liquidating loan lies much more within the practicable range of a bank manager's judgement than would a long-term direct investment in industry. British banks have often been criticized for their unwillingness to make longer-term advances, but it must be remembered that some short-term advances are renewed repeatedly and longer-term loans are also made through bank subsidiaries. In any case considerable changes are likely to occur in the practice of bank lending in the more competitive regime established by the new arrangements for credit control which are discussed in the next section and in Chapter 10.

3.5 THE ASSET STRUCTURE OF BRITISH DEPOSIT BANKS IN RECENT YEARS

In May 1971 the Bank of England made formal proposals for discussions with the banks on new techniques of monetary policy, and the proposals, which came into effect in September 1971, are likely to cause far reaching changes in the asset structure of banks in Britain. This section therefore describes, in the main, the asset structure of the deposit banks (mainly the London clearing banks) as it has existed in recent years, though an indication is given, where possible, of how the asset distribution may be affected by the new proposals. The Bank of England proposals are discussed in some detail in Chapter 10.

Discussion of the distribution of bank assets is complicated by the fact that deposits are not the only bank liability. As can be seen in Table 3.4 the liabilities of the clearing banks include capital, reserve funds, and provisions (including provisions for pensions, taxation, and dividends payable). Total bank assets therefore exceed total deposits, even after excluding the 'non-banking assets' of investments in subsidiaries and premises. A footnote to Table 3.4 draws the reader's attention to the meaning of *net deposits*. These are gross deposits less balances with, and cheques in course of collection on, other banks in the United Kingdom and the Republic of Ireland and less items in transit between offices of the same bank. Gross deposits

TABLE 3.4

LONDON CLEARING BANKS
LIABILITIES AND ASSETS: MARCH 1970

(£ million)

Capital		372	Cash and balance with B.E.	807
Reserve funds		771	Call and short money	1,352
Provisions		79	Bills discounted	750
Gross deposits*		9,785	Special deposits	205
Current accounts	5,169		Cheques for collection	378
Deposit accounts	4,394		Items in transit	169
Other accounts	222		Investments	1,153
			Advances	5,634
			Investments in subsidiaries	119
			Premises	441
		£11,007		£11,007

* Net deposits £9,239m, i.e. gross deposits (£9,785m) less items in transit (£169m) and cheques for collection (£378m).

therefore include an element of duplication. Table 3.5 shows the distribution in rather more detail of the 'banking assets' of the London clearing banks as at March 1970. The values of the main items are also expressed as percentages of gross deposits. The reader should beware of comparing banking statistics since the end of 1969 with statistics prior to that date. At the end of 1969 the London clearing banks and the Scottish and Northern Ireland banks made a number of accounting changes in connection with the full disclosure of profits and reserves. These changes have affected the statistics of gross deposits, investments, and advances. The reader is also reminded that the distribution will be rather different in the future now that the Bank of England proposals have taken effect.

We have seen that sound banking practice would require banks to keep some proportionate relationship between their holdings of cash and their deposit liabilities. But prior to 1946 the published cash ratios of some of the clearing banks were misleading. Books were made up on different days of the week so that it was possible for one bank to inflate its cash holding by borrowing cash, indirectly, from another bank which made up its books on a different day. This duplication of the same portion of cash was called 'window dressing'. From the end of 1946, at the request of the Bank of England, the

TABLE 3.5

LONDON CLEARING BANKS
DISTRIBUTION OF 'BANKING ASSETS' – MARCH 1970

	£ million		Percentage of gross deposits
Cash and balances with Bank of England		807	8·3
Cash in hand	610		
Balances with Bank of England	197		
Money at call and short notice		1,352	13·8
Discount market	815		
Other	537		
Bills discounted		750	7·7
Treasury bills	77		
U.K. commercial bills	308		
Other	365		
Total liquid assets		2,910	29·7
Special deposits with Bank of England		205	2·0
Investments		1,153	11·8
British govt. and govt. guaranteed	970		
Other	183		
Advances		5,634	57·6
Nationalized industries	104		
Other	5,530		

clearing banks agreed to dispense with window dressing; to make up all their books on the same day; and to keep the ratio of cash to gross deposits at approximately 8 per cent. In the new Bank of England proposals all banks will hold not less than 12½ per cent of their sterling deposit liabilities in certain specified reserve assets which are described below. No mention is made of a separate cash ratio requirement and, of the cash holdings, only the balance at the Bank of England is to be included among the specified reserve assets.

For very many years banks have sought to maintain a certain relationship between their holdings of liquid assets (including cash) and their gross deposits. The Chairman of the Midland Bank in evidence before the Committee on Finance and Industry (the Macmillan Committee Report published in 1931) stated that his bank sought to keep about one-third of assets in the form of cash, money at call and short notice, and bills. Later, in the 1930s the convention appears to have been accepted by the clearing banks generally of the minimum ratio of such assets to gross deposits of 30 per cent. When active monetary policy was resumed in 1951 minimum reserve requirements became a fulcrum of credit control. This involved an agreed convention of a minimum ratio, not only of cash to gross deposits, but also of total liquid assets to gross deposits. It also required a common definition of the assets to be regarded as liquid.

In 1951 the Bank of England intimated that a liquidity ratio (total liquid assets to gross deposits) of from 28 to 32 per cent would be regarded as normal and that no bank's ratio should ever fall below 25 per cent. Evidence given to the Radcliffe Committee indicates that by the mid 1950s the minimum acceptable ratio had become 30 per cent. But in the autumn of 1963 the Bank of England announced that this minimum ratio could be reduced to 28 per cent. One effect of the establishment of an agreed minimum liquidity ratio has been that in order to provide leeway for contingencies banks have sought to keep their liquid assets in excess of the minimum. The desirable amount of this excess has varied at different times of the year. Something like 40 per cent of tax revenue is paid during the first quarter of the calendar year. This causes a marked transfer of deposits to the public sector and an equal reduction in liquid assets, so that there has been a significant fall in the liquidity ratio during this quarter. To prevent the liquidity ratio falling below the minimum at this period of the year the banks required to build up the ratio well in excess of the minimum between April and December. The assets commonly agreed as falling within the liquid category included the following:

(1) Cash; that is, coin, bank notes, and balances with the Bank of England.
(2) Money at call and short notice: covering money lent to members of the London Discount Market Association; other short loans to non-clearing United Kingdom banks, stock exchange brokers and jobbers, and bullion brokers; specified foreign currency balances and foreign currency; and the banks' own holding of tax reserve certificates.
(3) United Kingdom Treasury bills.
(4) Other bills and re-financeable credits. These have included bills discounted for customers or bought in the market, and overseas Treasury bills. In February 1961 the Bank of England agreed to stand ready to re-finance instalments due for repayment within eighteen months on medium-term export credits guaranteed by the Export Credits Guarantee Department. This portion of export advances was therefore included in the liquid assets.

As mentioned above, the required liquidity ratio has now been replaced by a required minimum reserve assets ratio of 12½ per cent, applicable not only to the clearing banks but to all types of banks, including foreign banks and accepting houses. The reserve assets are to comprise cash at the Bank of England (but not banks' till money), British and Northern Ireland government Treasury bills, company tax reserve certificates, money at call with the London Money Market, British government securities with a year or less to run, local authority bills eligible for re-discount at the Bank of England, and, up to 2 per cent of eligible liabilities, commercial bills eligible for re-discount at the Bank of England.

It is perhaps worth emphasizing the main differences between the assets eligible for the reserve assets ratio and those eligible for the 28 per cent liquidity ratio. Excluded from the reserve assets are banks' till money, re-financeable export credits, commercial bills beyond the limit specified, and some elements of call money. Included for the first time are gilt-edged securities with less than a year to run. As the common reserve assets ratio has been fixed at 12½ per cent, the London clearing banks will find themselves holding more reserve assets than will be required. Of course these banks will wish to hold more than the minimum 12½ per cent of reserve assets in order to keep some leeway, and the authorities have taken steps to absorb some of the excess liquidity. Nevertheless the London clearing banks should have plenty of scope to substitute longer-dated securities and to meet additional demands for advances. Many other types of banks, which have traditionally held a very low proportion of liquid assets, will find themselves at some disadvantage in the new system.

Among the non-liquid assets listed in Table 3.5 the reader will notice *Special Deposits*. In April 1960 the Bank of England made the first use of a new technique of credit control by which the banks could be instructed to transfer cash to a Special Deposit at the Bank of England in amounts equal to a given percentage of their gross deposits, for example 1 or 2 per cent. Such a deposit is in effect frozen for a period of time at the discretion of the Bank of England, though interest is earned at the current Treasury bill rate. By calling for larger Special Deposits or by repaying them the Bank of England can influence the total liquid or reserve assets of the banks. This technique, including proposed modifications, will be further discussed in Chapter 10.

Investments formed a high proportion of assets in the early post-war years, but in recent years they have been around 10 to 13 per cent of gross deposits. This may be fairly close to what the banks would regard as a safe minimum for a second line liquidity reserve. Sales of investments have been the main defence against a fall in the liquidity ratio. By selling bonds to the public sector the banks obtain cash in exchange. By selling bonds to bank customers the banks reduce their deposit liabilities without reducing their liquid assets. In either case therefore sales of investments have raised the liquidity ratio. Advances of the clearing banks have fluctuated in recent years within a range of 47 to 58 per cent of gross deposits, under the influence of changes in the demand for advances and of variations in the extent to which advances have been controlled by the Bank of England. Generally speaking, if the proportion of advances falls, the proportion of investments rises. In other words investments are the main alternative asset to advances.

Bank assets in Tables 3.4 and 3.5 are listed in what is regarded as descending order of liquidity. But to some extent this order is misleading, since within each group of assets there is considerable variation in the degree of liquidity. For example, money at call and short notice includes loans as short as overnight and as long as one month. Some bills held will mature in a day or two, others may not mature for three months. Among the non-liquid assets there may be bonds which are almost due for repayment and which are more liquid than some of the bills held, while other bonds may not be due for repayment for, say, ten years. Similarly some advances will be due for repayment while others have only just been made.

The asset distribution of the Scottish banks has differed in several respects from that of the London clearing banks. In recent years the Scottish banks' liquid assets ratio has been very similar to that of the clearing banks. But within the liquid assets, cash has been a much larger item, generally about 17 per cent of gross deposits. This is because the cash holding has included cover for the Scottish banks' notes in circulation. The liquid assets have also included balances with, and cheques in course of collection on, other banks in the United Kingdom because these have been regarded as legitimate assets to the Scottish banks as a group. The investments ratio, at 18 per cent to 24 per cent, has been significantly higher than that of the clearing banks, with advances, at 43 to 51 per cent, significantly lower. Calls for Special Deposits from the Scottish banks, as percentages of gross deposits, have been half those called from the clearing banks. The asset distribution of Northern Ireland banks has been not dissimilar from that of the Scottish banks. There are, of course, many other types of banks in the United Kingdom, including accepting houses and overseas banks, but as their functions are very specialized they will be considered in a separate chapter. The reader is reminded that, as the new Bank of England proposals have now been put into effect, all banks will observe the same minimum reserve assets ratio, and the rate of call for Special Deposits will also be the same for all banks.

TABLE 3.6

LONDON CLEARING BANKS
ASSET DISTRIBUTION 1921 TO 1969
ANNUAL AVERAGE PERCENTAGES OF GROSS DEPOSITS

	Liquid assets	*Investments*	*Advances*
	%	%	%
1921–24	36	20	46
1925–31	32	15	54
1932–39	31	28	42
1940–51	27	27	24
1952–58	34	33	30
1959–63	33	19	45
1964–69	31	13	53

In conclusion it may be of interest to review briefly the changes which have occurred in the asset distribution pattern of the London clearing banks over the past fifty years. Table 3.6 shows the liquid assets, investments, and advances as percentages of gross deposits in a succession of fairly well defined periods since 1921. The percentages are in each case the annual average for each period. The reader should note that these percentages are not comparable with those from 1970 onwards because of the changes in accounting practice previously mentioned. They will be even less comparable with future banking statistics now that the new Bank of England proposals have come into effect.

The period 1921 to 1924 was one of intense post-war slump followed by gradual recovery, but the only noticeable feature from the point of view of asset distribution was a marked fall in the liquid assets ratio from 38 per cent in 1921 to 33 per cent in 1924. Between 1925 and 1931 was of course the period of the restored gold standard. The liquid assets ratio remained very steady but there was a marked shift in asset distribution from investments to advances as can be seen from Figure 3.1. The peak of the re-distribution was reached at the height of the post-war boom in 1929 when advances were 55 per cent

CURRENCY AND BANK DEPOSITS

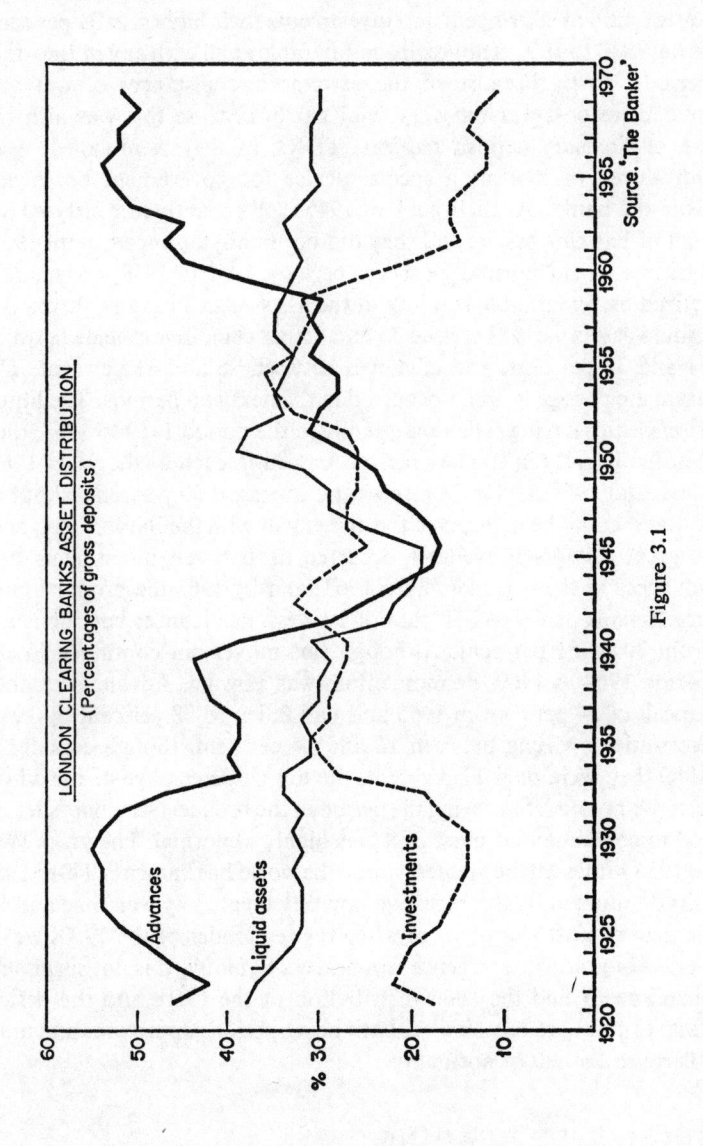

LONDON CLEARING BANKS ASSET DISTRIBUTION
(Percentages of gross deposits)

Source: "The Banker"

Figure 3.1

and investments 14 per cent. The next period was that of the great depression and of cheap money and was characterized by the reverse swing from advances to investments. In 1935 advances reached their lowest ratio at 39 per cent and investments their highest at 31 per cent. From 1940 to 1951 is not really comparable at all with any of the other periods, partly because of the extreme circumstances of war and immediate post-war recovery, and partly because this was also the era of Treasury deposit receipts. TDRs, as they were called, were introduced in 1940 as a special device for government borrowing from the banks. At their peak in 1945 they constituted nearly 40 per cent of banking assets, and they did not finally disappear until 1952. The first of the 'normal' post-war periods, 1952 to 1958, was characterized by remarkable stability in the asset distribution of the banks. Liquid assets varied between 33 and 35 per cent, investments between 31 and 35 per cent, and advances between 28 and 31 per cent. The dramatic change in trend occurred in the next two periods. The liquid assets ratio, having fallen marginally in the period 1959 to 1963, then fell significantly in the last period. Indeed in each of the years 1964, 1968, and 1969 the liquid assets ratio averaged 30 per cent, about as low as it could be in terms of the agreement with the Bank of England. A great scissors movement occurred as between investments and advances in the period 1959 to 1963; and by 1963 the proportion of investments held was half that of 1958 while advances had increased from 30 to 51 per cent. Although this movement continued in the period 1964 to 1969 the momentum was slowing. Advances reached a peak of 54 per cent in 1965 and had fallen to 52 per cent by 1969. Investments swung between 12 and 14 per cent, though actually in 1969 they were only 11 per cent, the lowest percentage of the whole fifty year period. Surveying the period in the broadest way one is tempted to conclude that most of it was highly abnormal. The years 1932 to 1936 witnessed the greatest slump the world has known; 1940 to 1951 was dominated by the excessive liquidity created by war-time and by immediate post-war finance; while the remainder of the 1950s was a period of gradual emergence from excess liquidity. It is not surprising therefore to find the asset distribution of the 1960s and the period 1925 to 1929 broadly similar, both being periods approximating most nearly to monetary normality.

SUGGESTED READING

R. S. Sayers, *Modern Banking*, 7th ed. (Oxford, 1967), chs. i, ii, v, vi, viii.

A. T. K. Grant, *The Machinery of Finance and the Management of Sterling* (Macmillan, 1967), chs. iii, iv.

R. S. Sayers, *Central Banking after Bagehot* (Oxford, 1957), particularly ch. viii.

M. Gaskin, *The Scottish Banks* (Allen & Unwin, 1965).

Bank of England Quarterly Bulletin, Mar. 1965, Mar. 1966.

4 The Theory of the Volume of Bank Deposits

4.1 FACTORS LIMITING THE CREATION OF DEPOSITS

In Chapter 3 we saw that changes in the volume of deposits in aggregate can occur through four different means: payments in or withdrawals of currency; transfers of deposits between the public sector and private sector; purchases or sales of securities by banks from or to bank customers; and increases or repayments of bank advances. We also saw that, although the banks play a passive role with regard to the first two, they have some degree of control over the latter two means. This raises the interesting question of the extent to which bankers, as a group, could increase the total volume of deposits by increasing their advances or by purchasing securities from bank customers.

One can distinguish three types of factors which can restrict bankers' ability to increase the volume of deposits on their own initiative. The first is the profitability of additional assets to the banks. The second is the willingness of customers to hold additional deposits. The third is the necessity for the banks to hold proportionate reserves of cash and of other liquid assets. To isolate the first two factors let us first imagine that the banks have reserves of cash and other liquid assets far in excess of minimum requirements and have no worry, therefore, on this score.

Banks can increase advances at given interest rates only so long as there is an unsatisfied demand for advances of the type that the banks regard as safe. The demand for advances will be influenced by the level of economic activity and of prices, and by the relationship between the interest charged and convenience of bank advances on the one hand, and the cost and convenience of alternative sources of finance on the other hand. It is true that an increase in bank advances will tend to stimulate greater economic activity so that to some extent the demand for advances will feed on the supply. But if banks try to expand advances continuously they are likely to find that at some point further demand for advances of a safe type can only be stimulated by a reduction in the rates of interest charged on advances. Given the marginal costs of administering a rising volume of bank deposits and the rates of interest that have to be paid on time deposits, reduction in loan rates would ultimately make further expansion of advances unprofitable.

Similar considerations would set an upper limit to bank purchases of securities from customers. The attractiveness of security purchases to banks depends either on the yield obtainable on such purchases, or upon prospects of capital gain in the event of security prices rising in the future. But, other things being equal, the more securities that the banks attempt to buy the higher the price they will have to pay; the lower will be the resulting yield and the less will be the probability that security prices will rise still higher in the future. Thus, ultimately, the return on additional security purchases would fail to cover the marginal costs of additional deposits.

The willingness of the public to hold additional deposits is of great importance. Here again, the demand for bank deposits is influenced by the level of economic activity and of prices. Since additional advances and additional security purchases from bank customers not only create additional deposits but also stimulate economic activity, the demand for bank deposits will also feed on the supply to some extent. Nevertheless, as we shall see later in this chapter, a continuous expansion of bank deposits is unlikely to be matched by an equal and contemporaneous expansion in the demand to hold wealth in the form of bank deposits. The recipients of additional deposits are likely to seek alternative and more rewarding ways of holding wealth at least with respect to some portion of the additional money holdings. For example, additional bank deposits may be transferred to non-bank intermediaries, such as building societies and finance companies, or they may be used to purchase bonds or equities. Such use of bank deposits does not necessarily destroy them. The additional bank deposits must remain in someone's ownership unless they are withdrawn in currency or transferred to another banking system. A transfer of a bank deposit to a private sector non-bank intermediary, in itself, merely involves a change in the ownership of the bank deposit. Similarly the use of bank deposits to purchase securities from other persons or institutions within the private sector merely means that ownership of bank deposits is transferred to the sellers of such securities. Nevertheless there will be further repercussions. An intermediary acquiring an addition to its bank deposit will be in a position to increase its lending and may compete successfully for loans which banks would otherwise have made. Additional demand for securities will tend to lower their yield, making such securities less profitable for banks to buy, while at the same time cheapening sources of finance which are alternative to bank advances. In other words the reluctance of the public to hold additional bank deposits will make it more difficult and less worthwhile for the banks to create further deposits by making advances or buying securities. It will bring nearer the point at which further expansion ceases to be profitable.

But the reluctance of the public to hold additional deposits may cause the destruction of some portion of the additional deposits created, or prevent some portion being created. To the extent that recipients of additional deposits transfer these to public sector intermediaries, such as the National Savings Bank, or acquire foreign securities, there will be a transfer of deposits to the public sector. Moreover since the creation of additional deposits is likely to be associated with a rise in national income and expenditure, it is also likely to be accompanied by larger withdrawal of currency, and larger transfers to the public sector to finance higher tax payments and higher imports. These aspects will be examined in more detail later in this chapter.

Even without any limitation set by reserve requirements there must always be some limit to the extent to which banks can expand deposits on their own initiative. The ultimate limit is set by the point at which further acquisition of assets by banks would be unprofitable, while, in practice, the creation of deposits would be further restricted by the induced 'leakages' of deposits by way of currency withdrawals and transfers to the public sector. The limiting point is largely conditioned by the intensity of the demand for bank advances and of the demand to hold additional bank deposits. This is not a static limit because both factors are influenced by the level of economic activity and of prices. In a growing economy the limit to the creation of bank deposits will be rising.

We must now turn to the third limiting factor, that is the need for banks to maintain minimum proportionate reserves in cash and other liquid assets. In Chapter 3 it was pointed out that the very existence of banking rests on confidence and, in particular, on confidence in the adequate liquidity of banks. Long ago bankers learned the necessity of maintaining an adequate proportion of their assets in a liquid form. In more recent years, as central banks have sought greater control and influence, such proportions have generally become fairly rigidly prescribed either by law or by agreement.

It was also argued in Chapter 3 that banks play a passive role as

THE THEORY OF THE VOLUME OF BANK DEPOSITS

regards the inflow and outflow of cash. Although they can normally get rid of surplus cash by buying securities from the public sector, they cannot rely on augmenting cash at will by selling securities to the public sector or by borrowing indirectly from the central bank. This limitation arises partly from the fact that the central bank reserves the right to decide what, if any, classes of securities it is prepared to buy, and reserves the right to charge a 'penal' rate on loans. It arises also from the fact that banks' holdings of securities of the types that the central bank would buy may not be sufficient to enable them to sell such securities for cash without reducing their holdings of money market assets below a prescribed minimum ratio, or indeed their holdings of investments below what the banks consider to be a safe ratio.

The limitation on the ability of banks to augment at will their holdings of cash, if coupled with an obligation to maintain a more-or-less fixed ratio of cash to deposits, can operate as an effective cut-off to any attempt of the banks to expand deposits by, say, increasing their advances. Suppose, for example, that bank cash holdings happen to be £1,000 million, that the banks are not able to increase these cash holdings significantly, and that they are obliged to maintain a ratio of cash to deposits of 8 per cent. It is obvious that in these circumstances the banks cannot allow their deposits to exceed £12,500 million, that is £1,000 million multiplied by 100/8. Any increase in bank advances would have to be offset by sales of investments to bank customers.

Such a cash reserve limitation may not always be operative. If as a result of heavy government expenditure there is a large and continuous transfer of deposits from the public sector to the private sector, there will also be (as we saw in Chapter 3) a continuous and equal transfer of cash to the banks. In such a situation it is unlikely that cash shortage would inhibit an expansion of bank advances and bank deposits. It might well be that expansion of advances is impeded either by inadequate demand or by government restrictions on bank lending. Then, in order to preserve the 8 per cent cash ratio, the banks would have to get rid of surplus cash by purchasing additional securities from the public sector. This sort of situation will be discussed at the end of this chapter and also in Chapter 5.

In the absence of the type of situation just described one can generally expect that attempts by banks to expand deposits on their own initiative will be impeded by their inability to increase their holdings of cash. In normal circumstances the cash reserve limitation will operate to cut off an expansion of bank advances or bank purchases of securities from customers well below the level at which further expansion would be unprofitable. One can conclude therefore that, of the three factors which restrict bankers' ability to expand deposits on their own initiative, it will usually be the third that is the operative limiting factor.

In Chapter 3 it was pointed out that the central bank can deliberately produce changes in bank cash holdings through open market operations. Does this give the central bank power to control the volume of bank deposits? We must now begin to examine this question.

4.2 INTRODUCTION TO THE THEORY OF CONTROL OF DEPOSITS

If banks maintain a fixed ratio between their holdings of cash and their deposit liabilities it is obvious that total deposits must always equal cash holdings multiplied by the reciprocal of the cash ratio. For example, if the fixed cash ratio is 8 per cent, then $D = C.100/8$, where D is total deposit and C is cash holdings. It also follows that if banks maintain a minimum ratio of all liquid assets or of specified reserve assets to deposits, then total deposits will never exceed these asset holdings multiplied by the reciprocal of the required minimum ratio. For example, if there is a required minimum liquid assets ratio of 28 per cent, then D cannot exceed $L.100/28$, where L is liquid asset holdings. Alternatively, if there is a required minimum ratio of specified reserve assets of, say, $12\frac{1}{2}$ per cent, then D cannot exceed $R.100/12 \cdot 5$, where R is holdings of reserve assets. But these are simply arithmetic relationships; they do not imply any causal relationship between cash and deposits or between other asset holdings and deposits. One cannot deduce, for example, that cash holdings determine deposits any more than that deposits determine cash holdings. If it could be shown, however, that banks cannot control the size of their cash holdings but that the authorities can do so, it would seem to follow that the authorities would have the power to control the total of deposits by manipulation of the cash base. Alternatively, if the banks cannot control their total liquid assets, or their holdings of specified reserve assets, whichever is required, but the authorities can control the relevant asset holdings, then the authorities would have power to control the upper limit of deposits by varying the supply of liquid assets, or of reserve assets, as the case may be.

In Chapter 3 we saw that from the 1950s the London clearing banks were required to maintain both a fixed cash ratio and a minimum ratio of all liquid assets. This led to an interesting academic controversy over which ratio in principle can call the tune. The reader will recall that in the new monetary policy techniques, which took effect in September 1971, the liquid assets ratio is replaced by a required minimum ratio of specified reserve assets, including Bankers' Balances at the Bank of England. No mention is made of cash ratio requirements, though no doubt banks will, in their own interests, maintain a fairly steady cash ratio. But this does not remove the issue of principle. The question is merely modified to whether deposits can be controlled through a reserve assets ratio or whether manipulation of the cash base, in conjunction with a stable cash ratio, remains the only effective mode of control. The controversy, therefore, still has relevance. Accordingly, the theory of control via the cash base is examined in the next section. Since this theory is based on the maintenance of a fixed cash ratio it is assumed, for illustrative purposes, that the required ratio is 8 per cent though, as we have seen, this is no longer applicable in Britain. In Sections 4.4 and 4.5 the historical controversy over control via the liquid assets ratio is reviewed; and the relevance of this controversy to the reserve assets ratio is discussed in Chapter 10.

4.3 THE THEORY OF CONTROL VIA THE CASH BASE

Open market sales by the Bank of England consist of sales in the market of either Treasury bills or government bonds. It is necessary to distinguish sales made direct to the banks, sales to the general public (normal bank customers), and sales made direct to the discount houses.

In Chapter 3 it was pointed out that Bank of England sales of securities to the banks simply result in a re-distribution of bank assets. The banks substitute securities for cash, and bank deposits are not affected directly. Clearly banks will only exchange cash for securities voluntarily if they consider their cash holdings excessive. In other words, Bank of England sales of securities to banks are merely a means of mopping up surplus cash.

Sales of securities by the Bank of England to bank customers are a very different matter. The first point to note is that such sales can always be made if a low enough price is offered. The second point is that such sales involve a double exchange of assets, one of which is voluntary and the other involuntary. As we have just seen, bank customers can be induced to exchange voluntarily bank deposits for securities by a sufficient reduction in the market price of securities. But the Bank of England is now in possession of cheques drawn on the deposit banks. These are exchanged by the Bank of England for part of the cash holdings of the deposit banks, in effect, by debiting Bankers' Balances at the Bank of England. The deposit banks have no option in the matter, since of course they are obliged to pay cash on demand. An open market sale of securities to bank customers leads, therefore, to an equal reduction in bank deposits and bank cash holdings. This implies a reduction in the ratio of cash to deposits. Suppose, for example, that initially deposits are £1,000 million, cash holdings £80 million, so that the cash ratio is 8 per cent. Then an open market sale to bank customers amounting to £1 million would reduce deposits to £999 million and cash holdings to £79 million. One can see that the cash ratio has been reduced to 7·9 per cent approximately. An open market sale of £10 million would have reduced the cash ratio to approximately 7·1 per cent.

Bank of England sales of securities to discount houses must be distinguished from sales to the general public because the former keep their main accounts with the Bank of England and should not therefore be regarded as customers of deposit banks for this purpose. It follows that sales of securities to the discount houses will not necessarily affect bank deposits. The security purchases by the discount houses presuppose one of three eventualities. The discount houses may buy the securities simply to get rid of surplus cash. Secondly, the banks may have lent surplus cash to the discount houses, enabling the latter to take up the security sales. The effect is then as though the banks had bought the securities directly, except that the banks exchange cash for call money instead of cash for securities. In neither of these cases are bank deposits directly affected, nor is it likely that bank cash holdings would be reduced below any required ratio. The third case, however, is quite different. The discount houses may obtain the funds to buy the securities either by selling other securities to bank customers, or by borrowing money from them. In either event there would be an equal reduction in bank deposits and bank cash holdings, and consequently a fall in the cash ratio. The effect of this third case is the same as though the Bank of England had sold securities direct to bank customers.

To summarize so far, open market sales by the Bank of England may simply mop up surplus cash held by the banks or by the discount houses, with no effect on bank deposits. But if neither the banks nor the discount houses hold surplus cash then such sales can only be absorbed by bank customers, either directly, or indirectly where bank customers absorb securities sold by the discount houses or where bank customers lend funds to the discount houses. One can conclude therefore that, when neither the banks nor the discount houses hold surplus cash, open market sales will cause bank deposits and bank cash holdings to fall equally and will cause the cash ratio to fall.

What would happen if open market sales caused the cash ratio to fall below an agreed minimum? The immediate obligation would be to restore the cash ratio. To do this without delay the banks must acquire additional cash. But one must note that restoration of the cash ratio does not necessitate complete restoration of the previous level of cash reserves, because the open market sales will also have reduced the level of deposits. The simple example used above can illustrate this point. We supposed that initially deposits were £1,000 million, cash reserves £80 million, and the cash ratio 8 per cent. Open market sales amounting to £1 million reduced deposits to £999 million, cash reserves to £79 million, and the cash ratio to 7·9 per cent approximately. To restore the 8 per cent cash ratio the banks must raise cash reserves to £79·92 million, which is 8 per cent of £999 million. The banks must therefore acquire £920,000 of additional cash.

The first line of defence of the banks, when they lose cash involuntarily, is to substitute money market assets for cash. They can do this in one of two ways. They may call in short loans made to the discount houses, and the latter will be obliged to obtain the necessary cash from the Bank of England by borrowing or re-discounting. Alternatively the banks can fail to replace their holdings of Treasury bills as they mature. The Treasury has to meet maturing bills by payment in cash, so the banks automatically recover cash by this means. Provided that the banks are holding sufficient Treasury bills which are about to mature they can quickly restore their cash holdings. But it has been the custom of the London clearing banks, when replacing Treasury bills, to buy them from the discount houses. This means that failure to replace Treasury bills would deprive the discount houses of cash which they would otherwise have obtained. In this second method, therefore, the discount houses would be equally obliged to obtain cash from the Bank of England.

In this model everything depends now on whether the Bank of England chooses to supply cash at current market rates of interest (through the 'open back door') or at the penal Bank rate (through the 'front door'). It is very important to note that the theory of control via the cash base assumes that the Bank of England supplies cash *only* at Bank rate. The effect of the Bank of England lending at current market rates will be examined later in this chapter.

Borrowing or re-discounting at Bank rate involves the discount houses in running losses because Bank rate is always maintained above the market rate of interest which the discount houses earn on their holdings of Treasury bills. Since these losses continue as long as the discount houses are in debt to the Bank of England, the former have an incentive to get out of debt as soon as possible. To do this the discount houses must acquire additional cash, but in the circumstances they clearly cannot borrow more from the banks. There are, however, three other possible ways. First, in theory, the discount houses could fail to replace their own holdings of Treasury bills as they mature, thus obtaining the cash from the Treasury. In this event the Bank of England would be forced to sell the new issues of Treasury bills, which the discount houses would otherwise have bought, to bank customers, and this would cause an equal fall in bank deposits and bank cash reserves, and thus a fall in the cash ratio. In practice this method is not available since the discount houses have an agreement with the Bank of England to 'cover the tender', that is they undertake to buy all the new issue of Treasury bills not sold elsewhere in the market. A second method would be for the discount houses to fail to replace their holdings of commercial bills as they mature. In so far as the maturing bills are drawn on British banks the settlement of the bills would cause a transfer of cash from the banks to the discount houses, an equal fall in bank deposits, and a reduction in the cash ratio. Finally, the discount houses could acquire additional cash by increasing their borrowing from bank customers or by selling bills or short bonds to such customers. Once again there would be an equal fall in bank deposits and bank cash, and a reduction in the cash ratio.

From this discussion it can be seen that each method that the discount houses employ to get out of debt to the Bank of England will deprive the banks of the cash they had gained and will reduce the cash ratio below the agreed minimum. In other words the banks cannot permanently restore their cash ratio, following an open market sale, by substituting money market assets for cash. They could, of course, keep repeating the operation of calling in short loans or failing to replace Treasury bills as they mature. But each time the discount houses succeed in getting out of debt to the Bank of England there is a further reduction in bank deposits, and each time also bank cash reserves fall back to the level to which they were initially reduced by the open market sales. One could

THE THEORY OF THE VOLUME OF BANK DEPOSITS 79

imagine equilibrium being restored eventually when deposits had been reduced to the level consistent with the reduced cash base.

The principle of the above process can be illustrated by the highly simplified example shown in Table 4.1. Stage 1 is the initial position.

TABLE 4.1

BANKS' ADJUSTMENT TO AN OPEN MARKET SALE
A simplified example

	Stage	1	2	3	4	5	6	Final position
Deposits	£m	2,000	1,990	1,990	1,980·8	1,980·8	1,972·3	1,875
Cash	£m	160	150	159·2	150	158·5	150	150
Cash ratio	%	8	7·53	8	7·57	8	7·6	8
Money market assets	£m	400	400	390·8	390·8	382·3	382·3	285
Investments and advances	£m	1,440	1,440	1,440	1,440	1,440	1,440	1,440

In Stage 2 there is an open market sale amounting to £10 million which reduces deposits and cash by £10 million and reduces the cash ratio to 7·53 per cent. In Stage 3 the banks restore the cash ratio to 8 per cent by calling loans amounting to £9·2 million from the discount market. This reduces bank holdings of money market assets to £390·8 million. In the meantime the discount houses obtain the funds to repay the banks by borrowing £9·2 million from the Bank of England. In Stage 4 the discount houses get out of debt to the Bank of England by, say, borrowing £9·2 million from bank customers, so that bank deposits and bank cash both fall by this amount and the cash ratio becomes 7·57 per cent. A similar sequence of events follows through successive stages. Each time the discount houses get out of debt to the Bank of England the cash reserves of the banks get pulled back to £150 million but bank deposits are further reduced. It can easily be seen that when bank deposits have been reduced to £1,875 million the cash ratio is restored to 8 per cent on the cash base of £150 million. This new equilibrium position could have been reached without all this to-ing and fro-ing had the banks responded to the open market sale of £10 million by selling investments to customers or calling in advances to the amount of £115 million, since this would have reduced deposits to £1,875 million. It must be emphasized that this example is not representative of what was likely to occur in real life. It is intended merely to illustrate the point that, on the assumptions made, the banks cannot escape adjusting deposits when open market sales reduce the cash base.

We must now examine the secondary consequences of an attempt to reduce bank deposits by open market sales, since these consequences may be such as to make the technique impracticable. It was mentioned at the beginning of this section that, to carry out open market sales, the Bank of England must be prepared to see the market price of securities fall sufficiently to induce the general public to substitute securities for bank deposits. Now a fall in the market price of a security is the same thing as a rise in its yield. Two examples can illustrate this. The first example is that of an undated bond which can be typified by $2\frac{1}{2}$ per cent Consols. The holder of a $2\frac{1}{2}$ per cent Consols bond nominally valued at £100 receives £2·5 a year indefinitely. If the market price of this bond is £50 then a purchaser, at this price, would have a yield of 5 per cent (£2·5 a year on an outlay of £50). If the market price falls to £40 the yield rises to $6\frac{1}{4}$ per cent. Since the rate of interest on new issues must be comparable with the market yield on existing securities a rise in yields implies a rise in rates of interest on new issues. The second example is of a bill of exchange. Suppose we have a £100 bill due to mature in three months. If the market price of the bill today is £99 then a buyer will earn £1 on an outlay of £99 over a period of three months – a yield of approximately 4 per cent per annum. If the market price of the bill falls to £98 the return, for a buyer, is £2 on £98 over three months, which is approximately 8 per cent per annum. From these examples the general conclusion can be drawn that a selling pressure in security markets which drives down security prices will also raise market yields and rates of interest.

Open market sales of securities by the central bank will therefore tend to raise yields or rates of interest, and rates must rise sufficiently to induce bank customers to substitute securities for bank deposits. If the central bank sells Treasury bills it will be short-term interest rates which primarily rise, while if it is bonds that are sold the rise in rates will tend to be at the longer end of the market. But that is not the end of the matter. As we have seen, the banks, in this model, restore the cash ratio by forcing the discount houses to obtain cash from the Bank of England. The discount houses, in turn, seek to get out of debt by selling bills or short bonds to bank customers or by borrowing from bank customers. Interest rates, therefore, have to rise still further to persuade bank customers to substitute bills, short bonds, or call loans for bank deposits. The question is how far must interest rates rise to persuade bank customers to acquire the additional securities sold, not only by the Bank of England, but also by the discount houses at the various stages of adjustment? This question can be put in another and more general way. If bank deposits are to be reduced customers must be persuaded to give up bank deposits in return for securities. How much must interest rates rise to induce any given reduction in the demand to hold bank deposits?

In principle a rise in interest rates can reduce the demand for bank deposits in two ways. In the first place a rise in interest rates may make securities relatively more attractive than before as a way of holding wealth alternative to holding bank deposits. This may induce some substitution of securities for bank deposits. In the second place higher interest rates tend to have a deflationary influence on the general level of expenditure. For example, the rise in the cost of borrowing may discourage expenditure on capital goods, durables, etc. If, as a result, the general level of expenditure falls, the public will have less need to hold money and may, in consequence, prefer to hold a smaller proportion of wealth in bank deposits and more in the form of securities.

As far as short-term rates of interest (e.g bill rates) are concerned it is widely believed that expenditure is insensitive to a rise in such rates. If this view is accepted, the reduction in the demand for bank deposits will depend on the extent to which a rise in short rates will directly induce a substitution of bills, short-term bonds, and call loans for bank deposits. It is sometimes argued that the market for such securities and loans is largely restricted to institutional operators who generally do not hold bank deposits in excess of minimum requirements. To take up more bills etc. such operators would have to reduce their lending elsewhere. In consequence, short rates might have to rise very high indeed to induce any significant reduction in the demand for bank deposits. This argument, however, seems to leave out of account the reactions of the more general public. Reduction in lending elsewhere by institutional operators will tend to cause a rise in a wide range of interest rates, including deposit rates offered by some non-bank intermediaries, such as finance companies. Even a moderate rise in interest rates offered by such intermediaries might induce a significant transfer of bank deposits to these intermediaries.

If the rise in interest rates spreads to the longer end of the market (e.g. long-term bond yields), there is a stronger prospect that the level of expenditure will be deflated, since longer-term rates probably play a more significant role in capital investment appraisal. However, there is generally a considerable, but variable, time lag between changes in interest rates and resulting changes in expenditure. In the short run, therefore, it is unlikely that there will be much reduction in the demand to hold money on this score. On the other hand a rise in longer-term rates of interest will impinge on a wide range of wealth-owners. One would therefore expect the substitution effect to be much more significant than where only short-term interest rates rise. Nevertheless one cannot always be certain even of the direction of portfolio adjustments because of the dominant influence of expectations in the short run. For example, if a rise in longer-term rates creates a general expectation that rates will rise still higher in the future, speculators and other investors may postpone purchases, or even sell securities, so as to avoid the prospective loss should security prices fall still further. This reaction of expectations is the more likely if it is known that the rise in rates has been instigated by the central bank.

From the above discussion it can be seen that there is much uncertainty as to the extent of the changes in interest rates which would result from attempts to control the volume of bank deposits by variations of the cash base. For a number of years the British monetary authorities have taken the view that the degree and unpredictability of interest rate fluctuations which would result from this type of policy are likely to be so serious as to conflict with other objectives of monetary and economic policy. Bank deposits could be controlled via control of the cash base but the price paid might not be worth the candle.

The analysis of this section has been conducted in terms of reductions in a cash base and open market sales. The reverse operations have been ignored partly in the interest of brevity and partly because policies of restraint are more relevant to the conditions experienced since the war. But the reader would find it useful to work out for himself the effects of increases in a cash base through open market purchases.

4.4 THE THEORY OF CONTROL VIA TOTAL LIQUID ASSETS

The view that the total liquid asset holdings of the banks, in conjunction with the required minimum liquid assets ratio, was the crucial regulator of bank deposits, first came to prominence in the middle 1950s. In a modified form this view also received support in the Radcliffe Report. But it has been a subject of considerable controversy, and in recent years it came under increasing attack.

An article by the late W. M. Dacey in *Lloyds Bank Review* of

April 1956 was influential in propagating what has been called the 'new orthodox' theory. It may be helpful, therefore, to outline the main features of the model on which Mr Dacey's argument rested. All models are based on arbitrary assumptions, and, in summary form, those of the Dacey model are as follows.

(a) The banks maintain fixed liquidity ratios – an 8 per cent cash ratio and a 30 per cent total liquid assets ratio.
(b) The total liquid assets of the banks consist solely of cash, short loans to the discount houses (call money), and Treasury bills.
(c) Discount house assets consist solely of Treasury bills, and their sole source of finance from the private sector consists of short loans from the banks.
(d) All Treasury bills in the private sector are held either by the banks or by the discount houses.

Assumptions (b), (c), and (d) imply that the only money market assets available to banks are Treasury bills, held either directly or indirectly via short loans to the discount houses, and that the banks and discount houses, taken together, are the sole market for Treasury bills.

It is easy enough to see that in this model the Bank of England would be precluded from reducing the cash base by open market sales of Treasury bills, since neither the banks nor the discount houses would buy extra bills if they held no surplus cash. However, the Bank of England can still make open market sales of bonds to bank customers, and this would reduce deposits and cash equally, causing a fall in the cash ratio. But the banks can recover their cash from the Treasury by failing to replace existing Treasury bills as they mature. Now if one assumes that (i) the government is unable to reduce its total borrowing by achieving a larger budget surplus or smaller deficit, and that (ii) the government is unwilling to reduce the portion of its borrowing by way of Treasury bill issues, then the Bank of England would be forced to reverse the open market operation to persuade the banks to replace their bill holdings. This amounts to saying that if the banking system, including the discount houses, is the sole market for Treasury bills, and if the Treasury bill issue is not reduced, the Bank of England is precluded from taking any action to reduce the cash base, since the Treasury bill issue could not then be placed.

This conclusion immediately suggests that control of deposits must be through variation in the Treasury bill issue. The issue could be reduced in two ways. In the first place the Treasury bill issue could be reduced if the government reduced its total borrowing, for example by curtailing its expenditure or by increasing taxation. In the second place the form of government borrowing could be changed. Larger bond sales could replace part of the Treasury bill issue. This is a device known as funding. The first method, that is via budgetary measures, involves more than monetary consequences, and clearly cannot be varied frequently or at short notice. But these difficulties do not apply to changes in the form of borrowing, hence this school of thought placed its faith in funding and unfunding operations as the appropriate method of control of bank deposits.

To make the theory clear it is worth tracing the repercussions of a funding operation. Suppose the authorities sell £x of bonds to bank customers and at the same time issue £x less of Treasury bills. As we have seen previously, the sale of bonds causes an equal fall in deposits and bank cash holdings. On the other hand, the reduction in the Treasury bill issue, in conjunction with the settlement of the bills currently maturing (i.e. of those issued three months previously), cause a transfer of cash from the Treasury to the banking system amounting to £x. The loss of cash due to the bond sales is therefore neutralized. At this point deposits are reduced by £x, cash holdings are at the original level, but Treasury bill holdings (or call money) are reduced by £x. Total liquid assets (cash plus Treasury bill holdings and call money) are therefore reduced by that amount. If deposits and total liquid assets are reduced by the same amount, the total liquid assets ratio must be reduced. On the assumptions of the model the ratio was initially at the required level of 30 per cent, so that the funding operation has pushed the liquid assets ratio below the required minimum. The banks are therefore forced to dispose of earning assets (investments or advances) until deposits have been reduced sufficiently to restore the 30 per cent ratio. It was admitted that, in practice, banks frequently hold liquid assets in excess of the required minimum. But this would not detract from the principle of control by funding since, if funding were pushed far enough, a reduction in the liquid assets ratio below the required minimum could be achieved.

The logic of the theory appears to be sound. The weakness lies in the assumptions of the model, notably the assumptions that the banking system provides the sole market for Treasury bills, and that Treasury bills (directly or indirectly held) are the sole non-cash liquid asset available to the banks. There is, in fact, an 'outside' market for Treasury bills. The existence of this market implies that the banking system cannot frustrate an attempt by the Bank of England to reduce cash holdings through open market sales, by refusing to replace maturing bills. Provided that the authorities are willing to allow bill rates to rise high enough, other buyers for the Treasury bill issue can be found among the institutional customers of the banks. On the other hand, banks need not be forced to reduce deposits by a reduction in the Treasury bill issue, due to funding, because if the banks and discount houses are willing to bid down bill rates far enough they can secure a larger share of the reduced Treasury bills available. Thus the existence of an 'outside' market for Treasury bills destroys the theory that the Bank of England cannot vary a cash base by open market operations; and it also destroys the theory that a reduction in the Treasury bill issue could enforce a reduction in bank deposits.

But the weakness of the 'new orthodox' theory was shown to be graver still when account was taken of the fact that bank liquid assets were not restricted to cash and Treasury bills holdings (directly or indirectly held). As we saw in Chapter 3 bank liquid assets included commercial bills, re-financeable export credits, short loans to the discount houses to finance the latter's holdings of commercial bills and short bonds, and short loans to the stock exchange. Moreover the banks are not the sole source of finance for the discount houses. There are 'outside' lenders. This means that banks can increase short loans to the discount houses if the latter reduce their 'outside' borrowing, or if the discount houses obtain a larger share of the Treasury bill issue from 'outside' investors. Thus a reduction in the Treasury bill issue did not necessarily exert pressure on the banks if other liquid assets could be found to replace the Treasury bills. Indeed, as W. T. Newlyn has pointed out, a funding operation actually made it easier for banks to secure liquid assets. The reduction in the supply of Treasury bills tends to cause a fall in bill rates (a rise in the market price of bills), and other short-term market rates tend to fall in sympathy. This reduction in short rates is likely to encourage greater borrowing by discount of commercial bills, increasing the supply of such bills available to the banks. At the same time the 'outside' demand for Treasury bills is likely to be discouraged, leaving the discount houses with a larger share of the total issue. The fall in short rates may also discourage 'outside' lending to the discount houses. For both reasons the banks may find it easier to expand short loans to the discount houses.

4.5 THE RADCLIFFE VIEW OF THE CONTROVERSY

It will be recalled that the theory of control via the cash base assumes that the Bank of England lends only at the penal Bank rate. We also saw in Section 4.3 that control via the cash base involves fluctuations in short-term and other rates of interest, and that these fluctuations might be very considerable.

The Radcliffe Report stated that 'Because the Bank of England wants reasonable stability in the Treasury bill rate, and believes that the market for these bills is narrowly limited, the Bank prefers to deal very freely between cash and Treasury Bills'.* The Report went on to argue that 'the Bank cannot restrain the lending operation of the clearing banks by limiting the creation of cash without losing its assurance of the stability of the rate on Treasury Bills.'* These quotations make it quite clear that control via the cash base was not employed because the authorities were not prepared to risk the instability of short rates which might result. The Bank preferred to supply cash normally at current market rates (through the 'open back door') rather than lend solely at the penal Bank rate. But the Radcliffe Report contended that 'It is because of this circumstance that the effective base of bank credit has become the liquid assets.'* This is a very different argument from that of the crude theory of control by funding, and we must now investigate this contention.

We saw in Section 4.4 that a funding operation did not necessarily have any effect on the total of bank deposits. In brief, the argument was as follows. A sale of £x of bonds by the Bank of England to ordinary bank customers caused both bank deposits and bank cash holdings to fall by that amount. But if, at the same time, the authorities repaid £x of Treasury bills, by issuing less Treasury bills than currently matured, bank cash holdings were fully restored. And if the banks acquired sufficient alternative money market assets they could re-expand their deposits to the former level by acquiring additional earning assets.

The authorities, however, did not need to restore fully the cash holdings of the banks. Indeed they could not do so if they wished to avoid a fall in short-term rates of interest. If the authorities had repaid Treasury bills by the full amount of the bond sales, the shortage of Treasury bills and the competition of the banks to restore their total liquid assets would have caused a fall in short-term rates of interest. To avoid this, the authorities had to prevent the full restoration of bank cash reserves. It was the attempt to keep short rates stable, at the time of a funding operation, which altered the situation.

The effects, in principle, of this type of operation can be demonstrated by means of a simplified model. This assumes that banks are required to maintain an 8 per cent cash ratio and a minimum liquid

* Radcliffe Report, Cmnd. 827, para. 376.

ratio of 28 per cent. The repercussions of the funding operation are here divided into four stages. In Stage 1 we assume that the authorities sell 100 units worth of bonds to bank customers. Bank deposits, bank cash holdings, and total liquid assets are each reduced by 100 units. The cash ratio is pushed below 8 per cent. In Stage 2 the banks take steps to restore the 8 per cent ratio. Since deposits are reduced by 100 units the ratio can be restored if the banks can recover 92 units of cash, so that cash reserves are reduced only by 8 units. The banks therefore call in loans from the discount market to the amount of 92 units. Now also in Stage 2 we assume that the authorities repay 100 units of Treasury bills in cash to the discount houses, but at the same time make open market sales of Treasury bills of 8 units to the discount houses. The latter therefore receive a net amount of cash from the Bank of England amounting to 92 units, just sufficient to repay the banks. The open market sale of 8 units was necessary to ensure that neither the banks nor the discount houses were left with any surplus cash at this stage.

Although the banks have restored their cash ratio they are still left with the problem, which arose in Stage 1, of the reduction in their total liquid assets of 100 units. They succeed in recovering 92 units of cash, but this was at the expense of an equal reduction in their call money. If we assume that prior to the funding operation their total liquid assets ratio was at the required minimum, and assume this to be 28 per cent, then the equal reduction of deposits and total liquid assets must have reduced the ratio below 28 per cent. How can they restore this ratio? They cannot attempt to buy additional money market assets from bank customers since such action would raise total deposits, and the cash position would prevent this. They have no option, therefore, but to reduce their total deposit liabilities by disposing of earning assets (selling investments or calling in advances). With total liquid assets reduced by 100 units, restoration of the 28 per cent ratio requires a further reduction in deposits of 257 units. This in conjunction with the initial reduction in deposits by the Bank of England sale of bonds will make a total reduction in deposits of 357 units. If total liquid assets are reduced by 100 units and deposits by 357 units the ratio of 28 per cent is maintained, since 100 is 28 per cent of 357. In Stage 3, therefore, we assume that the banks restore the required 28 per cent liquid assets ratio by disposing of 257 units of earning assets.

The banks, however, are still left with a problem because the cash ratio is now excessive. This can easily be demonstrated. If deposits are reduced by 357 units, maintenance of the 8 per cent cash ratio requires a reduction in cash holdings of 28·56 units, since 28·56 is 8 per cent of 357. But cash reserves have only been reduced by 8 units (the banks lost 100 units of cash from the Bank of England bond sales but recovered 92 units by calling in loans from the discount houses). The banks therefore hold 20·56 units more cash than they require and, within the total liquid assets, 20·56 units too few money market assets. In Stage 4 the banks attempt to correct this situation by increasing short loans to the discount houses by 20·56 units. But this would enable the discount houses to compete for additional bills and would cause a fall in short-term rates of interest. To prevent this (also in Stage 4) the Bank of England makes open market sales of Treasury bills of 20·56 units to the discount houses.

Banking equilibrium is now restored. Deposits have been reduced by 357 units. Total liquid assets have been reduced by 100 units (by the original funding operation), and the 28 per cent liquid assets ratio is restored. Bank cash reserves have been reduced by 28·56 units (in effect, by the open market sales of Treasury bills in Stage 2 and Stage 4), and the 8 per cent cash ratio is restored. And short-term rates of interest have been kept stable. It should be noted, however, that long-term rates will have been pushed up, not only by the initial sale of 100 units of bonds by the Bank of England, but also to the extent that the banks produced the further fall in deposits of 257 units by sales of investments.

As far as this crude model is concerned the funding operation has been associated with a reduction in deposits. It can be argued that it was the reduction of 100 units of liquid assets which caused the 357 unit reduction in deposits – a reduction equal to 100/28 times the funding operation. But it is also true that the cash base was reduced by 28·56 units as a result of open market sales of bills, and the reduction in deposits is equal to 100/8 times the fall in the cash base. One can therefore argue that the cause of the fall in deposits was the reduction in the cash base – a reduction selected to keep short-term rates of interest stable. The latter contention seems to be the better of the two because, were it not for the open market sales of bills, bank cash reserves would have been restored to the pre-funding level and the banks could have competed for sufficient additional money market assets to enable them to restore their deposits to the pre-funding level. But short rates would have fallen.

The conclusion from the rather lengthy discussion of these last three sections is that the authorities could, if they chose, exercise some deliberate control over the volume of deposits by variation of a cash base through open market operations. Moreover it seems that it is only a cash base, in conjunction with a required cash ratio, which can provide a firm fulcrum of control. In recent years, at least, the authorities did not choose to use this form of control for a variety of reasons which must be examined later.

4.6 THE THEORY OF THE BANK DEPOSIT MULTIPLIER

The reader will have noticed in the previous three sections of this chapter an implication that a given open market operation is capable of inducing a change in bank deposits which, in total, is several times greater. The reader may also have inferred that a change in bank cash holdings will necessarily cause a change in bank deposits which is some predictable multiple of the change in cash. What truth is there in this? Can one predict mechanically the change in the total of deposits which will follow the change in the cash base? To investigate these questions it is useful at the outset to construct two models in each of which a predictable deposit multiplier would operate. Both models are based on a number of artificial assumptions. Assumptions 1 to 4 inclusive are made merely to simplify analysis, but the other assumptions are essential to the operation of a predictable multiplier. The model assumptions are as follows.

1. Deposits are the only liabilities of the banks, and the only bank assets are cash and advances.
2. There are four banks of equal size. Payments of currency into banks by the general public are normally spread evenly between the four banks.
3. Each bank seeks to maintain an 8 per cent ratio of cash to deposits.
4. Bank advances are withdrawn by borrowers in currency. There is a lag of one time period between a borrower's withdrawal of an advance in currency and the re-deposit of currency by the ultimate recipients of the currency, also a lag of one period between a receipt of currency by banks and a subsequent increase in advances.
5. There is an unsatisfied demand for bank advances at current rates of interest.
6. There are no transfers of deposits or currency between the public sector and the private sector, other than that of a specific open market operation.
7. (*a*) In the first model the demand for currency by the general

public remains constant irrespective of changes in the level of bank deposits.

(b) In the second model the general public seeks, on average, to maintain a constant *proportion* of total money holdings in the form of currency. The proportion is 25 per cent.

The working of the first model is summarized in Table 4.2. Period 1

TABLE 4.2

ELEMENTARY MODEL OF THE BANK DEPOSIT MULTIPLIER
£ million

Period		Bank A	Bank B	Bank C	Bank D	Total
1	Deposits	2,000	2,000	2,000	2,000	8,000
	Cash	160	160	160	160	640
	Advances	1,840	1,840	1,840	1,840	7,360
2	Deposits	2,010	2,000	2,000	2,000	8,010
	Cash	170	160	160	160	650
	Advances	1,840	1,840	1,840	1,840	7,360
3	Deposits	2,010	2,000	2,000	2,000	8,010
	Cash	160·8	160	160	160	640·8
	Advances	1,849·2	1,840	1,840	1,840	7,369·2
4	Deposits	2,012·3	2,002·3	2,002·3	2,002·3	8,019·7
	Cash	163·1	162·3	162·3	162.3	650
	Advances	1,849·2	1,840	1,840	1,840	7,369·2
5	Deposits	2,012·3	2,002·3	2,002·3	2,002·3	8,019·2
	Cash	160·98	160·18	160·18	160·18	641·52
	Advances	1,851·32	1,842·12	1,842·12	1,842·12	7,377·68
6	Deposits	2,014·42	2,004·42	2,004·42	2,004·42	8,027·68
	Cash	163·1	162·3	162.3	162·3	650
	Advances	1,851·32	1,842·12	1,842·12	1,842·12	7,377·68
7	Deposits	2,014·42	2,004·42	2,004·42	2,004·42	8,027·68
	Cash	161·15	160·35	160·35	160·35	642·2
	Advances	1,853·27	1,844·07	1,844·07	1,844·07	7,385·48
8	Deposits	2,016·37	2,006·37	2,006·37	2,006·37	8,035·48
	Cash	163·1	162·3	162·3	162·3	650
	Advances	1,853·27	1,844·07	1,844·07	1,844·07	7,385·48
Final position	Deposits	2,038·75	2,028·75	2,028·75	2,028·75	8,125
	Cash	163·1	162·3	162·3	162·3	650
	Advances	1,875·65	1,866·45	1,866·45	1,866·45	7,475

shows the banking position prior to the disturbance to bank cash reserves. In Period 2 there is a deposit of £10 million additional cash in Bank A as a result of an open market purchase of securities which,

THE THEORY OF THE VOLUME OF BANK DEPOSITS 91

by chance, happen to be bought exclusively from customers of Bank A. Deposits and bank cash reserves in Bank A both increase by £10 million and the cash ratio is raised above 8 per cent. In Period 3 Bank A seeks to restore the 8 per cent ratio. The open market purchase has raised deposits in Bank A to £2,010 million and cash to £170 million. But 8 per cent of £2,010 million is £160·8 million so that the bank is holding £9·2 million more cash than is required. The bank therefore increases advances by £9·2 million. As, by assumption, the advances are withdrawn in currency, the cash holdings of Bank A fall to £160·8 million. In other words advances are substituted for cash. In the meantime, during this period, the additional £9·2 million of currency is in course of being spent by the borrowers. In Period 4, the additional currency having been spent, the recipients pay this currency into their respective banks. Because the banks are of equal size it is assumed that the recipients are divided equally, as customers, between the four banks, so that, of the £9·2 million, £2·3 million is paid into each bank. Deposits and cash in each bank rise by this amount and, in each case, the cash ratio is raised above 8 per cent. Each bank in fact is holding £2·12 million more cash than is required. In Period 5 each bank restores the 8 per cent ratio by substituting £2·12 million advances for cash so that, in aggregate, during this period there is additional currency amounting to £8·48 million in spending transit. In Period 6 a quarter of this currency is paid into each bank, and so on. The reader will notice that in each period after the disturbance the increase in deposits or the increase in advances gets smaller and smaller. This is a sequence which is converging towards a new equilibrium in which deposits in aggregate will have risen by £125 million, that is by 100/8 times the initial injection of cash.

The process of the changes in aggregate deposits and advances can be expressed more concisely.

Period 2 – deposits rise 10m   = initial injection
Period 3 – advances rise 9·2m = 10m (1 −0·08)
Period 4 – deposits rise 9·2m = 10m (1 −0·08)
Period 5 – advances rise 8·48m = 10m (1 −0·08)^2
Period 6 – deposits rise 8·48m = 10m (1 −0·08)^2
Period 7 – advances rise 7·80m = 10m (1 −0·08)^3
Period 8 – deposits rise 7·80m = 10m (1 −0·08)^3

The sequence of increases in deposits is therefore 10m + 10m (1 −0·08) + 10m (1 −0·08)^2 + 10m (1 −0·08)^3 ... which when summed to infinity is 10m (1/0·08) = 125m. The bank deposit multiplier in this model is 12·5, which is the reciprocal of the cash ratio.

One of the essential assumptions of this model is that the private sector banking system is virtually a closed circuit as far as cash is concerned. Once additional cash is injected into the system by, in this case, an open market purchase, the cash holdings of the banks remain permanently raised. The additional cash remains in the banking system except for temporary outflows and inflows. Similarly, in the opposite case of an open market sale, the cash reserve would be permanently reduced, at least until the next open market operation or other autonomous disturbance.

The reason why deposits change in a predictable multiple fashion is that since the banks have a preferred ratio of cash to deposits they also have a preferred ratio of cash to other bank assets. In this simple model where deposits are the only bank liability, with cash and advances the only bank assets, a preferred ratio of cash to deposits of 1 to 12·5 implies a preferred ratio of cash to advances of 1 to 11·5. When therefore banks experience a permanent addition to their cash holdings their preferred asset distribution is disturbed. To restore the preferred asset distribution the banks will seek to increase their advances by 11½ times the increase in their cash holdings. On the assumptions of the model they will have no difficulty in doing this because there is an unsatisfied demand for bank advances. Every increase in advances will raise deposits equally because, again on the assumptions of the model, there are no transfers of deposits out of the system or permanent withdrawals of currency. If advances are increased by 11½ times the initial deposit of cash, the ultimate increase in deposits must be 12½ times the increase in cash, that is, equal to the increase in cash plus the increase in advances. The important point to note is that deposits rise as an incidental consequence of the attempt of the banks to acquire additional non-cash assets so as to restore their preferred assets distribution.

The principle of the model can easily be extended to a more complex banking system in which there is a variety of non-cash assets, including money market assets and investments. The principle of the multiplier remains the same. A cash to deposit ratio of 1 to 12·5 still means a preferred asset distribution of cash to non-cash assets of 1 to 11·5.

It is time to examine the second model. We saw in Chapter 3 that there is some relationship between bank deposits in aggregate and the currency holdings of the general public. In the second model it is assumed that the relationship is one of fixed proportionality, i.e. that

THE THEORY OF THE VOLUME OF BANK DEPOSITS

the public seek, on average, to keep 25 per cent of their total money holdings in currency.

To illustrate this model with a numerical example would be rather cumbersome and we can avoid this by the use of algebraic symbols. Suppose that a is the fixed proportion of money holdings that the public seek to hold in currency and that d is the cash ratio that the banks seek to maintain. Period 1 is the stage before the disturbance of banking equilibrium. In Period 2 we suppose that the central bank makes an open market purchase of securities from the general public and pays for the securities in currency amounting to £x. Of this additional money the public retains the proportion a in currency, i.e. they retain £xa in currency. The balance, £$x(1-a)$, is deposited in the banks. Deposits and bank cash reserves therefore rise by £$x(1-a)$. In Period 3 the banks retain the proportion d of the newly acquired cash and lend the proportion $(1-d)$. Bank advances therefore increase by £$x(1-a)(1-d)$.

In Period 4 currency amounting to £$x(1-a)(1-d)$ has been borrowed from the banks and when this has been spent the recipients retain the proportion a in currency and deposit the proportion $(1-a)$. Bank deposits and cash rise by £$x(1-a)^2(1-d)$. In Period 5 banks lend the proportion $(1-d)$ of this additional cash so that bank advances rise by £$x(1-a)^2(1-d)^2$. In Period 6, after the borrowed currency is spent, the recipients retain the proportion a and deposit the proportion $(1-a)$. Bank deposits and cash rise by £$x(1-a)^3(1-d)^2$, and so on. There is, therefore, a sequence of increases in deposits £$x(1-a) + £x(1-a)^2(1-d) + £x(1-a)^3(1-d)^2 \ldots$ which when summed to infinity amounts to

$$\frac{£x}{(1-d)} \left[\frac{1}{1-(1-a)(1-d)} \right]$$

If we now substitute numerical values for the symbols we can calculate the increase in deposits and the size of the deposit multiplier. Suppose x is £10 million, a is 25 per cent, and d is 8 per cent, then the increase in deposits is

$$£10m \left[\frac{1}{(1-0.08)} \right] \left[\frac{1}{1-(1-0.25)(1-0.08)} \right]$$

which equals

$$£10m \left(\frac{1}{0.92} \right) \left(\frac{1}{1-0.69} \right),$$

which equals £10m multiplied by 3·5 approximately, i.e. £35 million approximately. The deposit multiplier is about 3½.

The size of the multiplier is determined by the combination of the asset distribution preferences of the banks and the money distribution preferences (as between deposits and currency) of the general public. The reader will notice that this multiplier is very much smaller than that of the first model. The reason is that part of the initial injection of cash leaks out of the banking system. The larger the proportion of money that the public prefers to hold in currency the greater will be the leakage of cash from the banking system as deposits expand. The smaller, therefore, will be the ultimate multiplier.

Both these models are of course extremely artificial. They are intended merely to demonstrate the nature of the multiplier process. It is worth pointing out however that, of the two models, the second is the less unrealistic since we know from experience that a very rough proportionality is maintained between currency holdings and bank deposits. For example, one can see from Table 4.3 that the proportion of the money supply held in currency in Britain remained

TABLE 4.3

MONEY HOLDINGS IN UNITED KINGDOM

(*Averages during the year*)

	Currency in circulation with public	Net deposits by U.K. residents with deposit banks	Sum of columns (1) and (2)	Column (1) as per cent of column (3)
	(1) £ million	(2) £ million	(3) £ million	(4) %
1963	2,240	7,800	10,040	22·2
1964	2,341	8,207	10,548	22·2
1965	2,517	8,585	11,102	22·6
1966	2,702	9,017	11,719	23·0
1967	2,796	9,456	12,252	22·8
1968	2,887	10,078	12,965	22·3

fairly steady at between 22 and 23 per cent in the years 1963 to 1968 (money supply is defined here as average currency in circulation plus net deposits by United Kingdom residents with deposit banks). Thus of the two deposit multipliers, that of the second model is much less unrealistic.

4.7 THE LIMITATIONS ON THE MULTIPLIER PROCESS

Although multiplier models of the types examined have their uses they can be very misleading as a guide to the behaviour of the banking system in practice. There is, in reality, nothing mechanical or predictable about the change that would occur in the level of bank deposits following an injection of cash. An increase in the volume of bank deposits involves the preferences and decisions of at least two groups – of the banks who acquire additional non-cash assets, and of the public who find themselves holding additional money.

We saw in the opening section of this chapter that banks will not acquire additional assets voluntarily unless it is profitable to do so. Generally speaking this means either that there is an unsatisfied demand at current interest rates for bank advances of the type that banks consider safe, or else that it remains profitable for banks to add to their holdings of investments. If banks had already expanded to the optimum, that is to the point at which the marginal revenue from bank assets is equal to the marginal cost of administering deposits, no further banking expansion would occur on the initiative of the banks. There would be no deposit multiplier in operation. The theory of the deposit multiplier implicitly assumes that bank expansion has been constrained below the optimum by a shortage of liquid reserves.

We also saw in the first section of this chapter that a reluctance of the public to add to their holdings of bank deposits can operate to restrain the growth of deposits. This is partly because such reluctance will tend to reduce the profitability of assets to the banks, and partly because it will induce leakages of cash from the banks to the public sector or into additional currency holdings. It will be useful now to carry this analysis a stage further by examining the secondary repercussions of an expansion of bank deposits.

Banks can take the initiative in expanding deposits either by making additional advances to customers or else by buying securities from bank customers. An additional bank advance can be used by the borrower for one of four purposes.

1. The borrower may buy existing financial or tangible assets, for example existing bonds or an existing house. The purchase will put some upward pressure on the prices of such assets to induce

the sale, and the seller or sellers will now hold additional bank deposits in place of such assets.
2. The borrower may pay off a debt. The recipient will now hold an additional bank deposit in place of a debt due.
3. The bank advance may be used to finance the construction of new capital goods. Those making the new capital goods find themselves holding an addition to their stock of wealth in the form of additional bank deposits.
4. The bank advance may be used to finance consumption of additionally produced consumer goods and services. The producers or providers of the additional commodities also find themselves holding an addition to their stock of wealth in the form of additional bank deposits.

In examples 1 and 2 the recipients have momentarily changed the form of part of their existing stock of wealth into bank deposits, while in examples 3 and 4 the recipients momentarily hold an addition to their stock of wealth in the form of bank deposits. If, in each of these examples, the recipients were content to continue holding wealth in this way there would be no further repercussions. But there is no reason to suppose that this would generally be the case. As a form of wealth-holding a current account bank deposit has a yield which can only be measured in convenience. Broadly speaking, one can say that the extent of this 'convenience' yield will depend on the level of income and expenditure of the holder of the bank deposit and, until the general level of income and expenditure has risen, one would not expect that recipients of additional bank deposits would, in general, want to hold more wealth in this form.

What can the recipients of additional bank deposits do if they do not wish to hold more wealth in this form? Clearly they can use the additional deposits for one or more of the four purposes for which a bank advance can be used. They can buy existing assets, pay off debts, finance the construction of new capital goods, or finance the purchase of additionally produced consumer goods. And the next round of recipients can do the same, and so on. There is one other use, and that is to transfer the bank deposit to the ownership of a non-bank intermediary, for example a building society, in exchange for a claim on that intermediary. But the intermediary is unlikely to wish to retain more than a fraction of the additional deposit, and will seek to increase its lending or purchase existing assets, thus passing on the deposit to other recipients.

Before attempting to trace the further consequences of this process it will be useful to examine briefly the repercussions of bank purchases of securities from bank customers. Customers are persuaded to sell by some rise in the price of securities. But it does not follow that the sellers will now be content to hold bank deposits instead. 'Keynesian' economists sometimes have argued that sellers of securities might be willing to hold money if they thought that the price of securities would fall again in the near future. This theory will be examined later in this book; it is sufficient to note at this juncture that, even if investors do expect security prices to fall again in the future, they are not obliged to hold money. They can, while waiting for the security prices to fall, transfer bank deposits to non-bank intermediaries where they will receive a positive yield. Alternatively, they may use the funds obtained from the sales of securities to purchase other assets the prices of which have not yet risen.

The conclusion to be drawn from the discussion so far is that so long as the public does not wish to hold, as additional average balances, the newly created bank deposits, there will be a continuously rising demand for existing financial and tangible assets, for new capital goods, and for additional consumer goods. The pressure of demand for existing assets will naturally cause asset prices to rise. This will intensify the demand for capital goods and consumer goods. A rise in the price of existing tangible assets, for example of houses, makes it more profitable to construct new ones. A rise in the price of financial assets, such as bonds and equities, implies a fall in interest rates and yields, making it more profitable to borrow and invest in the construction of new capital goods. Moreover the general rise in the price of assets will make owners feel wealthier and may induce them to raise their rate of consumption.

The picture, then, is one of rising expenditure, and therefore of rising prices and/or output. But the process is not likely to go on for ever, at least not in consequence of some given expansion of bank advances or some given bank purchase of securities.

There are two factors which will tend to raise steadily the demand to hold bank deposits. The rising level of expenditure and income will gradually raise the volume of bank deposits that the public will find convenient to hold. Less certainly, if yields on financial and tangible assets fall sufficiently, as a result of the pressure of demand for existing assets, some wealth-owners may come to feel that the yield no longer compensates adequately for the risks and inconvenience of holding such assets. They may prefer to hold money instead. Because of these two factors (or at least the first factor) the rise in expenditure would cease ultimately when the public, in aggregate, become content to hold the larger volume of bank deposits as average money balances.

But the process will operate actually to curtail the creation of additional bank deposits. We saw in the first section of this chapter that the transfer of unwanted additional bank deposits to non-bank intermediaries enables the latter to compete for lending that the banks might otherwise have made. We also saw that the use of additional bank deposits to purchase securities will, by reducing their yield, make bank purchases of securities less worthwhile and, by cheapening alternative sources of finance, reduce the demand for advances. The reluctance to hold additional bank deposits therefore tends to make banking expansion less profitable and, in some circumstances, might inhibit the expansion of deposits. But the more important reason why the reluctance of the public to hold more bank deposits will curtail the expansion is that the rising expenditure on assets and on output will induce cash leakages from the banks. As the level of expenditure rises the general public are likely to want to hold larger average amounts of notes and coin. Currency will be withdrawn from the banks leaving less of the initial injection of cash with the banks. The limiting effect of this factor on deposit expansion was demonstrated in the second model of the previous section.

The rising level of expenditure will also induce transfers to the public sector. Given the existing tax rates, the higher the level of income and expenditure the greater will be the flow of tax payment to the public sector. So long as the rise in the tax flow is not matched by a rise in the rate of government expenditure the effect will be to cause a greater net flow of deposits and cash to the public sector. Some part also of the increase in expenditure is likely to be on imports and foreign assets. To this extent there will be a higher rate of purchase of foreign exchange from the public sector (from the E.E.A.) which will also cause a larger flow of deposits and cash to the public sector.

Of course if, initially, public sector expenditure were exceeding public sector receipts or if the balance of payments were in surplus, the above developments might merely reduce the net flow of money from the public sector to the private sector. But to isolate the specific effects of the induced leakages to the public sector it is useful to assume that public sector expenditure and receipts and the balance of payments are initially in balance, or at least offsetting. It would then follow that the rise in the flow of tax payments and in expenditure on imports and foreign assets would induce a continuous flow of deposits and cash from the private sector to the public sector.

The effect of this development on the level of bank deposits will depend on what the government does with the continuing inflow of money. Normally the government will use net receipts of money to repay debt so as to reduce the total interest charge on the national debt. But the government can repay debt either to the central bank or to the private sector. Suppose that the expansion of bank advances has induced a flow of cash to the public sector amounting to £10 million per month. If the government chooses to repay debt to the private sector at the rate of £10 million per month an equal amount of cash per month will be transferred back to the private sector. There would be no reason why the induced transfers, via taxation and imports, to the public sector should curtail the expansion of bank deposits. On the other hand, if the government chooses to repay only £9 million of debt per month to the private sector, the balance being used to repay debt to the central bank, then cash holdings of the banks would be falling at the rate of £1 million per month. Ultimately this would force a contraction of deposits. Of course the contraction would not continue indefinitely because the fall in deposits would eventually cause a fall in the level of expenditure and income. This, in turn, would induce a decline in tax payments and in expenditure on imports and foreign assets.

The important point to note is that, since the government can choose whether to repay debt to the private sector or to the central bank, one cannot predict, without knowing that choice, what the effect of induced leakages to the public sector will be on the bank deposit multiplier.

4.8 SOME CONCLUSIONS

The theory of the bank deposit multiplier is concerned with the response of bank deposits to a disturbance to bank cash holdings. It may be useful, in this concluding section, to summarize the causes and implications of such disturbances. The main causes can be:

(*a*) changes in the public's preference as between holding currency and bank deposits;
(*b*) central bank dealings in assets;
(*c*) budgetary and balance of payments disturbances in conjunction with debt management.

We saw in Chapter 3 that weekly and seasonal changes in the public's preference for holding money as between currency and bank deposits occur regularly. But since these changes correct themselves fairly rapidly they do not produce significant disturbances to the level of bank deposits. More lasting changes in the public's preference do take place gradually and are an important long-term influence on the rate of growth of deposits. If the National Giro grows in popularity, the preference for deposits in the Giro may also become a significant influence on cash holdings and deposits in the ordinary deposit banks.

The central bank can induce changes in bank cash holdings by deliberate purchases or sales of assets. We have already discussed open market operations in securities in some detail in this chapter, and it is only necessary to recall some of the major implications. Open market sales will reduce cash holdings but, because the central bank is a lender of last resort, the banks can generally recover the lost cash, in the first instance, by borrowing from the central bank (via the discount houses). This facility does not destroy the central bank's control over deposits, but it does enable the banks to contract their deposits in their own time. A more important implication is that control of bank deposits by open market operations implies willingness by the authorities to accept whatever may be the resulting disturbance to interest rates. As we saw earlier in this chapter, an attempt to cause a significant change in bank deposits by open market operations may produce quite violent changes in interest rates. This may be especially the case if the knowledge that the central bank is trying to change the money supply in this way induces widespread expectation that security prices will be affected. For example, if central bank sales of securities cause speculators to believe that security prices are going to fall, speculators may attempt to unload their holdings of securities. The downward pressure on security prices and the upward pressure on interest rates will be magnified. It follows that, if the central bank is unwilling to allow sharp fluctuations in interest rates, it will be precluded from using open market operations to control bank deposits. Indeed if the policy of the authorities is to keep interest rates stable, then open market operations would have to be entirely passive. The operations would have to offset whatever changes should occur in the private sector's willingness to hold government securities.

One may mention in passing that the technique of Special Deposits, which was introduced in Britain in 1960, was designed to enable the Bank of England to reduce banking liquidity without having to sell securities. The technique was described briefly in Chapter 3 and will be examined in detail in a later chapter on monetary policy. It is sufficient to recall that a call for Special Deposits is simply an instruction to the banks to transfer part of their cash to a special deposit at the Bank of England. Since the deposit cannot be drawn upon the Bank of England can, by this means, reduce banking liquidity without having to sell securities. The technique, however, does nothing to prevent the downward pressure on security prices if the banks sell securities in order to restore the required liquidity ratios. The Bank of England may accompany the call for Special Deposits by an instruction to the banks to reduce advances rather than sell securities. But even this will not prevent some fall in security prices, since some customers, denied bank advances, will be forced to raise funds by selling securities.

In theory the central bank could attempt to control bank deposits, not by open market operations in securities, but by deliberate purchases or sales of foreign exchange. But just as deliberate open market operations imply acceptance of fluctuating interest rates, so deliberate dealings in foreign exchange to control deposits would imply acceptance of fluctuating foreign exchange rates. In practice the Bank of England is obliged to preserve stability of the exchange rate within a narrow range. Its foreign exchange dealings are therefore passive operations determined by the state of the balance of payments.

We must now examine briefly the implications of budgetary operations and debt management. The simple theory of control of bank deposits and of the deposit multiplier assumes implicitly that the monetary situation is not being disturbed by budgetary operations or by the balance of payments. The effect of balance of payments disturbances will be discussed in Chapter 5, so, to keep the present discussion as simple as possible, the influence of the balance of payments will be ignored. Strictly speaking this implies a 'closed' economy, i.e. a community with no foreign transactions.

We saw in Chapter 3 that when public sector expenditure is exceeding receipts from the private sector there will be a continuous transfer of money to the private sector. On the other hand when there is a net excess of public sector receipts there will be a continuous transfer of money the other way. In either case the effect on bank cash and bank deposits will depend on the nature of debt management.

Suppose that public sector capital and current expenditure is exceeding tax revenue and other current receipts from the private sector at the rate of £100 million per annum. This, in itself, is causing bank deposits and bank cash to rise at that rate. If the public sector finances this deficit by selling additional securities to the non-bank private sector at the rate of £100 million a year, the transfer of money will be exactly offset. Bank deposits and bank cash holdings will remain stable.

Such a continuous sale of securities would tend to depress security prices and raise interest rates. Indeed if the non-bank private sector was particularly unwilling to add to holdings of government securities, or perhaps trying to get out of them, the rise in interest rates might have to be formidable. If, in these circumstances, the government is unwilling to see such a rise in interest rates and in the cost of the national debt, it will have to finance part of the deficit by borrowing from the central bank.

Suppose that, within the range of increase in interest rates that the government is prepared to accept, it is only able to sell additional securities to the non-bank private sector at the rate of £50 million per annum. If the government borrows the remaining £50 million per annum from the central bank, then deposits and cash holdings in the commercial banks will be rising at that rate. The banks would now have surplus cash. If there were a required cash ratio of say 8 per cent then, with deposits rising at £50 million a year, bank cash holdings would only be required to rise at the rate of £4 million a year. The authorities would therefore attempt to mop up the surplus cash by selling securities of the right type to the banks at the rate of £46 million per annum. If they succeed in doing this the deficit of £100 million per annum is, in effect, financed as follows:

(i) sales of securities to non-bank private sector £50m p.a.
(ii) sales of securities to banks 46
(iii) borrowing from central bank 4

Total £100m p.a.

Bank deposits continue to rise at the rate of £50 million per annum and bank cash holdings at £4 million.

Suppose the government is prepared to allow interest rates to rise to a higher level at which it can sell securities to the non-bank private sector at the rate of £90 million per annum. Deposits and bank cash would then be rising at the rate of £10 million a year. With this rate of increase in deposits the banks only require cash to rise at £0·8 million per annum. The authorities therefore attempt to mop up the surplus cash of £9·2 million per annum by selling additional securities of this amount to the banks. If they succeed in doing this the deficit will be financed as follows:

(i)	security sales to non-bank private sector	£90m p.a.
(ii)	security sales to banks	9·2
(iii)	borrowing from central bank	0·8
	Total	£100m p.a.

Deposits will be rising at £10 million per annum and bank cash at £0·8 million.

In the limiting case in which the authorities are prepared to accept any rise in interest rates necessary to enable them to finance the whole deficit by sales of securities to the non-bank private sector, bank deposits and bank cash holdings would remain stable.

The government has, of course, another alternative if it wishes to control the rate of growth of bank deposits. That is by reducing its deficit. Suppose the authorities wish to limit the rise in interest rates to that which would enable them to sell £50 million additional securities to the non-bank private sector, and at the same time keep bank deposits stable. This can be achieved if the government can reduce the borrowing requirement of the public sector to £50 million by, for example, cutting public sector expenditure or by raising tax rates.

From these examples it can be seen that there are three variables which govern the behaviour of bank deposits in this context:

(*a*) the government's budgetary policy;
(*b*) the government's interest rate policy;
(*c*) the attitude of the non-bank private sector to holding government debt.

The government cannot control variable (*c*), though it can influence this attitude by, for example, the extent to which its policies succeed in controlling inflation. Aside from this influence, the government has the choice of controlling its deficit, or the level of interest rates, or the level of bank deposits. But it cannot control all three at the same time. One of the three must be the residual.

Even this analysis exaggerates the extent to which the authorities can control bank deposits, because the analysis assumes that the authorities can always mop up the surplus bank cash by persuading the banks to take up the required additional government securities. But if there were a strong demand for bank advances the banks might well prefer to expand advances rather than buy additional government securities. So long as the banks have surplus cash, and so long as there is an unsatisfied demand for advances, bank deposits can be expanded via an increase in bank advances. The only remedy left for the authorities would be to restrict advances by directive.

The existence of a large public sector deficit, at a time when investors are reluctant to take up additional government securities, makes it extremely difficult for the authorities to retain any real control over the rate of growth of the money supply. The situation, however, becomes entirely different if there is an overall public sector surplus. Budgetary forces would then be making for a fall in the money supply. The authorities would be in the powerful position of being able to choose between allowing bank deposits to fall, or preventing this by a sufficient repayment of debt. Nor are the authorities likely to be worried by any resulting fall in interest rates.

In a community in which there are vast transfers of deposits between the public sector and the private sector, where it is difficult for the government to keep a balance between public sector expenditure and receipts, where stability of interest rates is regarded as desirable, and where investors' appetite for government debt is unstable, it is clear that the level of deposits cannot be satisfactorily explained in terms of the simple deposit multiplier. The theory of the multiplier is of value to an understanding of the process of deposit creation. But it does not provide an adequate explanation of the money supply in contemporary Britain. We must turn to this problem in the next chapter.

SUGGESTED READING

D. D. Hester and J. Tobin (Eds.), *Financial Markets and Economic Activity* (Wiley, 1967), ch. i.

D. C. Rowan, *Output, Inflation and Growth* (Macmillan, 1968), chs. xv, xvi.

W. T. Newlyn, *Theory of Money*, 2nd ed. (Oxford, 1971), ch. ii.

T. Scitovsky, *Money and the Balance of Payments* (Unwin, 1969) ch. iii.

A. T. K. Grant, *The Machinery of Finance and the Management of Sterling* (Macmillan, 1967), chs. iii–v.

R. S. Sayers, *Modern Banking*, 7th ed. (Oxford, 1967), chs. v, viii.

A. B. Cramp, *Monetary Management* (Allen & Unwin, 1971), ch. ii.

A. D. Bain, *The Control of the Money Supply* (Penguin, 1970), ch. ii.

B. J. Moore, *An Introduction to the Theory of Finance* (Collier-Macmillan, 1968), ch. vi.

W. M. Dacey, *Money Under Review* (Hutchinson, 1960), ch. iii.

D. R. Croome, and H. G. Johnson, (Eds.), *Money in Britain 1959–1969* (Oxford, 1970), ch. iii.

5 Money Supply Statistics and Domestic Credit Expansion

5.1 THE CHANGE IN MONEY SUPPLY EQUATIONS

In the final section of Chapter 4 it was argued that, where there are large and variable flows of funds between the public sector and the private sector, changes in the money supply cannot be explained satisfactorily in terms of a simple bank deposit multiplier in relation to changes in a cash base. A more sophisticated explanation is required.

The Central Statistical Office publishes in 'Financial Statistics' the money supply and changes in money supply statistics for the United Kingdom. The statistical tables show a breakdown of the major components of the money supply outcome for each quarter and for each year. These components can be arranged in the form of equations which provide a useful framework for analysing the causes of the change in the money supply.

Before examining some of the actual statistics it will be useful to consider the principles underlying these equations and the usefulness of the equations for analytical purposes. At this stage it will be assumed, for simplicity of exposition, that the money supply consists of currency in circulation with the non-bank private sector plus bank deposits in the private sector; that bank deposits are the sole liabilities of banks; that all bank deposits are denominated in sterling and are owned by U.K. residents; and that the public sector bank deposits are all held at the Bank of England.

The causes of change in the money supply in some particular period of time can be classified under two main headings – the net transfer of funds from the public sector to the non-bank private sector, and the net acquisition of assets by banks from the non-bank private sector. The net funds transferred from the public sector can be held either as additional bank deposits or as additional currency, and when banks acquire assets from bank customers they give deposits in exchange and these can either be held or withdrawn in currency. It follows therefore that the net transfer of funds from the public sector plus the net acquisition of assets by banks from bank customers must equal the increase in deposits plus the increase of currency in circulation. The increase in bank deposits must, of course, be matched by an increase in bank assets, and these assets can be classified as either public sector assets or private sector assets. Hence the increase in the money supply must also be equal to the increase in bank holdings of public sector assets and private sector assets plus the increase of currency in circulation. Thus we can begin with three simple equations of the increase in the money supply:

Equation A
Net transfer of funds from the public sector to the non-bank private sector.
plus net acquisition of assets by banks from the non-bank private sector

equals

Equation B
Increase in bank holdings of public sector assets
plus increase in bank holdings of private sector assets
plus increase of currency in circulation

equals

Equation C
Increase in bank deposits
plus increase of currency in circulation

The next step is to subdivide the elements of Equation A. The net transfer of funds from the public sector during a particular period can be regarded as the outcome of three sub-elements:

(*a*) The public sector borrowing requirement (positive or negative).
(*b*) The net sales or purchases of foreign exchange to or from the private sector.
(*c*) The net sales or repayments of (non-currency) public sector debt to the non-bank private sector.

The public sector borrowing requirement is, in principle, the difference between the public sector's capital and current expenditure on the one hand, and its tax revenue and other current receipts on the other hand. A positive borrowing requirement implies that expenditure for the period has exceeded revenue and that there has been a net transfer of funds to the private sector.

The private sector buys foreign exchange from the public sector (the E.E.A.) to pay for imports and for net investment or lending abroad and sells to the public sector the foreign exchange receipts from exports. When, therefore, the total of private sector imports and net investment and lending abroad exceeds exports during the period, there is a net transfer of funds from the private sector to the public sector. Such a net transfer is a source of finance to the public sector and, indeed, this item is sometimes called 'external financing of the public sector'. The net amount of foreign exchange sold by the public sector to the private sector must either have been borrowed by the public sector from abroad (by selling public sector debt to the overseas sector) or else there must have been a reduction in the public sector's holdings of foreign exchange. Holdings of foreign exchange can be regarded as liquid claims on the overseas sector, so that the counterpart of the net sales of foreign exchange to the private sector is either an increase in the overseas sector's holdings of public sector debt or a reduction in liquid claims on the overseas sector. Hence net sales of foreign exchange by the public sector to the private sector can also be described as 'net acquisition of public sector debt by the overseas sector'. The reader should bear in mind, therefore, that 'net sales of foreign exchange by the public sector to the private sector', 'external financing of the public sector', and 'net acquisition of public sector debt by the overseas sector', all mean the same thing, and they each correspond in principle to the balance of payments deficit in the private sector. Of course when the balance of payments is in surplus each of these three aspects will have a negative value.

The net sales or net repayments of public sector debt to the non-bank private sector is simply the excess or deficiency of sales of debt over repayments during the period. Obviously when sales of debt to the non-bank private sector exceed repayments there is a net transfer of funds from the private sector to the public sector, and conversely in the case of net repayments.

The other major component of Equation A is the net acquisition of assets by banks from the non-bank private sector. This can be subdivided into net purchases (or sales) of public sector debt from (or to) bank customers, and 'bank lending to the private sector'. The latter includes net changes in bank advances, in commercial bills discounted, in call loans used to discount commercial bills, in refinanceable export credits, and in short loans to the stock exchange. A net increase in bank lending will of course increase the money supply.

Net purchases of public sector debt by banks from customers operate to increase the money supply, and net sales to decrease money supply. But as we have seen the public sector can also make net repayments or net sales of public sector debt to the non-bank private sector, and these transactions operate to increase and decrease the money supply respectively. Since the effects of both types of transactions are reflected in the non-bank private sector's holding of public sector debt the two sets of transactions are not distinguished in practice. The two are combined in the one item 'net acquisition of (non-currency) public sector debt by the non-bank private sector'. A positive net acquisition makes for a decrease in money supply since this means that the banks and the public sector taken together have made net sales of public sector debt to the non-bank private sector. A negative net acquisition makes for an increase in money supply.

Equation A can now be re-written as follows:

Item 1   Public sector borrowing requirement
less
Item 2   Net acquisition of public sector debt by overseas sector
less
Item 3   Net acquisition of (non-currency) public sector debt by non-bank private sector
plus
Item 4   Net increase in bank lending to the non-bank private sector

The reader should note that any of these items can be positive or negative.

Equation B remains as described previously except that it is usual to express the items as:

Item 5   Increase in bank lending to the public sector
plus
Item 4   Increase in bank lending to the private sector
plus
Item 6   Increase of currency in circulation

Equation C also remains as described previously, namely:

Item 7   Increase in bank deposits
plus
Item 6   Increase of currency in circulation

The three equations are of course accounting identities. Equation A indicates the sources of the increase in money supply in the period. Since an increase in money must be held either in bank deposits or in currency the sum of the items in Equation A must be identical with the sum of the items in Equation C. But the sum of the items in Equation B must also be identical with Equation C. The increase of currency is common to both. The increase in bank deposits of Equation C has a counterpart in the increase in bank assets of Equation B, i.e. the increase in public sector assets (bank lending to public sector) and the increase in private sector assets (bank lending to private sector).

The state of the net transfer of funds from the public sector (items 1 and 2 and part of 3) will have a bearing on bank lending to the private sector (item 4). If we assume an unsatisfied demand for bank credit, that additional lending remains profitable, and that lending is not constrained by Bank of England directives, then the limiting factor on bank lending will be the liquidity position. But the liquidity position of the banks is affected by the state of the net transfer of funds from the public sector. If the net transfer is positive the banks receive an addition to their cash holdings equal to the net transfer less any increase of currency in circulation. The banks are then free to determine what portion of the additional cash received they will retain by the amount of public sector debt they choose to buy from the public sector (directly or indirectly). Moreover all their holdings of public sector debt have some bearing on their liquidity position. Treasury bills, or short loans used to acquire Treasury bills, have been part of their conventional liquid assets and remain part of the new reserve assets. Bond holdings are a second line reserve and, if the authorities are supporting interest rates and if the bank's holdings of investments are above the minimum desired ratio, the banks can turn bonds into cash without much fear of loss either by selling bonds to the authorities or by refusing to re-invest as bond holdings mature. In these circumstances there is no serious liquidity constraint on bank lending to the private sector. The growth in such lending can become virtually demand determined. This is one reason why the authorities attempted to control bank lending by directives.

The situation is very different when the net transfer of funds from the public sector is substantially negative, particularly if this is due to a negative public sector borrowing requirement. The negative net transfer causes an equal fall in bank cash holdings, except to the extent that there is a change of currency in circulation. The banks have to restore cash by disposing of Treasury bills and other public sector debt or by calling in short loans etc. If this state of affairs continues banking liquidity can become seriously threatened and their ability to lend to the private sector undermined.

It may be helpful to illustrate the above situation by an imaginary example relating to a period of a month. The example in fact is somewhat similar to what occurred in March 1969. We suppose the equations for this month to have been as follows:

Equation A		£ million
Item 1	Public sector borrowing requirement	−1,200
plus		
Item 2	Net repayment of public sector debt to overseas sector	+200
plus		
Item 3	Net reduction of (non-currency) public sector debt held by non-bank private sector	+260
plus		
Item 4	Net increase in bank lending to private sector	+310
		−430

Equation B		
Item 5	Increase in bank lending to public sector	−790
plus		
Item 4	Increase in bank lending to private sector	+310
plus		
Item 6	Increase of currency in circulation	+50
		−430

Equation C		
Item 7	Increase in bank deposits	−480
plus		
Item 6	Increase of currency in circulation	+50
		−430

In this example public sector receipts from taxation etc. during the month exceeded public sector expenditure by £1,200 million. The borrowing requirement was therefore negative, representing a transfer of funds of £1,200 million from the private sector to the public sector. At the same time there had been a balance of payments surplus and £200 million of foreign exchange was sold to the public sector; and the authorities chose to repay £260 million of debt to the non-bank private sector; so these two sets of transactions produced a transfer of £460 million from the public sector to the non-bank private sector. The net transfer of funds to the public sector was therefore £740 million (£1,200 million minus £460 million). One can think of the net transfer as having caused a reduction in bank deposits and bank cash holdings of £740 million. But bank customers also withdrew £50 million in currency so that the total reduction in deposits and bank cash holdings from the net transfer of funds and the withdrawal of currency was £790 million. In the face of strong demand for bank credit, bank advances were increased by £310 million thus offsetting part of the reduction in deposits. The causes of change in bank deposits were therefore as follows:

	£ million
from net transfer to public sector	−740
from withdrawal of currency	−50
from increase in advances	+310
change in deposits	−480

With deposits reduced by £480 million the banks could allow cash reserves to fall by £38·4 million, i.e. by 8 per cent of £480 million, assuming that an 8 per cent cash ratio was obligatory.* But, as we have seen, the effect of the net transfer of funds to the public sector and the withdrawal of currency was to reduce bank cash by £790 million. The banks, therefore, had to recover £751·6 million of cash during the month by selling that amount of Treasury bills and bonds to the authorities (including calling in short loans to the discount market). One can suppose the changes in bank liabilities and assets to have been as follows:

Bank liabilities		Bank assets	
deposits	−£480m	cash	−38·4m
		treasury bills	−£96·0m
		investments	−£655·6m
		public sector debt	−£790·0m
		advances	+£310·0m
			−£480 m

If this type of situation, with a large negative public sector borrowing requirement, were to continue in subsequent months, the authorities would clearly be in a powerful position to control changes in the

* For purposes of simple illustration it has been assumed that all banks in 1969 were obliged to follow the 8 per cent cash ratio and 28 per cent minimum liquid assets ratio requirements. Since September 1971 these have been replaced by reserve asset requirements.

money supply if they so wished. So long as the negative borrowing requirement exceeds the balance of payments surplus, the authorities can exert greater downward pressure on the money supply merely by reducing the amount of debt repayment they choose to make to the non-bank private sector. Such action would increase the net transfer of funds to the public sector. Not only would this itself put greater downward pressure on the money supply, but since the net transfer of funds forces the banks to reduce their holdings of public sector debt, it would also reduce banking liquidity. A continuation of this state of affairs would make it increasingly difficult for the banks to increase their lending to the private sector.

5.2 THE ANALYTICAL VALUE OF THE EQUATIONS

The change in money supply equations provide a useful framework for examining the major causes of money supply disturbances; but it is important to be clear that the equations in themselves have a very limited explanatory and predictive value. We have emphasized that the equations are simply accounting identities. The totals of the three equations are equal in the sense that they represent different aspects of a set of events which have already happened. The sum of the items in Equation A must of necessity equal the change in currency and bank deposits because the latter change is the counterpart of the events depicted in Equation A. The equations in themselves do not imply anything about causation. Nevertheless it might be argued that Equation A does indicate the nature of the causative elements and indicates how changes in the money supply might be produced or controlled. For example, one might infer that the authorities could reduce the money supply by some given amount by reducing the public sector borrowing requirement. But the value of each item in Equation A is the result of a wide range of decisions made and preferences expressed during the period. Indeed this is true also of the values of the items in Equations B and C. Moreover the decisions which influence the outcome of one item may have repercussions on the outcome of another item. There is in fact an enormous number of factors which mutually determine the change in money supply. But, at the risk of gross over-simplification, it may be helpful to indicate the more important factors and how they react on each other. For convenience these will be considered under the headings of the various equation items.

The public sector borrowing requirement can be regarded as the outcome of public sector expenditure decisions on the one hand, and the nature of taxes and tax rates in conjunction with the level and distribution of national income and expenditure (though this leaves out of account other types of public sector receipts). The tax rates in conjunction with the level and distribution of income and expenditure determine the tax revenue of the public sector; and if this could be taken as given then the borrowing requirement would vary equally with public sector expenditure. But this is too simple a view. A reduction in public sector expenditure will tend to reduce national income, so that given existing tax rates, tax revenue will tend to decline. In other words the reduction in the borrowing requirement is likely to be less than the reduction in public sector expenditure. Similarly an increase in tax rates, by raising tax revenue, will tend to reduce the borrowing requirement, but the actual outcome will be complicated by the fact that the increase in tax rates will also tend to depress national income and expenditure. But many other factors can also influence the level of income and expenditure. For example an increase in exports relative to imports (item 2 of Equation A), and an increase in bank lending to the private sector (item 4 of Equation A) will both tend to raise the level of national income and expenditure, thus tending to raise tax revenue. Thus the borrowing requirement outcome will be influenced by the outcome of the other items in Equation A.

The net sales or purchases of foreign exchange to or from the private sector are the result of many factors some of which can be listed as follows:

(*a*) export competitiveness and the state of world demand
(*b*) import propensities and preferences
(*c*) the preferences and freedom of home residents to invest overseas and of foreign residents to invest here
(*d*) the level of private sector income and expenditure.

This list of factors is far from complete and each factor mentioned is the result of other factors. But at least the list gives an indication of the variety of factors which can influence the money supply through this particular item. Moreover it can be seen that factors which influence other equation items can also influence the outcome of this item. For example, an increase in public sector expenditure, by tending to raise national income and expenditure will also tend to induce a rise in imports and thus greater sales of foreign exchange to the private sector.

The third item in Equation A is the net acquisition of non-currency public sector debt by the non-bank private sector. The outcome of this item can be regarded as the result of the inter-play of the state of preference for holding public sector debt and the interest rate policy of the authorities. The size of this item can vary enormously from period to period. People can get out of public sector debt and into money easily, in large quantities, and without loss, by encashing national savings or by not re-investing the huge amounts received from debt redemptions. Theoretically the authorities could neutralize the effects of any changes in attitudes to holding public sector debt by allowing sufficient changes in the level of interest rates. But the fluctuations in interest rates might have to be so violent as to make such a policy impracticable. Changes in the non-bank private sector's attitude to holding non-currency public sector debt can therefore be a major cause of change in the money supply in any particular month. These changes of attitude are likely to be only modified in the short run by the sort of change in interest rates which has been experienced in recent years. Over a longer period of time however changes in interest rate policy may have a much more important effect. For example, a sustained policy of high interest rates may gradually overcome reluctance to hold public sector debt, thus reducing the rate of growth of money supply in the long run.

The outcome of this item will also be influenced by factors affecting the other equation items and by changes in the money supply itself. The state of the balance of payments has an important influence on attitudes to holding public sector debt since it affects expectations about the future level of interest rates. Expectations about the future course of inflation also have an important influence. Rising commodity prices reduce the real value of the interest earned from holding bonds. Inflationary expectations therefore induce a preference for holding equities and tangible assets the value of which tends to keep pace with inflation. An increase in the money supply, by inducing greater fear of inflation, can reduce the willingness to hold public sector debt, thus provoking a greater subsequent increase in money supply, unless the reduction in willingness is countered by a sufficient rise in interest rates. There is therefore some danger of a vicious circle.

The fourth item in Equation A, the increase in bank lending to the private sector, depends partly on the demand for bank credit and partly on the willingness and freedom of banks to add to their holdings of private sector debt. The demand for bank credit can be said to be determined on the one hand by the level of economic activity and prices and the future outlook for business, and on the other hand by the terms, ease, and convenience of bank credit compared with other sources of finance, including the running down of transactors' own money balances. Thus, among other things, the demand for bank credit will depend on comparative interest rates and the ratio of the stock of money to the value of national income. The willingness and freedom of banks to increase their lending will be influenced by the profitability of additional advances to the banks, by the extent to which bank lending is controlled by directives, and by the liquidity position of the banks.

The factors influencing bank lending have been discussed at some length in earlier chapters and it is sufficient here to note that the outcome of this item will be affected by factors determining other equation items. For example, since the level of economic activity and prices is affected by public sector expenditure, the demand for bank credit will also be affected. We have also seen that the net transfer of funds between the public sector and the non-bank private sector has an important influence on bank liquidity and therefore on the ability of banks to extend credit.

One further comment on this item is worth making. In theory the increase in bank lending to the private sector could be replaced by a statement of the total borrowing requirement of the non-bank private sector *less* the increase in private sector debt held by the non-bank private sector. The change in bank lending would then have been the residual. The total borrowing requirement of the non-bank private sector during a period is met partly by increased purchases of private sector debt by savers and partly by increases in bank credit. The statistics, by showing only the change in bank credit extended, fail to disclose or indicate the influence of the total borrowing requirement of the private sector and the influence of the attitude of savers to holding private sector debt. In this sense Equation A, by omitting the private sector borrowing requirement and changes in holdings of private sector debt, places an undue accent on the public sector borrowing requirement and on changes in the holdings of public sector debt.

From this discussion it can be seen that changes in the money supply are not caused in any simple way by the separate items of Equation A. Moreover it can be seen that one cannot predict precisely the effect on the money supply of a change in any one set of decisions or policies. One cannot, for example, predict the precise effect on the money supply of a given change in public sector expenditure or in interest rates. The equations, however, do bring out the point that the authorities can influence the direction of the change or the rate of change in money supply by changing such things as public sector expenditure, tax rates, or interest rates. If, however, the authorities are not prepared to alter budgetary policy or allow interest rates to change, it can be seen that they relinquish all control over the money supply.

In theory, the authorities could have complete control over the money supply were they prepared to accept any degree of change in interest rates. A public sector borrowing requirement or a balance of payments surplus, however large, could be prevented from causing a net transfer of funds from the public sector to the non-bank private sector, if sufficient additional non-currency public sector debt were sold to the non-bank private sector. And, if the authorities were to refuse to absorb any sales of public sector debt, the banks, with no means of increasing their cash, could only increase their lending to the private sector to the extent that they made room for such additional assets by selling investments to bank customers. The money supply would then be held constant. But interest rates would have to rise to whatever level should prove consistent with

(a) the pressure of demand to borrow by the public sector and the private sector;
(b) the willingness of the non-bank private sector to hold and add to holdings of public sector and private sector debt; and
(c) the state of the balance of payments.

Obviously, the greater the demand to borrow by both sectors and the less the willingness of the non-bank private sector to add to holdings of debt, the higher would interest rates have to rise.

At the other extreme, the authorities could aim at complete rigidity of interest rates. The money supply would then have to change to the extent consistent with

(a) the pressure of demand to borrow of the two sectors;
(b) the amount of non-currency debt of either sector that the non-bank private sector is prepared to hold at the chosen level of interest rates; and
(c) the state of the balance of payments.

In practice, the British monetary authorities have chosen a compromise policy – permitting some variation in interest rates and some variation in the money supply. They have attempted to moderate the rises in both money supply and interest rates by restricting the public sector borrowing requirement through budgetary policy (particularly by raising tax rates), and in the past by restricting bank lending to the private sector through directives. As a broad generalization one can say that from the war until about 1958, and to a lesser extent until about 1968, there was greater accent on stabilizing interest rates than on stabilizing the money supply. Behind this policy lay the belief that widely fluctuating interest rates are not compatible with the smooth management of the national debt. Moreover there was not much faith that control of money supply would provide effective control of national expenditure. At the same time the authorities did not believe that control of national expenditure was compatible with fixity of interest rates without undue budgetary restraint or undue restraint on bank lending. More recently the stress of policy appears to have shifted towards greater control over the money supply and less towards stability of interest rates. This change of stress is consistent with the change in the climate of economic thinking about the role of money. In 1969 there was a remarkable reduction in public sector expenditure in relation to public sector receipts so that there was a substantial negative borrowing requirement. As a consequence the growth of money supply was significantly reduced, interest rates actually fell for a time, and the liquidity of the banks came under pressure. Controls over bank lending became largely superfluous, and indeed, in the budget speech in April 1970, the Chancellor of the Exchequer indicated that credit regulation through control of bank liquidity might supersede direct controls over bank lending. This change of policy was carried a stage further in 1971 and is discussed in Chapter 10.

5.3. DOMESTIC CREDIT EXPANSION

We have seen that the change in the money supply that occurs in any period of time can be expressed in the form of three identity equations. The reader will recall that item 2 of Equation A is 'net acquisition of public sector debt by the overseas sector' and that this item is the same thing as 'external financing of the public sector'. Since the three equations are accounting identities it is obvious that we can omit the deduction of item 2 from Equation A and add this item on to Equation B and Equation C, and the three revised equations will still remain equal. The equations, when thus revised, are known as *Domestic Credit Expansion* or D.C.E. for short. The D.C.E. equations can therefore be expressed as follows.

D.C.E. Equation A
Item 1   Public sector borrowing requirement
less
Item 3   Net acquisition of (non-currency) public sector debt by non-bank private sector
plus
Item 4   Increase in bank lending to private sector

D.C.E. Equation B
Item 5   Increase in bank lending to public sector
plus
Item 4   Increase in bank lending to private sector
plus
Item 6   Increase of currency in circulation
plus
Item 2   External financing of the public sector

D.C.E. Equation C
Item 7   Increase in bank deposits
plus
Item 6   Increase of currency in circulation
plus
Item 2   External financing of the public sector

By omitting the 'external financing of the public sector' from D.C.E. Equation A we can regard this equation as representing the elements of change in money supply of internal origin only. D.C.E. Equation B can be viewed as a grouping of all the elements of additional lending by way of monetary expansion. While D.C.E. Equation C can only be regarded as an adjusted change in money supply.

The term 'domestic credit expansion' is perhaps rather misleading. Although, as we have seen, the D.C.E. Equation B can be regarded as the total increase in lending involving monetary expansion, it is not the total expansion of credit in the ordinary sense of the word. It does not include those forms of credit expansion which imply an acceleration of velocity of money. For example it does not include extension of trade credit, or extension of lending by non-bank intermediaries resulting from the transfer of bank deposits to the ownership of intermediaries.

5.4 THE PURPOSE OF THE D.C.E. EQUATIONS

The statistical presentation of the D.C.E. equations first appeared in May 1969 but the purpose was not made very clear. Nevertheless it is

MONEY SUPPLY STATISTICS

worth considering some of the possible purposes that the statisticians may have had in mind.

One purpose may be to give a clearer impression of internal monetary conditions. It can be claimed that the ordinary changes in money supply equations give a misleading indication of internal monetary conditions. When there is a balance of payments deficit the increase in the money supply will be less than would have resulted from internal expansionary factors taken alone, and conversely when there is an external surplus. This can be demonstrated with a simple example. Suppose that in the month of January external payments are exactly in balance, i.e. net sales of foreign exchange by the public sector to the private sector are zero, and suppose the items for Equation A of the change in money supply are as follows:

		£ million
1.	Public sector borrowing requirement	+400
2.	*less* Net acquisition of public sector debt by overseas sector	−0
3.	*less* Net acquisition of public sector debt by non-bank private sector	−50
4.	*plus* Increase in bank lending to private sector	+200
	Increase in money supply	+550

Now it is obvious that D.C.E. for January will also be £550 million because the removal of item 2 can make no difference to the total so long as it has a zero value. Suppose now that in February there has been an increase in public sector expenditure which, after allowing for induced changes in tax revenue, results in a public sector borrowing requirement of £480 million, i.e. £80 million more than in January. This increase in public sector expenditure will have caused some rise in national income and expenditure and is likely to have induced a rise in imports. There is no reason to expect that exports will have risen equally so that we may expect there to have been an external deficit in February. Suppose that this deficit amounts to £60 million; and, for simplicity, let us suppose that items 3 and 4 remain the same as in January. Equation A for the change in money supply is then: (1) £480m − (2) £60m − (3) £50m + (4) £200m = £570m. The increase in money supply in February is therefore only £20 million more than in January. But the D.C.E. Equation A will be as follows: (1) £480m − (3) £50m + (4) £200m = £630m, and this is £80 million more than the D.C.E. for January. Thus the internal expansionary factor is fully disclosed in the total for D.C.E. Not too much should be read into this conclusion because, as we saw in Section 5.2, the balance of payments outcome will have had some effect on the outcome of the internal items. Nevertheless it can be seen that if the authorities achieve a contraction in D.C.E. they will have achieved a contraction in the internal expansionary elements. This may be one purpose in setting a D.C.E. target for, say, a year ahead.

A second purpose, suggested in fact by the Bank of England, is that the D.C.E. statistics may provide an additional early warning device. In forecasting the effects of proposed changes in, say, budgetary policy, it should also be possible to forecast the effects of such a change in policy on D.C.E. statistics for some periods ahead. Since some of the D.C.E. statistics become available quickly it should be possible to get an early warning of the extent to which the more general forecast is being realized, thus permitting corrective action to be taken in good time. But it would seem that this advantage could also be obtained from the change in money supply statistics and that it is not an advantage peculiar to D.C.E.

A third purpose could be to use a constant D.C.E. target to provide an automatic balance of payments corrective. Suppose, for example, the authorities aim to keep D.C.E. at zero; and suppose that initially the external deficit is zero and the change in money supply zero. Thereafter any positive external deficit would create an equal positive D.C.E. if the change in money supply were to remain zero. To keep D.C.E. at zero the authorities would have to counterbalance the external deficit with an equal reduction in money supply. Similarly, to keep D.C.E. constant, any surplus on the balance of payments would have to be counterbalanced by an equal increase in money supply. The theoretical justification for such a policy is that a reduction in money supply would reduce expenditure. This in turn would moderate imports and, to the extent that internal prices fall, boost exports, thus reducing the external deficit. Similarly an increase in the money supply would lead to a reduction in an external surplus. This is, of course, only a disguised version of the former 'rules of the gold standard game'. In practice such a policy would compel the economy to suffer disturbances with every fluctuation in the balance of payments regardless of whether the external disequilibrium is temporary or lasting, whether it originates in current account or capital account transactions, or whether due to internal disturbances or to disturbances in other countries. Moreover experience shows that a reduction in money supply affects the price level only after a very long delay and that the main impact in the meantime is on output and employment. To attempt to correct an external deficit by an equal reduction in money supply would probably impose prolonged recession on the economy.

Finally mention should be made of a very theoretical argument that in the long run the size of D.C.E. determines the size of the balance of payments deficit or surplus. If this were so, of course, the authorities could control the balance of payments by controlling D.C.E. A very artificial model can be used to demonstrate the theory, based on the following assumptions:

(i) Changes in the money supply cause changes in the value of national income and the ratio of the value of national income to the money supply remains constant.
(ii) Changes in the value of national income cause changes in the value of imports and the ratio of imports to national income remains constant.
(iii) The value of exports is determined by quite separate factors (e.g. world demand).
(iv) Payments for imports and exports are the only elements in the balance of payments.

These assumptions imply that any increase in the money supply will cause a proportionate increase in the value of national income, and this in turn will cause a proportionate increase in the value of imports. Moreover any increase in imports will cause an equal deterioration in the balance of payments so long as the separate factors determining exports do not change.

Suppose we start from a position in which D.C.E. per month is zero and foreign payments exactly in balance, implying, of course, that the change in money supply is also zero. Suppose that subsequently there is an internal expansion, such as a higher rate of public sector expenditure, which causes D.C.E. to become a positive amount of, say, £100 million per month, at which level we suppose D.C.E. to remain constant. At the outset, for example in the first month, we can expect that the higher level of public sector expenditure will have caused only a modest rise in imports and therefore only a small balance of payments deficit. The greater part of D.C.E. in the first month will then consist of an increase in the money supply. For example, the D.C.E. of £100 million in the first month might consist of £90 million increase in money supply and £10 million external deficit.

But the balance between these two elements in D.C.E. will not remain stable as the months go by. The increase in the money supply will cause a proportionate rise in the value of national income, and this in turn will cause a proportionate rise in imports and therefore a larger external deficit (assuming that the separate factors do not cause a rise in exports). In fact so long as there is a positive increase in the money supply each month, national income will be rising, imports will be rising, and the external deficit will be growing larger. But as the external deficit grows larger the increase in the money supply must be growing smaller, as long as D.C.E. remains constant each month. Eventually when the external deficit has risen to £100 million per month, the deficit will constitute the whole of D.C.E. and the increase in the money supply will have become zero. As soon as the increase in money supply has become zero the value of national income will cease to rise (according to the assumptions of the model). Imports will therefore also cease to rise and the balance of payments deficit will become stabilized at £100 million per month. Similarly, if after this there is a further internal expansion which raises D.C.E. to £150 million per month there will be a further expansion of the value of national income until such time as the external deficit has risen to £150 million per month. The implication of the model is that there is a tendency for the external deficit to move to equality with D.C.E. It would therefore follow that to improve the balance of payments the authorities would have to take steps to reduce D.C.E.

Of course the model which has been sketched is extremely crude. The reader will have noticed that it is based on the quantity theory of money which is certainly not accepted universally. Not everyone by any means believes that an increase in money supply is *the* cause of an increase in the value of national income. The evidence is that the ratio of national income to money supply, which is another aspect of the velocity of circulation of money, is highly unstable in the short run at least. Nor is the ratio of the value of imports to national income particularly stable. Finally, balance of payments transactions include not merely imports and exports but also a whole range of international investment and lending transactions, and although it is generally agreed that there is a strong functional relationship between imports and national income, there is no clear-cut functional relationship between national income and international capital transactions. It is certainly possible that there is some long-term tendency for the balance of payments to be influenced by the average size of D.C.E., but we will need a very much longer series of D.C.E. statistics than is yet available to judge the extent of this relationship.

5.5 DEFINITIONS OF MONEY SUPPLY

In the opening section of this chapter a number of simplifying assumptions were made regarding the money supply so as to ease discussion of the principles underlying the money supply equations. In practice there are many complications. The public sector does not keep its bank accounts solely with the Bank of England. The public sector includes not only the central government but also local authorities and public corporations, and the bulk of public sector deposits are held with ordinary deposit banks. There are many types of banks, including accepting houses and overseas banks. There are also many types of bank deposits. Some are owned by overseas residents; some are denominated in foreign currency; and some are time deposits. These complications do not affect the essential nature of the causes of changes in money supply, but they impair the explanatory value of the published statistics. They also pose the question of how the money supply should be defined.

From an analytical and policy point of view the significance of money lies in its relationship to aggregate demand. How is money best defined from this viewpoint? This is not an easy question to answer. In the first chapter of this book we saw that it is impossible to define money clearly as a liquid store of value because there is no clear-cut division along the liquidity spectrum between assets which can be regarded as money and those which cannot. A tentative conclusion was reached that a clearer distinguishing feature lies in convenience for immediate debt settlement. In other words there is a case for defining money as those assets which can be used directly as a means of payment, while excluding from this definition all assets which require prior conversion into money before they can be used for debt settlement. On this criterion no one would dispute the inclusion of currency in the definition of money. The difficulty arises with bank deposits. Should all bank deposits be included or only certain types? An article in the Bank of England *Quarterly Bulletin* of September 1970 pointed out that bank deposits can be classified in four different ways: by type of bank, by denomination (sterling or non-sterling), by type of account (current or deposit account), by type of owner (private sector, public sector, overseas sector). If not all bank deposits are to be regarded as part of the money supply of the United Kingdom, which particular combination of these classifications should be so regarded? The answer to this question is unfortunately not clear. Whatever definition is chosen is bound to be arbitrary. Indeed more than one definition can be justified, depending on the purpose in mind.

Currently, in the United Kingdom, there are three official definitions of money supply published, known as M1, M2, and M3. The narrowest definition is that of M1 which is restricted to currency in circulation plus the total of chequable current accounts with all types of banks (including Giro) which are owned by private sector residents and denominated in sterling, and after deduction of items in transit. M2 consists of M1 plus private sector sterling deposit accounts with deposit banks and discount houses. While M1 is probably closer to the commonsense view of a means of payment, M2 has the advantage that it takes some account of the difficulty in practice of distinguishing between current and deposit accounts as means of payment. Public sector deposits are excluded from both definitions on the grounds that public sector deposits are not closely related in amount to public sector spending. Moreover government can, in effect, create money.

TABLE 5.1

MONEY SUPPLY – AVERAGE AMOUNTS OUTSTANDING
(£ millions)

	M1	M2	M3
1964	7,070 (100)	10,508 (100)	11,376 (100)
1965	7,270 (103)	11,099 (106)	12,100 (106)
1966	7,508 (106)	11,651 (111)	12,919 (114)
1967	7,750 (110)	12,194 (116)	13,665 (120)
1968	8,044 (114)	12,977 (124)	14,978 (132)
1969	8,075 (114)	13,144 (125)	15,618 (137)

M3 is a much broader definition, covering currency in circulation plus all categories of bank deposits owned by United Kingdom residents. It therefore brings in deposit accounts held for specified periods with accepting houses and overseas banks; it brings in accounts denominated in foreign currency; and it brings in public sector deposits. Of all the possible classifications of deposits the only one excluded from this definition of money supply is deposits owned by non-residents. The advantage of M3 is that it is a definition which is easily reconciled with the aggregate of bank assets, and therefore with the total of bank lending and domestic credit expansion. But as a definition of the means of payment of the community M3 is far from satisfactory. There is no more justification for including fixed-term deposits with accepting houses and overseas banks or deposits in foreign exchange than deposits with building societies or with savings banks, etc., indeed perhaps less justification. M3 is a complete hybrid. From an analytical point of view there would be a better case for attempting to aggregate all highly liquid assets.

Table 5.1 shows the behaviour of each version of money supply from 1964 to 1969, with index numbers based on 1964 in brackets.* The growth rates per annum of M1 and M2 were 3 to 4 per cent and 5 to 8 per cent respectively, except that neither experienced significant growth in 1969. M3, on the other hand, had growth rates varying from 6 to 12 per cent per annum, and even in 1969 M3 increased by 5 per cent. Which of these growth rates should the policy maker have regard to? Did the money supply increase significantly in 1969 or did it not?

Table 5.2 shows the ratios of gross national product to each version

TABLE 5.2

RATIOS OF G.N.P. AT MARKET PRICES TO MONEY SUPPLY

	M1	M2	M3
1964	4·70	3·16	2·92
1965	4·92	3·22	2·96
1966	5·06	3·26	2·94
1967	5·16	3·28	2·92
1968	5·33	3·30	2·86
1969	5·65	3·47	2·91

of money supply, that is to say the table compares the income velocities of each definition of money. The income velocities of M1 and M2 both rose steadily, though that of M2 more slowly. The behaviour of the income velocity of M3 however was quite different. There was some rise and fall, but the variation was modest, and the income velocity could be reasonably described as constant. One might be tempted to suppose that this relative constancy of income velocity implies that M3 is the best definition of money. But a moment's reflection disposes of that supposition. This was a period in which interest rates and deposits with non-bank intermediaries rose rapidly, and on both counts one would expect velocity to have risen steadily. The reason for the difference in the behaviour of income velocity is made clear by Table 5.3. The first two columns make up M1 and the addition of column three gives M2. The main part of the difference between M1 and M2 on the one hand and M3

* *See also* **Figure 5.1.**

126   AN INTRODUCTION TO FINANCIAL ECONOMICS

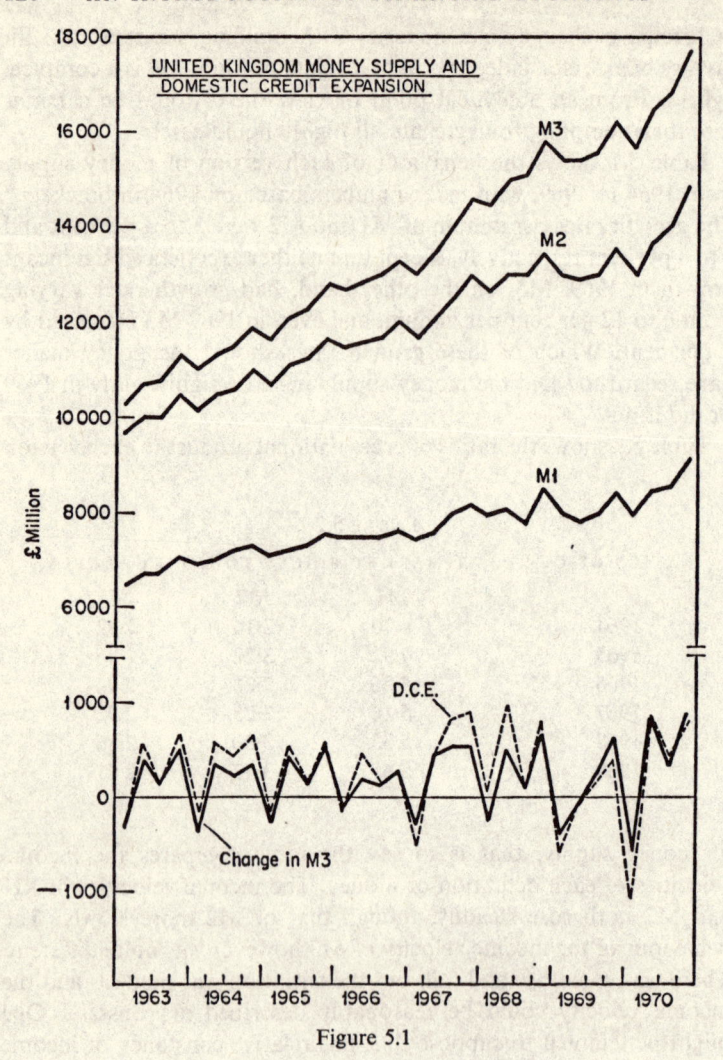

UNITED KINGDOM MONEY SUPPLY AND DOMESTIC CREDIT EXPANSION

Figure 5.1

on the other hand lies in the behaviour of column four (M3 also includes public sector deposits but these remained broadly stable). Although there were significant differences in the growth rates of the first three columns they were all of the same order as the growth of gross national product (37 per cent from 1964 to 1969). But the increase in column four of 300 per cent over this period is an entirely different order of magnitude. Moreover time deposits with accepting houses and overseas banks, which make up column four, are in no

MONEY SUPPLY STATISTICS

TABLE 5.3

VARIOUS COMPONENTS OF MONEY SUPPLY

(£ millions)

	Currency in circulation	Current accounts all banks	Sterling deposit accounts with deposit banks and discount houses	Sterling and non-sterling deposit accounts with other banks	G.N.P. at market prices (1964=100)
1964	2,328 (100)	5,308 (100)	3,438 (100)	491 (100)	100
1965	2,488 (107)	5,397 (102)	3,829 (111)	619 (125)	108
1966	2,678 (115)	5,524 (104)	4,143 (121)	821 (167)	114
1967	2,765 (119)	5,659 (107)	4,444 (129)	1,010 (206)	120
1968	2,851 (122)	5,882 (111)	4,933 (144)	1,568 (319)	129
1969	2,903 (125)	6,009 (113)	5,069 (147)	1,975 (401)	137

sense means of payment. Yet it is the growth of these deposits which accounts for the stability of the income velocity of M3.

Are there any grounds for preference as between M1 and M2 as definitions of money supply? One argument in favour of M2 over this particular period of time is that the relatively slow growth rate of current accounts in all banks (column two) may have been due to the exceptional rise in deposit rates of interest which occurred and which may have induced an exceptional transfer to time deposit accounts. This would suggest that columns one, two, and three, taken together, would give a less distorted picture of the trend of money supply than columns one and two alone. Against this it must be mentioned that recent research conducted in the Bank of England provides some evidence that a narrower definition of money supply is more strongly correlated to changes in gross domestic product than is a broader definition. On the other hand, since depositors are free to move between current accounts and time deposits, M1 is not an aggregate that is controllable by the authorities.

5.6 MONEY SUPPLY EQUATIONS AND D.C.E. EQUATIONS IN PRACTICE

Table 5.4 gives the actual change in money supply equations for 1968 and 1969. The first point to note is that money supply is the M3 definition. Although, as we have seen, M3 is a somewhat misleading concept of money, it is the definition chosen for these equations because this definition can be reconciled with changes in bank lending with the minimum of adjustments.

TABLE 5.4

MONEY SUPPLY EQUATIONS IN PRACTICE

(£ million)

	1968	1969
A.		
Public sector borrowing requirement	1,318	−473
less net acquisition of public sector debt by overseas sector	−1,114	+594
less net acquisition of non-currency public sector debt by non-bank private sector	−79	−340
plus net increase in bank lending to the non-bank private sector	685	553
	810	334
Adjustments		
less increase in non-deposit liabilities	+25	−34
less increase in deposits of non-residents	+240	+154
	1,075	454
B.		
Increase in currency in circulation	52	146
plus increase in bank lending to public sector	73	−365
plus increase in bank lending to private sector	685	553
	810	334
Adjustments		
less increase in non-deposit liabilities	+25	−34
less increase in deposits of non-residents	+240	+154
	1,075	454
C.		
Increase in currency in circulation	52	146
Increase in net deposits of U.K. residents	1,023	308
Change in money supply (M3)	1,075	454

The reader will note that these equations are identical in pattern with those discussed in Section 5.1 except for the two adjustments made to Equations A and B. The total of Equation A is equal to the increase in currency in circulation plus the increase in bank assets (or bank lending). This is because the portion of the public sector borrowing requirement not financed by sales of foreign exchange or of public sector debt to the non-bank private sector must be financed by bank lending to the public sector; and bank lending to the private sector is the remaining item. Equation B is also, of course, the increase in currency in circulation plus the increase in bank assets. The increase in bank assets must be equal to the increase in bank liabilities, but the latter need not equal the increase in bank deposits owned by United Kingdom residents. In the first place some portion of the increase in bank assets may be matched by an increase in non-deposit liabilities. To derive the increase in deposits from Equations A and B one must deduct the increase in non-deposit liabilities (or add a decrease). In the second place some portion of the increase in deposits may be owned by non-residents so that one must deduct such increase to derive the increase in U.K. owned deposits (or add a decrease). The reader should note the contrast between 1968 and 1969 in the behaviour of the three equations, with the discussion in Sections 5.1 and 5.2 in mind.

TABLE 5.5

D.C.E. IN PRACTICE

(£ million)

	1968	1969
A.		
Public sector borrowing requirement	1,318	−473
less net acquisition of non-currency public sector debt by non-bank private sector	−79	−340
plus increase in bank lending to private sector	685	553
	1,924	−260
Adjustments		
plus increase in bank lending in £ to non-residents	139	150
less increase in bank lending in foreign currency to residents for investment abroad	−155	−70
	1,908	−180
B.		
Increase in currency in circulation	52	146
plus increase in bank lending to public sector	73	−365
plus increase in bank lending to private sector	685	553
plus external financing of public sector	1,114	−594
	1,924	−260

Adjustments	*1968*	*1969*
plus increase in bank lending in £ to non-residents	139	150
less increase in bank lending in foreign currency to residents for investment abroad	−155	−70
	1,908	−180

C.

Increase in currency in circulation	52	146
plus increase in net deposits of U.K. residents	1,023	308
plus external financing of public sector	1,114	−594
	2,189	−140

Adjustments		
plus increase in non-deposit liabilities	−25	+34
plus increase in deposits of non-residents	−240	−154
plus increase in bank lending in sterling to non-residents	139	150
less increase in bank lending in foreign currency to residents for investment abroad	−155	−70
	1,908	−180

Table 5.5 shows the actual D.C.E. equations for 1968 and 1969 and it can be seen that there are rather more adjustments. Neither of the adjustments that are made to the money supply equations (A and B) are made to the D.C.E. Equations A and B because D.C.E. is regarded primarily as a lending total. These adjustments must therefore be made in reverse to D.C.E. Equation C. But two other adjustments are made to all three equations. An increase in bank lending in sterling to non-residents is added on the grounds that such lending is mainly to finance United Kingdom exports and is therefore indistinguishable from lending to United Kingdom exporters. An increase in bank lending in foreign currency to United Kingdom residents is deducted because it is regarded as entrepot business.

The justification for all the adjustments to the D.C.E. equations is that D.C.E. is regarded primarily as a lending concept rather than as a currency plus deposit concept. But the effect is to impair the simple view of D.C.E. as the change in money supply adjusted for the external deficit. Moreover the adjustments in aggregate are very large and very erratic as can be seen from Table 5.5 and they must seriously distort interpretation of changes in D.C.E. The behaviour of D.C.E. over the period 1963 to 1969 is shown in Table 5.6 and can be com-

TABLE 5.6

MONETARY CHANGES 1963–1969

(£ million)

	Increase in money supply		D.C.E.	Public sector borrowing requirement	External finance of public sector
	M2	M3			
1963		697	1,040	824	104
1964	480	597	1,514	999	657
1965	686	915	1,131	1,190	99
1966	320	536	789	965	415
1967	1,015	1,309	1,766	1,826	505
1968	673	1,075	1,908	1,318	1,114
1969	80	454	−180	−473	−594

pared with the changes in M2 and M3. The reader should note the dominating influence of the public sector borrowing requirement on D.C.E.

SUGGESTED READING

Bank of England Quarterly Bulletin, Sep. 1969: Supplement on Domestic Credit Expansion, Sep. 1970, Dec. 1970.

Economic Trends (H.M.S.O., May 1969).

M. J. Artis and A. R. Nobay, 'Two Aspects of the Monetary Debate', *National Institute Economic Review*, Aug. 1969.

D. Kern, 'The Implications of DCE', *National Westminster Quarterly Review*, Nov. 1970.

'Money Supply and the Banks', *Midland Bank Review*, Feb. 1969; 'Another Look at Money Supply', Nov. 1970.

6 Financial Intermediaries

6.1 THE NATURE OF FINANCIAL INTERMEDIATION

The functions of financial intermediaries were discussed briefly in the first chapter and it may be helpful, at the outset, to recapitulate and elaborate on that discussion. A financial intermediary is an institution which stands between ultimate borrowers and ultimate lenders. Just as money permits the process of exchange to be split into separate transactions of sale and purchase so financial intermediation permits the lending-borrowing process to be split into separate transactions. An intermediary borrows from ultimate lenders and, as a separate transaction, lends to ultimate borrowers. And just as the intermediation of money enormously facilitates exchange so financial intermediation enormously facilitates lending and borrowing. Intermediation involves a double exchange of claims. The intermediary offers a claim on itself (a secondary security) to lenders in exchange for money and uses the money to acquire claims on ultimate borrowers (primary securities). Both sets of transactions are interdependent. The intermediary cannot acquire primary securities unless lenders acquire its own secondary securities; and the intermediary will not willingly borrow from lenders unless it can profitably use the funds to acquire primary securities.

As we saw in Chapter 1 the function of intermediation is performed by many different types of institution. Banks offer deposits and lend by way of advances; building societies offer deposits and share liabilities and lend on mortgage; pension funds offer pension rights and acquire marketable securities, and so on. As regards the essential function of intermediation there is no distinction between banks, finance houses, insurance companies, building societies, investment trusts, or any other type of intermediary. The distinguishing features lie in the nature of the claims and services offered to lenders and in the nature of the claims acquired and services offered to borrowers. In these respects there are very wide differences between intermediaries. But there is nothing static about these differences. Under pressure of competition financial intermediaries are continually seeking new ways of attracting funds and new outlets for profitable lending, not only to capture business from other intermediaries but also to meet the changing needs of society.

It would be wearisome to categorize in detail the differences between financial intermediaries, but it may be helpful to indicate broadly how they differ. As regards the claims and services offered to lenders there are three major groups. There are those institutions which offer an outlet for contractual saving and cover against specific risks, including insurance, life assurance, and pension funds. Then there are institutions which offer forms of wealth-holding with varying combinations of convenience, security, repayability, interest, and prospect of capital appreciation. This group would include building societies, saving banks, finance houses, investment trusts, and unit trusts. Finally there are banks which offer a means of debt settlement and a wide variety of other services. But, in offering interest bearing time deposits, banks also straddle the second group. As regards the claims acquired and services offered to borrowers the differences between intermediaries largely speak for themselves. To some extent the nature of the claims acquired will be influenced by the nature of the claims offered to lenders. Thus pension funds, for example, which are concerned with liabilities in the distant future, will tend to acquire longer-term securities. At the other extreme, banks, conscious of the obligation to repay current account deposits on demand, tend to specialize in short-term advances.

One would expect financial intermediaries as a whole to expand with the growth of wealth and income since they provide an important outlet for the growth of saving. Moreover the demand for finance grows with economic activity. But the rate of expansion of different types of financial intermediary has not been equal by any means. There are a number of reasons why growth rates may differ. Clearly those institutions which are more efficient and more enterprising are likely to grow at the expense of the inefficient and conservative. The level of interest rates, the state of equity markets, and the rate of inflation are all factors which can affect the relative attractiveness of different intermediaries. When interest rates are high those intermediaries in which the offer of interest is a major attraction will have an advantage, particularly as against intermediaries which offer claims on which no interest is paid. Thus at a time of high interest rates one would expect banks to expand more slowly than many other financial intermediaries. Unit trusts and investment trusts are likely to flourish when equity prices are rising and are expected to rise further, but are likely to lose business to other intermediaries when the equity market is weak and falling. Inflation tends to create a bias against intermediaries which offer a yield fixed in money terms unless the yield is sufficiently high to compensate for expected inflation. Finally, the monetary and other policy measures of the authorities may have a biased effect on different intermediaries. For example, banks are likely to suffer relatively to other financial intermediaries if the authorities rely heavily on controls on bank lending as a means of restraining inflation.

6.2 THE ECONOMIC SIGNIFICANCE OF FINANCIAL INTERMEDIATION

It was remarked in the previous section that there is a parallel between the effect of intermediation of money on the scope and efficiency of exchange and the effect of financial intermediation on the scale and efficiency of lending and borrowing. In splitting the lending-borrowing process the intermediary is usually able to offer lenders more attractive outlets for savings and borrowers more convenient and cheaper provision of finance than would otherwise be possible. As we saw in Chapter 1 intermediaries are in a position to offer advantages to both parties because they are able to exploit economies of scale. Unit costs of financial transactions are reduced; lending risks are reduced by diversification; liabilities can be made highly liquid because where there are a large number of depositors withdrawals become statistically predictable and the maturity of assets can be scheduled to meet claims; the employment of experts becomes profitable; and so on.

In the absence of financial intermediaries the lending-borrowing process is seriously impeded, partly because the riskiness and maturity of the primary securities that ultimate borrowers can offer will appeal only to a limited number of potential lenders, and partly because of the difficulties and costs of direct communication between ultimate lenders and borrowers, particularly in the case of small-scale lenders and borrowers. Intermediaries, collectively, offer to lenders a very large range of assets. There are all sorts of combinations of convenience, repayability, security, and interest. It is easy therefore for each wealth-owner to adjust his portfolio according to his individual taste for liquidity, risk-aversion, ease of access, scale of investment, and yield. Because of this, intermediaries are in a position to tap the current saving and spare money balances of the greater part of the community. To borrowers, they offer a wide range of financial facilities which are generally more convenient and cheaper than the direct issue of primary securities. Borrowers too are in a position to adjust their sources of finance according to their individual requirements.

We saw also in Chapter 1 that the more direct methods of obtaining finance become easier and cheaper with the development of intermediaries. Trade credit is more readily extended when traders have access to the funds of intermediaries. New issues of primary securities are easier and cheaper when intermediaries are among the buyers and act as underwriters. Moreover, by satisfying more fully the community's need for liquid and secure assets, intermediaries probably encourage wealth-owners to be more willing to acquire the less liquid and riskier primary securities.

Intermediaries offer to lenders claims that are more attractive than the claims they themselves acquire from borrowers; they thus transmute the comparatively unacceptable claims on ultimate borrowers into highly acceptable claims on themselves. What is the economic significance of this? In the first place, by enabling savers to satisfy more fully their portfolio wants, intermediaries probably help to raise the marginal utility of saving. Secondly, because they collectively offer such a wide and attractive range of claims, intermediaries are able to tap an enormous area of saving at comparatively low cost. By thus reducing the cost of finance to borrowers they help to stimulate real investment. Intermediation, therefore, helps to raise the proportion of resources released from consumption and encourages the use of such resources in real investment. The net effect is to raise the average ratio of investment to gross national product thereby helping to raise the rate of economic growth. Thirdly, the easing of the supply of finance, which results from the development of intermediation, also eases the constraint of income and net worth on expenditure. It becomes much easier for ordinary consumers to enjoy the enormous convenience of spending in anticipation of income. More important still, it is easier for those with enterprise, ability, and know-how to acquire physical capital and engage in roundabout methods of production. Intermediation therefore encourages the accumulation of wealth in a productive form, and helps to raise the community's productivity and output. Finally, through their experience, judgement, and expertise, financial intermediaries help to ensure that the flow of saving is directed into the most productive uses.

But although the development of intermediation has clearly contributed enormously to output, economic growth, and general convenience, it has also posed some difficulties, We have seen that intermediation reduces the constraint of income and net worth on expenditure. By the same token intermediaries may help to stoke the fires of inflation at a time when productive resources are fully utilized. A highly developed system of intermediaries also probably increases the difficulty of control of the economy. For example, restriction of money supply may be offset by expansion of intermediaries. The money they attract is generally money which is surplus to spending requirements – 'idle money', as it is sometimes called. But this formerly idle money is now lent to borrowers for the purpose of adding to expenditure and so moves into the active spending circuit. In short, an expansion of intermediation implies a more intensive use of the existing stock of money. The authorities may attempt to restrain expenditure by reducing the stock of money (or by reducing its rate of growth), but this policy may be thwarted by an expansion of intermediaries which permits a more intensive use of the reduced stock.

6.3 THE MULTIPLE CREATION OF FINANCIAL CLAIMS

It is sometimes said that the feature which distinguishes banks from other financial intermediaries is that the former have the power to create deposits by additional lending whereas other financial intermediaries have no such power. They can only lend, it is claimed, what is deposited with them. The ability of the banks to create their own deposits is demonstrated by the theory of the bank deposit multiplier. By implication therefore, if other financial intermediaries cannot create their own liabilities there can be no non-bank financial intermediary deposit multiplier. This is the issue to be examined in this section.

The multiple creation of bank deposits results from the interplay of the asset preferences of the public and the asset preferences of the banks, following some disturbance to equilibrium. Suppose, for example, that the initiating disturbance is a change in asset preferences of the public, resulting in an additional deposit of cash in a bank. Since banks do not choose to hold 100 per cent of their assets in cash, this additional cash will disturb the equilibrium of the bank's portfolio. In seeking to restore the preferred distribution of assets the bank will substitute additional advances or investments, etc. for part of the cash received, provided that there are profitable opportunities to acquire such assets. Such advances or investment purchases will return cash into the hands of the public, but no multiple creation of deposits will occur unless the public are willing to re-deposit part or all of this cash. Provided this does happen the re-deposit of cash in the banks will again disturb banking portfolios. The sequence of events will keep repeating until such time as portfolio equilibrium is restored. When one says that banks can create deposits, one is really saying that when they acquire assets from the public the latter are induced to hold more wealth in bank deposits.

In principle this process of multiple creation of claims is applicable to any financial intermediary. The same conditions apply. The disturbance to the liquid asset holdings of the intermediary must induce that intermediary to substitute other assets. This implies that the intermediary chooses to hold less than 100 per cent of its assets liquid and that there are profitable opportunities to acquire other assets. Finally, the acquisition of assets by the intermediary must induce, directly or indirectly, the public to become willing to hold more wealth in the form of the liabilities of that intermediary.

It may be helpful to illustrate this principle with an example, though the reader should be warned that, for simplicity of exposition, the assumptions in the example are extremely unrealistic. Suppose that, for some unspecified reason, a change occurs in the asset preferences of a group in the community. The group decides to hold less wealth in bank deposits and more in building society deposits (this might be the result of building society advertising). For illustrative purposes let us suppose that the amount of this transfer is £100,000 in total. At this point in time all that has occurred is an exchange of claims. The public have acquired £100,000 building society deposits in exchange for bank deposits; the building societies have acquired £100,000 additional bank deposits in exchange for additional claims on themselves. Bank deposits in aggregate are unchanged; but there is a change in ownership – the general public hold £100,000 less and the building societies £100,000 more. But the change in asset preferences has created £100,000 more building society deposits.

The acquisition of £100,000 additional bank deposits will have disturbed the portfolio equilibrium of the building societies, since these societies do not choose to hold all their assets in bank deposits. Purely for illustrative purposes let us suppose that the preferred asset distribution of the building societies is 5 per cent in bank deposits and 95 per cent in loans. The societies will then seek to increase their loans by £95,000. Suppose all the £95,000 lent is used to finance the construction of new houses, this sum of money being transferred into the ownership of the various participants in the housing construction. At this point in time the building societies have substituted £95,000 of additional loans for bank deposits, and £95,000 of bank deposits have been transferred back into the ownership of the general public.

To the recipients, the £95,000 is additional income. If these recipients were to save the whole of this additional income there would be no further direct repercussions on expenditure. Suppose, however, that on average, they save only one-fifth of the additional income, i.e. £19,000, and spend the remaining £76,000 on additional consumption. In this event there will be a secondary rise in income. If we again suppose that on average one-fifth is saved (£15,200), and the balance (£60,800) spent on additional consumption, and that this process keeps repeating itself, it can be seen that the expenditure repercussions get smaller and smaller, and at each round the stock of saving rises. Finally, when the stock of saving has risen by £95,000, the direct expenditure repercussions will cease. The increase in real wealth (houses in this case) must generate a counterpart increase in the stock of saving, i.e. in the volume of financial claims which are firmly held. From our point of view the important thing is not whether this occurs immediately or after a series of income-expenditure repercussions; the important thing is the type of financial claim in which the additional saving is held.

An extreme assumption would be to suppose that the whole of the additional stock of saving is placed in building societies. On this supposition building society deposits would rise a further £95,000, reflecting a transfer back of the £95,000 bank deposits previously loaned out. Building societies would retain 5 per cent of the bank deposits received, amounting to £4,750, and would lend the remaining £90,250 for more house construction. If we keep making the extreme assumption that the whole of the resulting additional stock of saving is placed in building societies, not only in this round, but also in succeeding rounds, it is fairly easy to see that a predictable multiple expansion of building society deposits will occur. The process comes to an end when building society deposits have expanded by an amount equal to the initiating additional deposit of £100,000 multiplied by the reciprocal of the building society bank deposit reserve ratio, i.e. the reciprocal of 5 per cent (or one-twentieth). At the conclusion, therefore, building society deposits would have risen by £2,000,000; while, on the assets side, bank deposit reserves of building societies would be up £100,000 and their loans by £1,900,000.

This multiplier model is exactly parallel to that of the simplest version of the bank deposit multiplier, and in practice it is subject to the same types of limitation. The assumption that the whole of every addition to the stock of saving will be held in building societies (or any other type of intermediary) is obviously quite unrealistic. Additional saving will take the form of a demand for all sorts of financial claims, including currency, bank deposits, claims on the whole range of non-bank financial intermediaries, and marketable securities. Nevertheless some portion of the additional saving may well be placed in building societies and to this extent some multiple expansion of building society deposits will occur. Moreover, in so far as additional saving increases the demand for marketable securities, the resulting fall in their yield may induce a greater preference for claims on intermediaries whose interest rates remain unchanged or are relatively inflexible. This would include claims on building societies.

It is important to emphasize that the process of multiple expansion of claims is not restricted to claims on building societies. These societies have been used merely to represent any type of non-bank intermediary. One should also point out that building societies' asset preferences are not, in practice, those assumed in the model. As indicated earlier, the model is intended only to illustrate the process of multiple creation of claims. It is also important to emphasize that the process of multiple claim creation is not restricted to cases where there is an increase in the stock of wealth, or to cases where the initiating disturbance is a change in the asset preferences of the general public. To take the first point, in the model which we have just examined we might have assumed that building society loans are used to finance, not the construction of new houses, but the purchase of existing houses. On this assumption, the recipients of additional bank deposits, i.e. the sellers of existing houses, have not received an addition to income, but have merely changed their form of wealth-holding from houses to bank balances. But of course there is no reason to assume that the house sellers wish to hold more wealth in the form of money, other than transitionally. If the sellers choose to place some portion of the proceeds in building society deposits there can be some multiple expansion of building society deposits. Generalizing, we can say that where a non-bank financial intermediary uses funds received to acquire existing assets (financial or real), such purchases will disturb existing wealth portfolios, and where the response to such disturbance takes the form of an additional demand for claims on the intermediary concerned, then there will be some multiple expansion of claims on that intermediary.

The initiating disturbance need not be a change in the asset preferences of the public. It may be due to a change in the supply of existing assets. For example it may be due to a change in the supply of money, resulting perhaps from open market purchases of the central bank, or perhaps from an additional government expenditure financed by the creation of money. The increase in the money supply will disturb the distribution of assets that the public are required to hold. The public may well respond by substituting other financial claims for the additional money they find themselves holding. If these include claims on non-bank financial intermediaries the multiplier process previously described will be set in motion. The initiating disturbance may be the decision by one group in the community to add to its stock of saving by cutting expenditure in relation to current receipts. The counterpart to additional current saving is additional demand for financial assets. If these include claims on non-bank financial intermediaries a multiple expansion of such claims can be initiated. But the outcome of this last example is complicated by the fact that the increase in saving by one group, unaccompanied by an increase in the real investment of the community, may reduce the income and saving of other groups. The additional demand for financial assets by the saving group may be matched by reduced demand for financial assets by other groups. Clearly the effect on financial intermediaries would be unpredictable. The general point which emerges from all this discussion is that a multiple expansion of claims on a non-bank financial intermediary is set in motion because of a shift in the asset preferences of the public in favour of that intermediary, whether this shift in preference is spontaneous or induced by some other disturbance. The subsequent expansion occurs because the intermediary is induced to substitute other assets for the money received, and because such substitution induces the public to hold more wealth in the form of claims on that intermediary.

Although the process of the multiple expansion of claims on non-bank intermediaries is identical in principle to that of multiple expansion of bank deposits, there is likely to be a difference in degree between the two processes. The non-bank intermediary deposit multiplier is likely to be much smaller than the bank deposit multiplier. One reason lies in the fact that bank liabilities are money, and claims on other intermediaries are not. When bank deposits are increased by a receipt of cash the additional cash will remain in the banking system (apart from temporary outflows) except to the extent that the public prefer to substitute currency for bank deposits as a form of money, and except to the extent that there are larger net transfers to the public sector banking system. Aside from these exceptions, additional lending by the banks does not cause any permanent loss of cash by the banks as a group. Loans are made in money, and bank deposits are money. If loans are made in banks' own liabilities (e.g. by crediting the borrower's account) there is clearly no loss of cash. Even if loans were made in notes and coin, such currency would be returned to the banks because, generally speaking, bank deposits are superior to currency as a form of money (except for small change purposes). And because bank deposits are money the attempt by the public to substitute other assets does not destroy bank deposits nor cause cash leakages (apart from the two exceptions previously noted). If the public substitute goods or other assets for bank deposits, the deposits merely move into the ownership of the sellers. Reluctance to hold bank deposits does not reduce them. It initiates an expansion of expenditure on output and on other assets, and the process continues until the rise in the value of output and the fall in the yields on alternative assets overcome the reluctance of the public to hold the existing stock of bank deposits.

The case is very different with non-bank intermediaries. Their loans, or other asset acquisitions, must be made in money and, unlike the banks, cannot be made with their own liabilities. Any increase in lending by such an intermediary will be matched by an equal reduction in its holdings of money. And since there are many alternative ways of holding wealth only a small portion of this money can be expected to flow back to the intermediary so as to raise its liabilities further and permit further lending. Moreover, in contrast to the case of bank deposits, reluctance by the public to hold the liabilities of a non-bank financial intermediary will destroy such liabilities. If the public wish to hold less of these claims money is simply withdrawn and the claims on the intermediary cancelled. One reason therefore for expecting a non-bank intermediary deposit multiplier to be smaller than the bank deposit multiplier is that leakages from an intermediary occur more easily than from the banking system, because the liabilities of a non-bank intermediary are not money whereas those of banks are.

A second reason for difference in the deposit multipliers may lie in the marginal profitability of assets to the institutions concerned. Banks are generally more subject to rigid reserve requirements than are non-banks. Frequently also they are inhibited from competing for additional deposits by variation of interest rates offered. Deposit banks in Britain, for example, offer no interest on current account, and the interest offered on time deposits has been tied to Bank rate in the past. The combination of these factors means that bank expansion is normally cut off by shortage of reserves well below the point at which further expansion would cease to be profitable, i.e. where the marginal yield on bank assets is equal to the marginal cost of administering deposits. When banks receive an accretion to their reserves their subsequent expansion is unlikely to be impeded by considerations of profitability. The expansion is likely to proceed until the required ratio of reserves to liabilities is restored. This is less likely to be the case with non-bank financial intermediaries. Some of these institutions, less subject to reserve requirements, and free to compete for additional reserves and deposits by interest rate variation, are likely to operate much closer to their optimum than are the banks. When an intermediary, in such a position, receives an accretion of deposits, the attempt to substitute loans or investments for the money received may cause a fall in the yield on such assets sufficient to make the expansion unprofitable. Indeed the intermediary may find it unprofitable to encourage a growth in its deposits. It may also be the case that bank advances, being very flexible in use, enjoy a higher elasticity of demand than do the more specialized loans of non-bank financial intermediaries. This would imply that the yield on bank advances is less likely to fall during an expansionary process than the yield on the loans of non-banks. There are, therefore, various reasons for supposing that a multiple expansion of bank deposits is likely to occur in greater degree than in the case of the claims on non-bank financial intermediaries. But the reader is reminded of the discussion in Chapter 4 in which it was pointed out that the bank deposit multiplier in practice is not likely to be large, or predictable, or even relevant in some circumstances.

6.4 COMPARATIVE GROWTH RATES OF DEPOSIT BANKS AND OTHER FINANCIAL INTERMEDIARIES

We saw in Section 6.1 that growth rates of financial intermediaries may differ because of differences in efficiency and enterprise, because of changes in the level of interest rates etc., and because monetary policy may have a more biased effect on some intermediaries than on others. We also saw that high interest rates and restrictive monetary policy are more likely to restrict bank expansion than the expansion of many other types of financial intermediary. In addition to these factors one would expect the pattern of asset preferences to change with the growth of wealth. As the stock of saving rises it is likely that the demand for liquid assets which offer a significant yield will rise faster than the demand for money. There is some statistical evidence

FINANCIAL INTERMEDIARIES

of this. Since the First World War the average annual rate of growth of building society shares and deposits has been about three times that of deposits with commercial banks. Funds of life assurance companies also grew at about twice the rate of bank deposits.

Since 1958 there has been an exceptionally fast rate of growth in certain types of claims on financial intermediaries. Table 6.1 shows that deposits with deposit banks (London clearing banks, Scottish

TABLE 6.1

DEPOSITS IN A SELECTION OF FINANCIAL INTERMEDIARIES

	Dec. 1958	Dec. 1969	1969 % of 1958
	£ million	£ million	%
Deposit banks	7,462	11,140	149
Savings banks	2,806	4,156	148
Building societies	2,479	8,652	349
Finance houses	128	636	496
Accepting houses, British overseas and Commonwealth banks:			
Total deposits	785	6,629	844
Sterling deposits of non-bank U.K. residents*	140	1,334	950
American and foreign banks:			
Total deposits	332	11,308	3,406
Sterling deposits of non-bank U.K. residents*	30	408	1,360

* Estimated figures for sterling deposits of non-bank U.K. residents in December 1958 based on the proportion of these deposits in 1962.

banks, and Northern Ireland banks) increased by about 50 per cent between 1958 and 1969. This is substantially less than the 90 per cent increase in Gross National Product over this period. In contrast, building society shares and deposits increased more than threefold, deposits with finance companies fivefold, deposits with accepting houses and British and Commonwealth overseas banks more than eightfold, and deposits with foreign banks thirtyfold. Deposits with the last two groups include very large holdings by overseas residents and United Kingdom banks. Sterling deposits of non-bank United Kingdom residents are only a small part of the respective totals, nevertheless their growth rates have been extraordinary. Of the claims on financial intermediaries included in the table, only deposits with savings banks have experienced a growth rate as moderate as those with deposit banks. Of course deposits with deposit banks are still very large in absolute terms though as a proportion of total liquid assets their importance is probably only half what it was in 1958.

The relative decline of the deposit banks was undoubtedly due, in part at least, to the factors already mentioned. Monetary policy was increasingly restrictive after 1958 and, with the heavy reliance on controls on bank lending, had a disproportionate effect on deposit banks. There was also a phenomenal rise in interest rates. Short-term interest rates which were around 3 to 4 per cent in 1958 and 1959 had risen to around 8 per cent in 1969, and the rise was equally great at the longer end of the market. Banks have sometimes been blamed in the past for failing to show as much enterprise as some other intermediaries in seeking to meet or to anticipate the fast changing financial requirements of modern society. They have also been blamed, rather unfairly, for not breaking free earlier from the tied relationship between the rates of interest they offered on deposit accounts and Bank rate, so as to compete more freely with other intermediaries for deposits. Undoubtedly some intermediaries, such as accepting houses, overseas banks, and finance companies, have taken advantage of their freedom in this respect. Finally, the more rapid growth rate of non-bank financial intermediaries reflects, in part, a completion of the portfolio adjustment following the excessive liquidity of the early post-war years.

It is sometimes argued that expansion of other financial intermediaries can itself be a cause of the relative decline of deposit banks. In principle this could occur in either of two ways. Expansion of other intermediaries could cause deposit banks to lose cash or, more generally, could reduce banking liquidity. Expansion of other intermediaries could also reduce the profitability of bank expansion.

An increase in the liabilities of a non-bank intermediary generally implies a transfer of bank deposits to that intermediary. In considering the effect of this on banking liquidity one should distinguish between public sector and private sector financial intermediaries. A transfer of bank deposits to a public sector intermediary, such as the National Savings Bank or a trustee savings bank, generally causes a transfer of funds to the public sector banking system since the bank deposits received are likely to form part of the flow of lending to the government. In this event there would be an equal fall in bank deposits and bank cash holdings. But if the government borrows more through this channel it is likely to reduce its borrowing through other sources. For example, it is quite likely that the issue of Treasury bills will be reduced. If the repayment of government debt is equal to the transfer of bank deposits to the public sector intermediary, then cash holdings of the banks will be fully restored and there may be no squeeze on banking liquidity. But competition for the reduced supply of Treasury bills is likely to cause a fall in Treasury bill rates. If the authorities wish to avoid this they are likely to reduce the issue of Treasury bills by an amount somewhat less than the transfer of deposits to the public sector intermediary, the balance of the funds being used to repay debt to the Bank of England. In this event the cash of the banks will not be restored fully and there will be some degree of contraction in banking liquidity. But of course one cannot predict what the policy of the authorities will be, so one cannot predict the net effect on banking liquidity of a transfer of bank deposits to a public sector intermediary. It is true that such a transfer does in itself destroy or reduce bank deposits in the private sector. But if bank reserves are fully restored by the repayment of government debt there is no reason why bank deposits should not be re-expanded to their former level. But if reserves are not fully restored neither will be bank deposits. The most we can predict is that the effect of a transfer of bank deposits to a public sector intermediary will strengthen the ability of the authorities to control the growth of bank deposits.

A transfer of bank deposits to a private sector intermediary will have no direct effect on the level of bank deposits or on bank cash. All that happens initially is a transfer in the ownership of the bank deposits, for example from the ownership of householders to the ownership of, say, building societies. Nevertheless there may be indirect effects on banking liquidity. In the first place the intermediary may use the funds to buy government securities (Treasury bills or bonds). Such purchases tend to drive down interest rates. But if the authorities aim to stabilize interest rates they will sell additional debt equal in amount to the purchases of the non-bank intermediary. Such sales by the authorities will cause an equal fall in bank deposits and bank cash, and so reduce banking liquidity. But here again one cannot predict the policy of the authorities; one can only predict that the power of the authorities to control bank deposits is strengthened. In the second place private sector non-bank intermediaries do keep some cash reserves. If an expansion of their liabilities induces these intermediaries to hold larger cash reserves, such additional cash will be drawn from the banks. It is worth noting that were non-bank intermediaries to maintain the same reserve ratios as deposit banks, any net transfer in ownership of bank deposits to these intermediaries would compel banks to reduce their deposit liabilities by the same amount as the liabilities of the other intermediaries rise. It is only because other intermediaries keep very much smaller reserve ratios that an increase in their liabilities is not matched by a decrease in bank deposits. In the third place a transfer in the ownership of bank deposits to non-bank intermediaries tends to cause an increase in expenditure, as we saw earlier in this chapter. A rise in the level of expenditure may induce the general public to hold larger amounts of currency, drawing the additional currency from the banks. But more important than this, the rise in expenditure is likely to induce the authorities to apply a more restrictive monetary policy. And such policy, as we have seen, tends to harm banks more than other intermediaries.

The alternative way in which expansion of other intermediaries can harm deposit banks is through the effect on the profitability of bank expansion. A greater preference by the general public for claims on non-bank intermediaries implies that the latter are now able to obtain funds on easier terms. They can therefore offer better terms to borrowers and can compete for loans that the banks might otherwise have made. If the non-bank intermediaries use the additional funds to buy securities, the yields on these will tend to decline. This will cheapen alternative sources of finance and so reduce the demand for bank advances. It will also make investments less profitable for banks to buy. In general, the greater the preference of the public for claims on non-bank intermediaries in comparison with bank deposits the greater will be the ability of these intermediaries to compete with the banks.

As we shall see in more detail in Chapter 10 the major constraints on bank competition have been abandoned with effect from mid-September 1971. No doubt this will have profound effects on bank expansion but, at the time of writing, it is too soon to forecast the repercussions. It has been argued, however, that one cause of the previous relative decline of banks may have been their failure to compete actively enough for deposits. It is said that if the banks had broken free from the agreement to tie their deposit rates to Bank rate, and if they had competed vigorously for deposits by variation in interest rates offered, they could have attracted deposits away from non-bank intermediaries. Lending by the latter would have been reduced and expenditure would have declined. It is contended that, on the assumption that the authorities seek to maintain a given level of economic activity, contraction of non-bank intermediaries can induce the authorities to adopt a less restrictive monetary policy. The squeeze on bank liquidity may be eased so permitting a more rapid growth in bank assets and in bank deposits. In other words, bank deposits can be larger, consistent with government aims, the more attractive bank deposits are made in relation to the liabilities of other intermediaries. Moreover if banks offer special rates for longer-term deposits, they are in a position to diversify their lending and capture business undertaken by specialist intermediaries, for example, instalment credit and mortgage loans.

The main arguments brought against this view were, first, that deposit banks cannot compete effectively against each other by deposit rate variation. There are too few banks for this. If one bank increases its deposit rate the others are forced to adopt an identical policy. Although higher deposit rates attract business away from other intermediaries they also make deposit accounts more attractive in comparison to current accounts. The cost of a significant transfer of funds from current account to deposit account may therefore more than offset any profits from business gained from other intermediaries. On the other hand, by operating through their subsidiaries the banks compete for larger fixed-term deposits without disturbing the rates offered in the parent banks on the very large volume of small deposits. Secondly, confidence in the liquidity and safety of banks is more easily maintained if business such as medium and long-term lending and equity participation is clearly divorced from the normal banking function and left with specialist subsidiaries. Thirdly, since much of the business of the specialized subsidiaries requires expertise, the scarcity of which necessitates high rates of pay, to bring this business within the parent bank risks disturbing the normal salary structure of the bank.

The implication of these arguments is that it is more profitable for banks to allow normal banking business to decline relatively to that of other intermediaries and to counter the effects of such decline by vigorous expansion of their subsidiaries. There is something in this but the case is not convincing. Although banks could, through their subsidiaries, have shared some of the expanding business of non-bank intermediaries, it is likely that they would have lost an increasing amount of business to the independent intermediaries. In any case the general public stands to gain from a more competitive financial regime.

6.5 NON-BANK FINANCIAL INTERMEDIARIES, MONETARY POLICY, AND VELOCITY

We saw earlier in this chapter that by offering a wide range of assets combining, in varying proportions, liquidity, convenience, safety, and yield, non-bank intermediaries encourage wealth-owners to hold wealth in these assets rather than in idle money balances, and encourage savers to accumulate their savings in these assets. At the same time because these intermediaries are able to tap funds at comparatively low cost they are able to provide funds to borrowers on terms that are easier and cheaper than would otherwise be possible. They therefore help to stimulate real investment. In brief, non-bank intermediation makes for a more intensive use of the stock of money and for a more effective flow of saving into real investment.

Non-bank intermediaries also make the supply of finance more responsive to changes in demand, and the demand for finance more responsive to changes in supply. An increase in the demand for finance causes market rates of interest to rise. Those intermediaries whose interest rates are flexible offer more attractive terms. The gap between the interest rates offered by these intermediaries and the zero rate on bank current accounts widens and, in the past, if Bank rate remained unchanged there was a wider gap between the competitive rates offered by the non-bank intermediaries and the rates of interest on bank deposit accounts. There is a tendency, therefore, for a larger flow of funds to these other intermediaries. They are also encouraged by the pressure of demand for finance to advertise more and to experiment in new forms of intermediation so as to attract more money and a larger portion of the flow of saving. Finally, intermediaries may obtain additional funds by selling their holdings of marketable securities to holders of idle money balances. In these various ways the supply of finance becomes more responsive to an increase in demand.

But non-bank intermediaries also help to make the demand for finance more responsive to changes in the supply. In a community where non-bank intermediaries are the established recipients of a substantial portion of the community's saving, any increase in aggregate saving will be reflected in a stronger demand for their liabilities. A receipt of additional funds by an intermediary will be an embarrassment unless such funds can be converted into earning assets. An increase in saving will therefore put pressure on intermediaries to seek new outlets for lending and to stimulate demand for finance. This point can be put in a different way. In a community where the development of non-bank financial intermediaries is no more than rudimentary much of the stock of saving will be accumulated in money. But when saving is accumulated in money it gives no signal to the economic system to encourage a greater demand for finance. Of course if saving takes the form of an additional deposit of currency in a bank, additional bank lending will be encouraged. But saving is more likely to take the form of holding on to bank deposits instead of transferring them in the process of expenditure. Such additional saving simply makes bank deposits idle which were previously circulating. This saving does not add to bank deposits or to bank liquidity; it merely reduces the turnover of bank deposits. But in a community where non-bank financial intermediaries are highly developed, additional saving is less likely to consist of holding on to bank deposits instead of spending them, and more likely to take the form of transfer of ownership of bank deposits to non-bank intermediaries. And in this case, as we have seen, intermediaries will be under pressure to stimulate demand for finance.

By making demand for and supply of finance more responsive to each other the non-bank intermediaries also help to make investment plans and saving plans more responsive to each other. This should reduce the instability of aggregate demand. On the other hand the fact that these intermediaries make the supply of finance more responsive to demand also implies that they make the velocity of circulation of money more variable. It may be argued that this reduces the significance of the supply of money. A reduction in the quantity of money may be offset or partially offset by an increase in its velocity. For example, if bank lending is curtailed by restrictive monetary policy, borrowers may turn to other intermediaries, and the latter will have an incentive to attract idle bank deposits. The stock of bank deposits may be reduced by restrictive monetary policy, but a larger portion of that reduced stock may be drawn into circulation by being transferred to the ownership of non-bank intermediaries. The ability of the banks to create money is important, but so too is the ability of non-bank intermediaries to draw money into active circulation. It was for reasons such as these that the Radcliffe Committee chose to play down the importance of the quantity of money and to substitute the importance of the whole liquidity position of the economy.

One must accept the argument that a well-developed system of non-bank intermediaries tends to make the velocity of money more variable. But how much more variable? If the variability of velocity remains moderate and reasonably predictable the quantity of money will still exert an important influence on expenditure; monetary policy remains effective, though stronger measures may be needed to produce a given result. The degree of variability of velocity will depend on the elasticity of substitution between different types of claims. At one extreme, if the general public regard deposits of non-bank intermediaries as perfect substitutes for bank deposits, and if borrowers regard loans from non-bank intermediaries as perfect substitutes for bank advances, the variability of velocity would be extremely high. A reduction in bank deposits and in bank advances would be easily neutralized by an increase in the deposits and loans of non-bank intermediaries. Borrowers, deprived of bank advances, could switch without difficulty to loans from non-bank intermediaries because the latter would have no difficulty in attracting a transfer of bank deposits. On the other hand the less readily these claims can be substituted for each other the more difficult will it be for an expansion of non-bank intermediaries to neutralize the effect of a contraction in bank deposits and in bank lending. And there is one very good reason for believing that claims on non-bank intermediaries are far from being perfect substitutes for bank deposits – the latter are means of payment, the former are not.

Not only is it implausible that the elasticity of substitution between bank deposits and claims on other intermediaries is so high as to render the quantity of money unimportant and traditional monetary policy ineffective, but the actual behaviour of some non-bank intermediaries tends to reinforce rather than neutralize the effects of changes in the money supply. Building societies, for example, aim to keep their rates of interest as stable as possible, and their rates are changed far less frequently than Bank rate. When monetary supply is reduced market interest rates tend to rise (in the short run at least). Building society deposits become less attractive and, after a time lag, the building societies are forced to reduce their lending. Restrictive monetary policy is also likely to have an adverse effect on the equity market. Unit trusts and investment trusts attract less funds. Then there are intermediaries which are unlikely to be affected either way by changes in money supply or in monetary policy. These intermediaries include life assurance companies and pension funds which depend largely on contractual saving. Of course it is true that there are intermediaries such as finance companies, accepting houses, and overseas banks which compete actively for deposits by means of interest rate variation, and whose behaviour will tend to offset the influence of changes in deposits of commercial banks. All-in-all, the conclusion is that although a highly developed system of non-bank intermediaries increases the variability of velocity of money, this degree of variability is unlikely to be sufficient to make the supply of money of little significance.

SUGGESTED READING

R. S. Sayers, *Modern Banking*, 7th ed. (Oxford, 1967), chs. vii, x.

B. J. Moore, *An Introduction to the Theory of Finance* (Collier-Macmillan, 1968), chs. vi, vii.

Radcliffe Report (H.M.S.O., 1959), chs. iv, v.

National Board for Prices and Incomes (H.M.S.O., May 1967), Report No. 34, *Bank Charges*.

N. J. Gibson, 'Financial Intermediaries and Monetary Policy', *Hobart Paper* (No. 39, 1967).

D. R. Croome and H. G. Johnson, *Money in Britain 1959–1969* (Oxford, 1970), part iv.

G. Clayton, 'British Financial Intermediaries in Theory and Practice', *Economic Journal*, Dec. 1962.

A. N. McCleod, 'Credit Expansion in an Open Economy', *Economic Journal*, Sep. 1962.

E. L. Furness, 'Income Flows and Financial Asset Holdings', *Oxford Economic Papers*, Mar. 1969.

J. G. Gurley and E. S. Shaw, *Money in a Theory of Finance* (Brookings Institution, 1960), particularly ch. vi.

D. D. Hester and J. Tobin (Eds.), *Financial Markets and Economic Activity* (Wiley, 1967), ch. i.

7 Money and Economic Activity: an Introduction

7.1 INTRODUCTORY SURVEY

The feature that distinguishes money from all other assets is its function as a medium of exchange and, no doubt, it is because of this unique function that money has attracted so much attention in economic literature. In any case it is understandable that the supply of money should have been thought important in the days when financial innovation was yet rudimentary. In those days money, if not the sole financial asset, was certainly an important element in personal wealth. But the significance of the money supply is perhaps more open to question in a modern economy characterized by intensive financial innovation.

The longest held theory concerning the role of money in economic activity is the *quantity theory*. There have been many versions of this and probably the only element common to all has been an insistence on the importance of the money supply. Many accounts have also shared a belief in the causal relationship between the quantity of money and the general level of prices. There is some evidence that this belief was held in very ancient times, but the first post-Renaissance expression of this view is usually attributed to Jean Bodin who, writing in 1568, argued that the cause of the rise in prices had been the abundance of gold and silver. It is doubtful whether any economist has thought that changes in the quantity of money cause exactly proportionate changes in the price level in some automatic manner. Earlier writers who considered the transmission mechanism frequently regarded the rate of interest as the important link. It was thought that an increase in the quantity of money would cause a fall in interest rates which would stimulate speculation in commodities, leading in turn to greater expenditure and a rise in prices; but it was also thought that by the time the price level had adjusted fully, the rate of interest would have been pulled back to the natural level as determined by the demand for and supply of capital.

Economists of the nineteenth century (and later) became particularly concerned with the formal analysis of resource allocation, product distribution, and relative prices. The ultimate determinants were usually thought to be 'real' forces such as tastes, factor supplies, thrift, time preference, and state of technology. Given these real forces, it was thought that there would be a particular equilibrium distribution of resources, set of relative prices, and level of output to which the economy would tend to move. The role of money was regarded as providing the measuring element in which relative prices would be expressed. A change in the quantity of money would cause a disturbance but this could only be temporary because, so long as the state of the real forces of tastes, factor supplies, etc., remained unchanged, the equilibrium allocation of resources, set of relative prices, and level of output would also remain unchanged. Since the economy would always tend to move to this equilibrium, the ultimate effect of a change in the quantity of money could only be a proportionate change of the number of units of money in which relative prices were expressed. In equilibrium, real forces would determine output and relative prices; the quantity of money would simply determine the absolute level of prices.

There is however a logical inconsistency in a theory which separates the determination of relative prices and of absolute prices. Classical economists appeared to be saying on the one hand that relative prices are determined entirely by real forces and that supply of and demand for commodities are determined by relative prices only; yet on the other hand that an increase in the quantity of money raises the price level because it induces greater expenditure on commodities. How can a change in money supply affect expenditure if demand depends only on real income and relative prices? The solution to this quandary is generally attributed to A. C. Pigou, the celebrated Cambridge economist. Pigou argued that wealth is one of the determinants of demand and that 'real' money balances are a part of individual wealth holdings. Real money balances are balances measured in terms of the volume of commodities that the money commands. This monetary command can rise for two reasons, either because of an increase in the nominal quantity of money, with commodity prices unchanged, or alternatively because of a fall in the commodity price level, with the nominal quantity of money unchanged. In either event money balances will be worth more in terms of commodities. A fall in real money balances occurs for the opposite reasons. The initial effect therefore of an increase in the nominal quantity of money is to raise real money balances. Since people feel wealthier there is a rise in demand for commodities and the price level is pushed up. But as the price level rises the real value of the enlarged stock of money declines. Eventually, when the price level has risen in the same proportion as the quantity of money, real money balances are reduced to their former level and the stimulus to higher demand ceases. This is sometimes called the 'Pigou effect' or the 'real balance effect'.

This classical theory of the transmission mechanism has been criticized for failing to distinguish between *outside* money and *inside* money. Broadly speaking these terms refer to the distinction between money originating *outside* the private sector and money originating *inside* the private sector. From an operational point of view the significant distinction is not place of origin but whether or not the creation of the money adds to the net wealth of the private sector. Outside money adds to net wealth; inside money does not. Money which originates in government purchases of current output from or transfer payments to the private sector adds to the assets of that sector without simultaneously reducing other assets of the sector or increasing its liabilities. This is outside money. But money can also be created when commercial banks buy securities from or make advances to the non-bank private sector. In these cases the additional money is matched by an offsetting reduction in holdings of securities or by an offsetting increase in the liabilities of the non-bank private sector. The same is true of money created by central bank open market purchases. Money the creation of which involves a counterpart reduction in other assets or increase in the liabilities of the non-bank private sector, is termed inside money. The distinction between outside money and inside money is clearly very relevant to the real balance effect. An increase in the quantity of outside money unequivocally increases the real value of the wealth of the private sector. A reduction in the commodity price level also raises the real value of outside money balances, and conversely. In either case one would expect the repercussions on expenditure to be predictable. But the real balance effects on expenditure of an increase in the quantity of inside money are far from clear. The real balance effect on inside money of a change in the commodity price level is equally doubtful. A rise in the price level reduces the real value of inside money but it also reduces the real value of the debts owed to banks. Since, in a modern community, the proportion of the money supply which can be regarded as 'inside' usually predominates, the real balance effect must be regarded as a rather doubtful explanation of the manner in which the quantity of money influences the level of expenditure. The 'portfolio effect' provides a much more promising explanation, but that is the subject of a later chapter.

A major development in monetary theory came in the 1930s with the publication by John Maynard Keynes of the General Theory of Employment Interest and Money. Whereas earlier economists had been more concerned with the analysis of long-term equilibrium (when everything is assumed to be fully adjusted to everything else), Keynes was primarily concerned with the analysis of shorter-term disturbances. Price inflexibilities and uncertainty play a paramount part in his theory. Keynes regarded the supply of money as important but chose to explain its influence as operating indirectly through the rate of interest. An increase in the quantity of money would tend to lower the rate of interest and this would stimulate expenditure. Whether this would result in higher prices or larger output would depend on the prevailing state of employment. The closer to full employment the more important would be the price response, and the higher the level of unemployment the more important the output response. Keynes thought that in certain circumstances even a large increase in the quantity of money may exert only a small influence on the rate of interest, and in these circumstances changes in money supply could have little effect on expenditure. Some disciples of Keynes came to treat these special circumstances as of general application, and added also the contention that even if changes in interest rates did occur the response of expenditure would be slight. This left no way in which the quantity of money could exert a significant influence on economic activity. To some 'Keynesians' money did not matter.

A reaction to this view came to the fore in the 1950s with the emergence of the monetarist school led by Professor Milton Friedman of the University of Chicago. Like Keynes, the monetarists are concerned less with hypothetical long-term equilibrium than with the impact of money on economic activity in practice, both in the shorter term and in the longer term. Their work is characterized by historical research and the application of statistical techniques to historical data from which they claim to have established a strong and consistent correlation between the behaviour of money supply and that of economic activity. Their conclusions are that money plays an important causal role in the determination of output and the price level, and that money exerts its influence on expenditure directly as well as indirectly through the rate of interest.

This introductory sketch does no more than draw attention to a few of the theories which have made an impact on monetary thinking.

An attempt will be made in this chapter to convey in a little more detail the substance of some of the 'classical' theories, and attention will be given to the work of Keynes and the monetarist school in separate chapters. Before embarking on this it will be advisable to examine the meaning of the velocity of money, a concept which figures prominently in all monetary literature.

7.2 THE VELOCITY OF CIRCULATION OF MONEY

The velocity of circulation is a formidable sounding term yet in essence it is very simple. It is the ratio between a stock of money and the value of monetary transactions conducted during a period of time, usually a year. If the stock of money in a community is, say, £10,000 million and the value of monetary transactions in a year amounts to, say, £50,000 million, then the velocity of circulation is 5. In other words velocity is equal to the value of transactions divided by the stock of money.

For purposes of comparison it is obviously necessary to have a consistent definition of the stock of money. In the first place there is the question of which assets are to be included. Clearly the ratio of transactions to the stock of currency will be very much higher than to the stock of currency plus bank deposits. For some purposes it may be useful to calculate the velocities of differently defined stocks of money. In the second place there is the question of the point in time to which the stock relates. Since the size of the stock of money is a changing factor one must decide whether the transactions of the year are to be divided by the stock at the beginning of the year, the average stock of the year, or even the average stock of the previous year.

It is also necessary to have a consistent definition of the value of monetary transactions. A complete coverage of all monetary transactions in the year would include not only the final stage purchases of current output but also all the intermediate stage purchases of the entire production process. Indeed it would also include every exchange of existing assets, both real and financial, and some assets change hands many times during the year. Perhaps fortunately, we do not have much choice of definition because reliable statistics of total monetary transactions are not available. We do, however, have reasonably reliable estimates of the value of final stage purchases of current output each year. These include the purchases of current output by households, government, and the overseas sector, and the additions to stocks of real capital, and these together constitute the national product or national income. The ratio of the value of national income to the stock of money is known as the income velocity of money or, simply, *the* velocity of money.

For illustrative purposes let us suppose that the stock of money remains constant during a year at £10,000 million and that the value of national income (gross national product) is £30,000 million. Income velocity is 3, that is £30,000 million divided by £10,000 million. Another way of looking at this is to say that a stock of £10,000 million of money has been used to make purchases during the year worth £30,000 million. Some units of money may have been used many times, some only a few times, and some not at all, but the average use of each pound during the year is 3. Income velocity therefore tells us the average frequency with which each unit of money is used during the year to make final stage purchases of output. If each unit of money is used on average 3 times during the year for this purpose, then the average interval of time between each use is 4 months (12 months divided by 3). Income velocity therefore also tells us the average period of time between each use of money, excluding the uses of money for intermediate transactions and for the exchange of existing assets. The term velocity is derived from this notion of average frequency of use or average time interval between use. But this concept can be rather misleading. Suppose, continuing with the same example, that in a subsequent year the stock of money remains constant at £10,000 million but that the value of national income rises to £40,000 million. Income velocity is now 4 and this may give an impression that most units of money are being used more frequently. But, as we shall see presently, the time interval between uses of money for final stage purchases depends mainly on the payment habits of society and these generally change only slowly. A much more likely explanation of the rise in velocity is that a larger portion of the stock of money is changing hands.

It is helpful to an understanding of velocity to think of the stock of money as being divisible into active and idle balances. One can regard active money balances as the normal minimum amounts which transactors require to hold to finance output transactions. Each transactor needs a certain minimum buffer stock of money because receipts and payments seldom synchronize. The size of this required stock will depend partly on the payment habits and credit facilities of society and partly on the value of the payments being made per period of time. We can say therefore that, given existing payment habits and credit facilities, the demand for active money balances will be a function of the value of national income.

The total stock of money is normally well in excess of the required minimum. One can regard this excess as idle money; idle in the sense that output transactions could be conducted without such excess balances. Why should anyone wish to hold more money than is necessary to meet normal payments? A full answer to that question would be very involved, but the short answer is that the yields on alternative assets are not regarded as sufficiently attractive to justify the trouble and risks of investing the excess money balances.

An individual does not normally distinguish between that portion of money which is the required minimum or active balance and that portion which is the excess or idle balance. But to illustrate the significance of active and idle money it will be helpful to assume that transactors do make such distinction. We could suppose, for example, that active balances consist of currency and current accounts, and that all idle balances are held on deposit account. On this assumption let us now suppose that the total stock of money is £10,000 million of which £2,000 million is active money (currency and current accounts) and £8,000 million is idle money (deposit accounts). If the value of national income for a particular year is £30,000 million the velocity of the total stock of money is 3; but the idle money is not used at all, and the average turnover of the active money is 15 (£30,000 million divided by £2,000 million). Suppose next that in a subsequent year the total stock of money remains at £10,000 million but that £1,000 million is transferred from idle deposit accounts to active current accounts, making the latter £3,000 million (including currency). If the income velocity of active money remains unchanged at 15, total expenditure on output will amount to £45,000 million. Now although the money actively circulating is still used at the rate of 15 times a year for making purchases, the income velocity of the total stock of money has risen to 4·5 (£45,000 million divided by £10,000 million). The rise in velocity may give the impression that money is typically used more frequently, yet what has happened is that a larger portion of the total stock of money is circulating.

In the example just described velocity rose because £1,000 million was transferred from idle balances to active balances. Alternatively one can say that the cause of the acceleration of velocity was a decision by transactors to reduce the ratio of idle balances to national income from 8:30 to 7:30 (i.e. from 0·26 to 0·23). Why should transactors choose to reduce the ratio of idle balances? One possible reason could be that opportunities to spend emerge which were previously not available. A notable example of this occurred in the early post-war period. War-time rationing had severely curtailed spending opportunities and 'involuntary saving' accumulated in idle money balances. When rationing was removed and peace-time products became available large amounts of idle money moved into active circulation. A less extreme example of this sometimes occurs when a state of economic depression is succeeded by a period of recovery; money balances which were idle during the slump become active when spending prospects are brighter. The more normal cause of a reduction in the ratio of idle money is a rise in interest rates. Those who want to spend more attempt to borrow idle money, either directly by selling securities or indirectly via intermediaries. Interest rates are pushed up until sufficient holders of idle balances are induced to shift wealth out of money and into the now more rewarding securities or claims on intermediaries.

Changes in the desired ratio of idle money to national income are the usual cause of change in velocity. But income velocity can also change because of a variation in the required ratio of active money to national income. The frequency with which incomes are received is a very important factor. Where wages are paid weekly the required ratio of active money to income will tend to be smaller than where they are paid monthly. Suppose we imagine a community in which all employees are paid weekly. The typical employee might hold all his weekly pay as a money balance on pay day and might run down this balance to zero prior to the next pay day. But as each employee runs down his balance over the week, each employer would have to accumulate money in preparation for the next pay day. Employees and employers taken together will require to hold money balances at least equal to the total weekly wage bill. By a similar line of reasoning the total required active balances in a community in which all employees are paid monthly would be at least equal to the total monthly wage bill, i.e. a sum approximately 4 times as great as where all employees are paid weekly. These examples do not take account of all the factors influencing the demand for active money and are intended only to illustrate the effect on required balances of changes in the frequency with which incomes are received. As a generalization, we can say that the less frequently incomes are received, on average, the greater will be the community's demand for active money, and conversely. In a similar manner the frequency with which debts are settled will also have a bearing on required active money. The less frequently debts are settled, *ceteris paribus*, the larger will need to be the accumulation of money balances to meet such settlements. In a community in which the grocers' bill, for example, is typically settled weekly there will be a smaller demand for active money than where it is typically settled monthly.

Credit facilities and financial innovation are also important influences on the required ratio of active money to income. Trade credit facilities, credit cards, etc., make it easier for transactors to synchronize debt settlement with receipts of money (from income or from sales), and there is less need to accumulate or hold a money balance over the interval between successive receipts of money. In general, the easier, the cheaper, and the more accessible are the facilities for short-term borrowing the less will be the need to hold stocks of money. But credit facilities can only obviate the need for active balances to the extent that the timing of immediate needs for money to settle debts differs. This is because credit facilities merely enable money which is not immediately required by one set of transactors to be put at the disposal of another set whose needs are immediate. Near money assets such as building society shares and deposits with savings banks, etc., can also be expected to reduce the need to hold money balances to meet unforeseen payments or to meet debts due in the near but not immediate future. The process of financial innovation is therefore also likely to reduce the demand for active balances.

The payment habits of society and the state of financial innovation are fundamental influences on the required ratio of active money but these are influences which normally change only slowly in the course of time. In the shorter run, changes in the demand for active balances are more likely to be attributable to very marked increases or decreases in interest rates. When interest rates rise very high there will be an inducement for business firms and other transactors to economize on active balances. For funds not required for immediate payment there is a trade-off between the trouble and cost of investing and then liquidating funds over a short period, and the interest that can be earned in that period by investing the funds. The higher is the rate of interest the more is the balance tilted in favour of investing rather than holding the funds liquid over the short period of time. The lower is the rate of interest, on the other hand, the greater will be the weight attached to the trouble and cost of investment and liquidation. But although high interest rates give more encouragement to the investment of active balances which are awaiting use they also discourage reliance on short-term borrowing. The net effect on the demand for active money is therefore not entirely predictable.

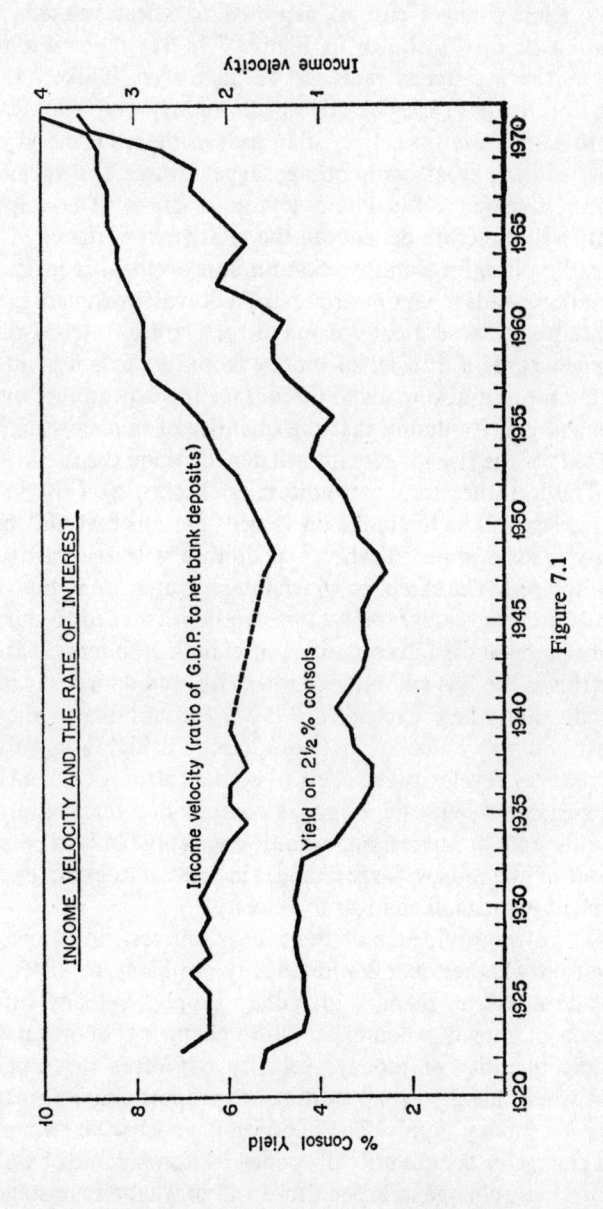

MONEY AND ECONOMIC ACTIVITY: AN INTRODUCTION 161

INCOME VELOCITY AND THE RATE OF INTEREST

Figure 7.1

Since changes in interest rates negatively influence the demand for idle money, and may also negatively influence the demand for active money, such changes can be expected to affect velocity, and an indication of this is shown in Figure 7.1. But there is a two-way effect. A rise in interest rates, as we have seen, is likely to induce transactors to hold less wealth in idle money and may encourage them to economize on active balances. On the other hand a rise in interest rates may also discourage expenditure. The former effect accelerates velocity; the latter acts as a brake. The response of velocity will therefore depend on the relative importance of the two effects. Suppose, for example, that an improvement in general profit expectations leads to an upward revision of real investment plans and, in consequence, to a greater demand for finance. Interest rates rise. This encourages a transfer of money from idle balances into active circulation but it also tends to discourage the expenditure on capital equipment etc. Assuming that the quantity of money is unchanged, the extent of the rise in velocity will depend upon the rise in expenditure. The less, therefore, expenditure is checked by a rise in interest rates the less will be the brake on velocity; in other words, the rise in velocity is least impeded when expenditure is least sensitive to the rate of interest. The extent to which interest rates rise in this situation depends on how readily transactors can be persuaded to shift wealth out of idle balances into securities or claims on intermediaries. The easier this is the less will interest rates rise, and conversely. One can conclude that where expenditure is very insensitive to the rate of interest and where demand to hold money is highly sensitive, then large changes in velocity are likely to be associated with small changes in interest rates. With the opposite combination (expenditure sensitive to the rate of interest and wealth-owners difficult to persuade to shift out of idle money) large changes in interest rates are likely to be associated with small changes in velocity.

This two-way influence of the rate of interest on velocity has a bearing on whether changes in velocity are likely to offset or reinforce the effect of changes in money supply. Velocity offsets the influence of money when expenditure changes proportionately less than the quantity of money; velocity reinforces the influence of money when changes in expenditure are proportionately greater than changes in money supply. The question is under what circumstances will a change in the quantity of money be accompanied by a smaller proportionate change in expenditure and in what circumstances by a larger proportionate change? Suppose the money supply is reduced by open market sales. Interest rates must rise to persuade wealth-owners to substitute securities for money. Now if wealth-owners are easily persuaded the rise in interest rates will be very slight, and if at the same time expenditure is insensitive to changes in the rate of interest the level of expenditure will be scarcely affected by the reduction in money supply. In this combination of circumstances the rise in velocity will have offset the effect of the change in the quantity of money almost completely. If, however, wealth-owners are very reluctant to substitute securities for money, interest rates will have to rise very sharply to persuade them to do so. If at the same time expenditure is highly sensitive to changes in interest rates, the contraction in expenditure may well be proportionately greater than the reduction in money supply. The change in velocity will have reinforced the change in the quantity of money. In the technical jargon of economists, the relationship between the rate of interest and velocity is influenced by the relationship between the interest-elasticity of substitution of money and other assets and the interest-elasticity of expenditure. The higher the former elasticity and the lower the latter the more likely is it that changes in velocity will tend to neutralize the influences of changes in money supply.

7.3. SOME CLASSICAL VERSIONS OF THE QUANTITY THEORY

The final section of this introductory chapter on the relationship between money and economic activity will be devoted mainly to a brief look at two 'classical' versions of the quantity theory of money. Irving Fisher's equation of exchange must be included in this survey, if only because his equation has become so identified with the classical quantity theory. The Cambridge equation deserves examination because it provided the foundation on which was built the theories both of Keynes and the monetarist school.

Irving Fisher's influence on monetary thought is partly attributable to the vivid simplicity of his equation of exchange – $MV = PT$. Indeed, to this day, many elementary textbooks give the impression that this *is* the quantity theory. The equation is so well known that it is unnecessary to give more than a brief account. Fisher acknowledged the equation to be simply a truism or accounting identity. MV stands for the stock of money multiplied by its average velocity of circulation. It is therefore the total monetary expenditure in the year (or other period of time). PT is the volume of transactions multiplied by the average price of each transaction and is therefore the total value of monetary transactions in the year. The equation states the obvious that the total money spent in a year equals the total value of things bought in the year. Of course, as we saw in Section 7.2, it is necessary to define the term T. If this is defined to include all monetary transactions then V will be total transactions velocity and P will represent a hybrid average of prices relating not merely to goods and services but also to stocks and shares and all kinds of assets exchanged during the year. If, on the other hand, T stands for the volume of final stage purchases of current output, P will be the average price level of current output, PT the value of national income (gross national product or GNP), and V will be income velocity.

As indicated above, the equation is not a theory at all. It is merely a vivid way of highlighting the variables that must be involved if a change in the quantity of money occurs. Looking back at any completed period of time one is bound to find that a change in M has been accompanied by an equal proportionate change in some combination of V, P, and T, because MV must equal PT. Thus, for example, if the average stock of money in a period has doubled, the value of purchases (PT) can only have remained unaltered if the velocity of money has halved; if velocity has remained unaltered then the value of purchases must have doubled; if velocity and the volume of purchases remain unaltered the average price must have doubled. But there is nothing in the equation to imply direction of causation. Fisher, however, was not concerned merely with providing a framework designed to indicate the variables involved with monetary change. He believed the quantity of money to be the causal factor determining changes in the price level. He argued that in the long run, and on the average in a large community, velocity remains stable because it is rooted in the customs and payment habits of society. The volume of output (T), he thought, would not be affected by monetary factors in the long run because it depends ultimately on real factors such as physical capacity and the state of technology. Finally, he regarded the price level as the dependent variable and did not believe that changes in prices could cause changes in the quantity of money. On these assumptions it follows that changes in the quantity of money must in the long run cause proportionate changes in the price level (allowing, of course, for any long-term changes in velocity or in output due to changing social customs and technological conditions etc.).

It is interesting to compare the Fisher equation with that of the Cambridge school, originating in the lectures of Alfred Marshall. There are several versions of the equation, some of which are rather complex; but the essence is sufficiently conveyed in the simplest version – M = KPR. Two advantages may be claimed for this equation over that of Fisher. The Cambridge equation can be regarded, not as an accounting identity, but as a condition of equilibrium; and it expresses the determination of the price level in a theory of value form. M is the supply of money, KPR is the demand for money. In equilibrium the price level (the inverse of the value of money) must be at that level at which the supply of money is equal to the demand.

In this equation M is the stock of money, as in the Fisher equation. Pigou described R as the resources of the community, which could mean the stock of real wealth; but most economists have interpreted R as the volume of output or real income and P as the price level of that output. On this interpretation PR is the value of national income. The novel symbol is K. This is the demand for money expressed in terms of liquid command over a fraction of real income. If, for example, K is one half, the implication is that the community wishes to hold money balances equal in purchasing power to half the annual output. In the Cambridge equation, therefore, the demand for money is a demand to hold a stock of real purchasing power. Of course the nominal amount of money that the community wishes to hold will depend not only on the fraction K, but also on the volume of real income and the price level. If PR is, say, £20,000 million and K one half, then the demand for nominal money balances will be £10,000 million; in other words, KPR is the demand for money expressed as a nominal sum of money. So long as K remains unchanged, the demand for nominal balances will vary proportionately with the value of national income, regardless of whether changes in this value are due to price change or to change in the volume of output.

If one assumes not only that K is a constant, but also that the economy is continuously at full employment so that R (the volume of output) changes only slowly with the growth in resources and productivity, then the main variables are M and P. Assuming also P to be the dependent variable one can conclude that P must always move to bring the demand for money into equality with any changes in the supply.

A simple account of the adjustment process would be as follows. We assume that equilibrium is disturbed by an increase in the quantity of money. The community now finds itself holding more money than is desired and will attempt to substitute investment goods and consumer goods. The additional expenditure does not of course reduce the nominal quantity of money but it pushes up the price level. The demand for nominal money balance rises with the price level until eventually prices reach that level at which demand equals the enlarged supply. The theory can easily be extended to include variations in output as well as in prices. Suppose, for example, the economy is at less than full employment. An increase in the quantity of money induces an attempt to substitute investment goods and consumer goods. The extra expenditure now causes an increase in output in addition to, or in place of, a rise in prices. Assuming K remains constant, the demand for nominal balances will rise with the value of national income, and when PR has risen in the same proportion as M the demand for money will equal the enlarged supply. In this more general version the quantity theory holds that changes in the quantity of money cause proportionate changes in the value of national income.

The reader will have noted the parallel between the assumption of a constant K in the Cambridge equation and of a constant V in the Fisher equation. In each equation the proportionate relationship between the quantity of money and the value of national income depends upon the assumption of constancy in K or V respectively. Indeed in equilibrium, K of the Cambridge equation is simply the reciprocal of V in the Fisher equation (where V stands for income velocity). Provided that in the Fisher equation T is interpreted as real income and V as income velocity the equation could be re-written $MV = PR$, or $M = \frac{1}{V} PR$. As M, P, and R are identical in both equations K must be identical with $\frac{1}{V}$, or, alternatively, V must be identical with $\frac{1}{K}$. In other words, in equilibrium, income velocity is the reciprocal of the fraction of real income over which the community wishes to hold monetary command. This throws some new light on velocity. It is not just a random value. In equilibrium it is determined by the community's choice as to the proportion of output over which purchasing power is held.

It is sometimes implied that earlier economists of the Cambridge school assumed K to be a constant. Pigou, in fact, assumed no such thing. He argued that each transactor will wish to hold a money balance sufficient to conduct ordinary transactions without trouble and to secure him against unexpected demands. Given the payment habits of society, the credit facilities, the degree of industrial integration, and the state of price change expectations, the required money balance of the average transactor will bear some relationship to the resources enjoyed. But this is not a fixed proportion. A money balance provides an imputed yield in terms of convenience and security, and the size of the marginal imputed yield depends upon the plenitude or scarcity of the money balance relative to income and other forms of wealth. As the ratio of the stock of money to income and wealth rises the marginal imputed yield of money falls, and conversely. What will be the optimum ratio of money to income and wealth for each transactor? Pigou's answer was that it will be that ratio for which the marginal imputed yield is equal to the explicit yield on alternative forms of wealth. He took this to be the yield on productive capital. This implies that K will vary inversely with the rate of return on capital. When this rate of return is high transactors will seek to hold a stock of money with an equally high imputed yield, i.e. the community will seek to maintain a low ratio of money to income and wealth. The size of K will fall as the rate of return on capital rises, and conversely.

In practice, choice of wealth holding is not confined to money and tangible capital, and for the typical wealth-owner financial assets are the more natural alternative to money. This implies that K will vary inversely with the rate of interest (the yield on financial assets) as well as with the rate of return on capital. In practice, too, an increase in the quantity of money is likely to induce substitution of financial assets as well as substitution of investment goods and consumer goods (indeed some economists argue that substitution is restricted to financial assets). Prices of financial assets will therefore rise causing a fall in the rate of interest. But if an increase in the quantity of money normally causes a fall in the rate of interest it must also normally cause a rise in K. This seems to imply that the change in PR is normally proportionately less than the change in M. If this is so then the quantity theory, in its cruder form, is invalid. But the quantity theory is not necessarily refuted if the change in interest rates is merely transitory.

In the classical tradition changes in the money supply have no long-run effects on the rate of interest. This conclusion seems logical enough if one assumes all bonds and bills, etc. are issued by the private sector to finance purchases of capital goods. According to the quantity theory an increase in the money supply, as we have seen, creates an excess demand for commodities and, assuming no increase in output, commodity prices must rise until the increase in the demand for money matches the increase in the supply. It also creates an excess demand for financial assets and, initially at least, prices of these assets must rise, causing a fall in the rate of interest. But the fall in the rate of interest cannot be permanent because the volume of bonds and bills, etc. cannot be assumed to remain unchanged. Indeed the issue of financial assets must keep pace proportionately with the rise in commodity prices to enable entrepreneurs to raise sufficient finance to meet the rising price of capital goods. In the new equilibrium the volume of financial assets will have increased in the same proportion as commodity prices and in the same proportion as the money supply. The rate of interest will therefore have been pulled back to its former level. One should note, however, that this conclusion is not applicable to government debt, the supply of which is unaffected by changes in commodity prices, for example, debt incurred in past wars.

At the level of abstraction of long-run equilibrium analysis a logical case can be made for the classical quantity theory, i.e. for the view that, in the long run, changes in money supply cause proportionate changes in the price level. But the logic is valid only if one ignores the many complications of reality, such as economic growth, the distinction between outside money and inside money, the existence of government debt, and the possibility that the money supply can be the dependent variable. The relevance of the crude quantity theory to the world of reality is indeed highly debatable, and it is to the problems of the world of reality that we must turn in the remaining chapters.

SUGGESTED READING

E. Dean (Ed.), *The Controversy over the Quantity Theory of Money* (Heath, 1966).
W. T. Newlyn, *Theory of Money*, 2nd ed. (Oxford, 1971), ch. iv.
H. G. Johnson, *Essays in Monetary Economics* (Allen & Unwin, 1967), part i.
R. F. Harrod, *Money* (Macmillan, 1969), chs. ii, vi.
Sir J. Hicks, *Critical Essays in Monetary Theory* (Oxford, 1967), ch. ix.
A. A. Walters, 'Money in Boom and Slump', *Hobart Paper*.
M. J. Artis and A. R. Nobay, 'Two Aspects of the Monetary Debate', *National Institute Economic Review*, Aug. 1969.

8 The Role of Money in the Economics of Keynes

8.1 AN INTRODUCTION TO THE ECONOMICS OF KEYNES

Keynes' work is usually studied in the context of macro-economic theory. Considerations of space prevent such an approach in this book, and the reader unfamiliar with macro-economics is strongly advised to read one of the many excellent textbooks on this subject. Nevertheless it would be unsatisfactory to discuss the role of money in the economics of Keynes without prefacing this with at least an outline introduction to his theories. There have been many interpretations of Keynes and many attempts to formalize his contribution to economics. In this process much of Keynes' vision and insight has been obscured and forgotten. A recent scholarly work by Axel Leijonhufvud, entitled *On Keynesian Economics and the Economics of Keynes*, has done much to recapture and clarify this vision. The outline which follows owes much to this important work.

It was pointed out in Chapter 7 that, in his General Theory of Employment Interest and Money, Keynes was concerned essentially with the problems of short period economic disturbance. Over short periods of time inflexibilities and uncertainty can be of crucial importance. It is therefore difficult to make a meaningful comparison between the economics of Keynes and that of classical economists concerned with the analysis of long period equilibrium because, if a long enough view is taken, inflexibilities and uncertainty cease to be significant. The General Theory was a challenge to the validity of applying orthodox economics to the problems of short-run disturbance. It was a challenge to theory based on the assumption that the market mechanism is capable of co-ordinating the plans and decisions of innumerable transactors in such manner that resources are always fully employed; there are defects in the market mechanism inherent in the nature of a money-using economy.

8.11 *The Defects of a Money-using Economic System*

We saw in Chapter 1 that money has contributed immeasurably to productivity in the widest sense. It has facilitated the development of a system of production and distribution of which the decision-making process is astonishingly diffused and in which the plans and preferences of a host of individual consumers, producers, and owners of productive services are utterly interdependent. The co-ordination of the system depends basically on the price mechanism. Disturbance of one set of decisions and preferences must be accompanied by more-or-less instantaneous adjustment of other decisions and preferences if the innumerable plans of transactors are to remain mutually consistent in the aggregate. Since it is price movements which provide both the information basis and the incentive for the adjustment of plans, prices must change with sufficient speed and by a sufficient amount to produce the necessary quick adjustment of plans. But the nature of a money-using economy impairs the corrective mechanism.

In an imaginary barter economy any offer for sale of commodities or of labour service is always accompanied by a counterpart demand for commodities or services. That is the nature of barter. When men offer their services for employment they simultaneously demand output. When employers offer output for sale they simultaneously demand labour service. In such an imaginary economic system one would not expect involuntary unemployment to exist more than momentarily. Any increase in the offer of labour service would also constitute an increased demand for output; wage rates would tend to fall and commodity prices tend to rise making it profitable to employ more labour. But in a money-using economy the situation is very different. Commodities and labour services are sold for money, and money is required to buy output. An additional offer of labour service is a demand for money, not a demand for additional output. There is a downward pressure on wage rates, but there is no simultaneous upward pressure on commodity prices. Output responds to an offer of money, to what Keynes called *effective* demand; it does not respond to the potential demand of unemployed labour. One reason, therefore, why involuntary unemployment may persist is that the mechanism for translating the offer of labour service into demand for output is defective.

Money, by permitting exchange to be split into independent decisions of sale and purchase, separate in time, thereby also introduces uncertainty. When disturbances occur in demand-supply relationships corrective forces are set in motion which bring pressure to bear on the pricing system, but there is no automatic market mechanism which ensures that prices will adjust immediately to the requirements of the new equilibrium. No doubt in a long enough period the interplay of market trial and error would normally produce the requisite adjustment. In the short run, transactors, living in a world of uncertainty, are guided by expectations which are often strongly influenced by the recent past. Price adjustments are often delayed while transactors seek alternative markets, and only after a considerable period will expectations be adjusted to the realities of the changed supply-demand situation. In the meantime productive resources are idle and commodities remain unsold. But the problem, as Keynes saw it, is not just one of temporary frictional unemployment. The failure of the price system to adjust with sufficient speed and to a sufficient extent to the emergence of excess supply results in a decline in output and income which will have a feed-back effect on demand. This magnifies the excess supply and distorts the corrective forces operating through the price mechanism.

Leijonhufvud maintains that the revolutionary element in the General Theory was that Keynes reversed the assumptions about speed of quantity and price adjustment. In place of the orthodox assumption that output and employment in aggregate remain broadly stable with prices adjusting rapidly to correct disturbances in demand and supply, Keynes assumed price and wage rate adjustment to be slow, with fairly rapid changes in output and employment taking the brunt of disturbances. The Keynes model does not rest on special assumptions of rigidity in prices and wage rates, but merely on the assumption that output and employment respond more rapidly than prices and wage rates.

8.12 *The Stable Level of Output*

In a classical model in which price adjustment is assumed to be sufficiently rapid to keep resources fully employed, the aggregate volume of output is determined by such factors as the volume and efficiency of resources and the state of technology. Output is stable; it increases only slowly with economic growth. But if price adjustment in the short run is not sufficiently rapid to ensure continuous full employment, what does determine the volume of output in the short run, when resources are less than fully employed? Keynes' answer was that aggregate output will tend to move to that level at which it is equal to aggregate effective demand. If output is less than demand producers will tend to expand output and employment. If output is in excess of demand commodities will be unsold and output and employment will decline. Hence the position of short-run stability must be when aggregate demand and output are equal. This position of stability can exist at any level of employment, but it can only be short-run stability so long as there is involuntary unemployment because the latter will exert a longer-run downward pressure on wage rates. In the Keynes model, therefore, the thing that matters is the level of aggregate effective demand, and it is to the determination of this that we must now turn. The analysis of aggregate demand can be conducted on various levels of complexity but for the purpose of indicating Keynes' ideas the simplest concept of aggregate demand will suffice, i.e. where it consists of two components only – consumption and real investment.

8.13 *The Consumption Function*

It is reasonable to suppose that in the short-run the effective demand of consumers will be constrained by their income; hence Keynes assumed that aggregate consumption would depend on aggregate real income. Since income is generated by output one can equally say that consumption depends on output. If real income rises people will consume more, and conversely. But when real income rises people can also afford to save more so that the rise in consumption will tend to be less than the rise in real income. Similarly, when real income falls people cannot afford to save as much, and the reduction in consumption will tend to be less than the decline in income. Consumption therefore has a peculiar dependent relationship with income; it will tend to change with income but by less than the change in income. This relationship is known as the consumption function. Although this simple relationship cannot be expected to hold in a predictable fashion in the long run, Keynes believed that, in the short run and in the aggregate for the community, the functional relationship between consumption and income would remain reasonably stable, though it might be influenced by changes in interest rates.

8.14 *The Determination of Investment*

As for the other component of aggregate demand, Keynes argued that real investment would depend on the relationship between the long-term rate of interest and what he termed the *marginal efficiency of capital.* The economic significance of a capital good to its owner consists of the flow of net earnings which the owner expects to derive from the asset over its life (net earnings are gross earnings less additional running costs involved). The marginal efficiency of capital is that rate of discount which, when applied to the expected flow of net earnings, will equate their discounted value to the cost of the capital good. It can be regarded as the rate of return over cost expected from the asset. Keynes maintained that so long as this rate of return over cost exceeds the long-term rate of interest by a margin sufficient to compensate for the risk involved, the purchase of the capital good will be worthwhile. From the point of view of the economy as a whole one can conclude that a rise in the average marginal efficiency of capital relative to the long-term rate of interest can be expected to cause a rise in real investment, and conversely.

An alternative, and perhaps easier, way of explaining this is to say that the demand for new capital goods depends on the relationship between the cost of newly produced capital goods and the value of such goods in the eyes of purchasers. Given the cost of capital goods, the higher the value of these goods the greater is real investment likely to be. The value of a capital asset to a purchaser depends in the first instance on the expected flow of net earnings to be derived from the asset over its life. These expectations are based on such factors as the prospective state of market demand for the product on which the capital asset is to be employed, the physical productivity of the new capital good, the size of the existing stock of capital goods in relation to the supply of labour, and the state of competition. These factors can be labelled *investment expectations.* In the economy as a whole there can be widespread changes in investment expectations, associated sometimes with a generally pessimistic or generally optimistic outlook. But the present value of a capital good cannot be obtained simply by adding up the expected annual net earnings over the life of the asset because a pound in the future is worth less than a pound today, and the more distant is a prospective net earning the less is its present worth. The reason for this is that a present pound can be invested in a financial asset and, at some given future date, will be worth more than a pound at that date by the compound interest earned over the intervening period. Putting this the other way round one can say that a pound at some future date is worth less than a present pound by the amount of the compound interest that can be earned up to that future date. To find the present value of an amount of money due at a future date it is therefore necessary to discount by an appropriate rate of interest. It also follows that the present value of a flow of earnings over a period of time ahead will be the sum of the series of discounted earnings. Keynes believed the appropriate rate for discounting purposes to be a long-term rate of interest because he assumed that the typical capital good has a long life. On this assumption it follows that the long-term rate of interest will be an important influence on the present value of new capital goods in general. Indeed, given the cost of capital goods and the state of investment expectations, one could say that investment demand would be a function of the long-term rate of interest. A rise in the rate of interest would lower the present values of all expected flows of net earnings from capital assets since such earnings have now to be discounted by a larger factor. And if the values of all new capital goods are lowered in relation to their cost, the purchase of new capital assets will be discouraged. Similarly, given the cost of capital goods and the state of investment expectations, a fall in the long-term rate of interest will give general encouragement to real investment. In Keynes' view the long-term rate of interest is of great importance to the level of aggregate investment demand.

8.15 *The Determination of Output*

To summarize the argument so far, we can say that consumption is determined by the level of income or output, given the nature of the consumption function; and real investment is determined by the long-term rate of interest, the state of investment expectations, and the cost of new capital goods. We know therefore the determinants of the components of aggregate demand but we have still to discover how, in the Keynes model, these components combine to determine the short-run stable level of output or income. Suppose that investment demand (as determined by the rate of interest, investment expectations, and cost of capital goods) together with the existing level of consumer demand gives an aggregate demand which exceeds current output. In this situation stocks of commodities will be falling and producers will have an incentive to raise the level of output. As the level of output (and therefore of real income) rises consumption will also rise but by a smaller amount (in accordance with the consumption function). It follows, therefore, that the gap between aggregate output and consumption will steadily widen as the level of output rises. Eventually the gap will be just equal to investment demand. At this point consumption plus investment will exactly equal the value of aggregate output. Output then stabilizes at this level since the expansionary incentive of excess aggregate demand no longer exists.

Suppose, on the other hand, that investment demand, together with the existing level of consumer demand, falls short of aggregate output. Some output remains unsold; stocks begin to pile up; producers have an incentive to reduce the level of output. As the level of output (and of real income) falls, consumption falls but not by as much. The gap between aggregate output and consumption therefore steadily narrows until it is just filled by investment demand. Aggregate demand then equals aggregate output, and a stable level of output is reached. One can conclude from this discussion that the stable level of output, or the level of output towards which the economy will always tend to move, is determined by investment demand in conjunction with the consumption function. In other words output will always tend to move to that level at which the consumption which results, together with investment demand, is just equal to that output. This can be put in yet another way. Since output, or income, will be stable when it is equal to the sum of investment and consumption, it can also be said that income will be stable when the portion of income not spent on consumption is just equal to investment, i.e. when planned saving is equal to investment demand. Income will therefore always tend to move to that point at which the planned saving which results is just equal to investment.

8.16 *The Investment Multiplier*

Up to this point we have seen that the stable level of output is determined by the level of investment and the consumption function. Keynes believed the consumption function to be reasonably stable, at least in the short run. But investment, determined as it is by the long-term rate of interest, investment expectations, and the cost of capital goods, is by no means stable. Hence, in Keynes' view, it is to changes in investment that the initiating changes in output and employment are mainly due. What sort of response in output will a change in investment produce? Suppose some disturbance causes a worsening of general investment expectations and that in consequence investment demand declines to a lower rate per annum. The impact effect is that investment plus existing consumption now falls short of output. Producers thereupon reduce the rate of output and this causes an equal reduction in real income; the effective demand of households is therefore curtailed and consumption is reduced, though by a smaller amount. This secondary decline in sales can be assumed to cause an equal reduction in the rate of output and therefore in real income. In turn, this leads to a further fall in consumption, though by a smaller amount than previously. The tertiary decline in sales causes a further decline in real income, and so on. Because of the nature of the consumption function, the decline which occurs in consumption at each stage of the process is less than the decline in output. The gap between aggregate output and consumption therefore steadily narrows. Eventually this gap is just equal to the reduced level of investment demand; aggregate demand is once more equal to aggregate output; a new position of stability is reached. The total reduction in the rate of output per annum will be equal to the initiating reduction in the rate of investment *plus* the induced reduction in the rate of consumption. The total change in output is therefore greater than the initiating change in investment. Indeed it follows from the nature of the consumption function (at least so long as it remains stable) that a change in investment demand will always tend to cause a change in the value of output of a greater amount. The ratio of the total change in output to the initiating change in investment was termed by Keynes the *investment multiplier*.

8.17 *Liquidity Preference and the Rate of Interest*

In the Keynes model the behaviour of investment is the main cause of disturbance to income and employment; investment, in conjunction with a stable consumption function, also determines the stable level of output. But, as we have seen, investment is a function of the long-term rate of interest (given the state of investment expectations and the cost of capital). Hence the long-term rate of interest plays a crucial role in Keynes' theory. How is this all-important regulator determined?

Keynes argued that the rate of interest is determined by the supply of and demand for money. The supply is assumed to be controlled autonomously by the monetary authorities. The demand for money is assumed to be a function of three motives – transactions, precautionary, and speculative. The transactions motive arises from the need to hold a stock of money to bridge the gap between receipts and payments. Given society's payment habits, the stock of money desired for this purpose will vary with the value of transactions, i.e. with the value of national income. The precautionary motive reflects the need of the community to hold a stock of money to meet unforeseen payments. This motive was also thought to vary with the value of national income. In Keynes' opinion neither motive is likely to be sensitive to the rate of interest.

The novel element in Keynes' analysis of the demand for money is his speculative motive. This can be regarded as the preference for holding wealth in the form of money rather than in bonds – hence the term *liquidity preference*. Why should anyone prefer to hold money, i.e. more money than is required to satisfy transactions and precautionary needs? The answer is that money may be regarded as preferable either because of the uncertainty of the future price of bonds (i.e. uncertainty about the future rate of interest), or because some wealth-owners expect the price of bonds to fall in the near future (i.e. rate of interest to rise). Keynes thought that the strength of the speculative motive would be a function of the current long-term rate of interest. The higher the rate of interest the greater is the compensation for holding an asset of uncertain capital value; the less, therefore, is likely to be the preference for holding money instead of bonds. Moreover the higher the rate of interest in relation to what is generally thought to be the norm, the fewer are likely to be the speculators who expect the rate to rise still higher in the near future and the larger the number who expect the rate to fall in the future (i.e. bond price to rise in the future). If the predominant market sentiment favours the expectation that bond prices will rise in the near future the prospect of capital gain to be derived from holding bonds is likely to reduce the preference for holding money.

8.18 *Causes of Change in the Rate of Interest*

Suppose that the supply of money is increased by the monetary authorities, so that the supply exceeds the demand to hold money as determined by the three motives at the existing level of income and the existing rate of interest. Since transactors find themselves holding more money than they wish, it is argued that they will attempt to substitute bonds for the surplus money. This does not get rid of the surplus money but the greater pressure of demand for bonds will drive down the rate of interest. As the rate of interest falls two things will happen. In the first place the speculative demand for money will increase. In the second place investment expenditure, and therefore income, will rise, increasing the transactions and precautionary demands for money. At some point the rate of interest will reach the level at which the community is content to hold the enlarged supply of money. Equilibrium will be restored at a higher level of income and a lower level of the rate of interest. In a similar manner a reduction in the quantity of money would cause a fall in the level of income and a rise in the rate of interest.

The rate of interest can also be disturbed by a change in the demand to hold money which is not offset by an equal change in the supply. A re-appraisal of investment expectations, for example, may cause a change in investment expenditure and therefore in the level of income. If the level of income rises, the resulting increase in the transactions and precautionary demands for money will cause the rate of interest to rise until a new equilibrium is reached at which the larger transactions and precautionary demands are balanced by a reduced speculative demand for money. A change in the demand for money may also emanate from the speculative motive. This will occur if the market takes a new view about the general norm of the long-term rate of interest. Suppose, for example, that the market begins to take the view that the average level of the long-term rate of interest will be higher in the future, i.e. that the general level of bond prices will be lower. In this event there will be a stronger preference for holding money by bear speculators seeking to avoid a capital loss. The attempt by such speculators to get out of bonds and into money will of course drive up the current rate of interest.

To summarize all this discussion, we can say that the basic determinants of the Keynes model are the state of investment expectations, the cost of capital goods, the consumption function, the supply of money, the demand functions for money, and expectations about the future norm of the rate of interest. Given these basic determinants the stable level of income and the rate of interest will be mutually determined.

8.2 THE EFFECT OF CHANGES IN THE QUANTITY OF MONEY

In the usual interpretation of the Keynes model changes in the quantity of money affect output, employment, and the price level only indirectly through the resulting changes in the rate of interest. The typical chain of events is as follows. An increase in the quantity of money causes a fall in the rate of interest; this leads to a rise in investment which in turn induces a 'multiplier' increase in consumption; this rise in aggregate demand causes an increase in the level of output and employment, and if the economy is close to full employment there will be a rise in the price level. But there are many qualifications which must be applied to this simple sequence of events.

It is useful to distinguish two types of change in money supply which can be described as exogenous and endogenous. An exogenous change can be thought of as a change deliberately produced as a part of monetary policy. An endogenous change is one which occurs in response to an increase in aggregate demand. The best example of this is additional government expenditure financed by an increase in money supply. It is obvious in this case that the increase in the quantity of money is not the cause of the additional expenditure though undoubtedly it facilitates the rise in expenditure. Since we are concerned mainly with the independent influence of money on economic activity it will be more helpful to concentrate attention of the effects of exogenous changes in money.

In a modern economy an exogenous increase in money supply is normally achieved by means of central bank open market purchases. These purchases will have some direct effect on the rate of interest and they will also create excess banking liquidity. The banks will seek to restore their normal distribution of assets and, in the absence of an unsatisfied demand for advances, they will do so by purchasing bonds. The money supply will increase to the extent that these are bought from the private sector. This amounts to saying that the money supply rises because wealth-owners are induced to hold bank deposits in place of bonds, and the rate of interest must fall by whatever amount is necessary to persuade wealth-owners to make the required substitution. On the usual interpretation of Keynes, aggregate demand will only be affected indirectly to the extent that the fall in the rate of interest induces greater investment expenditure and to the extent that this leads to a rise in consumption. The effect on aggregate demand of a given increase in the quantity of money depends, therefore, on the amount by which the rate of interest has to fall to induce the public to substitute the required amount of money for bonds and the extent to which investment and consumption respond to such fall in the rate of interest.

8.21 *The Inflexibility of the Long-term Rate of Interest*

Although Keynes regarded long-term rates of interest as of great importance, the basic problem of the economic system in his view is that long-term rates are not sufficiently flexible. The cause of this inflexibility, argued Keynes, lies in the influence of expectations on the speculative motive. He thought that past experience of the behaviour of long-term rates exerts a very powerful influence on market expectations about the future behaviour of long-term rates, and that this inhibits the flexibility of the rate of interest. Suppose that a majority of speculators believe firmly that long-term rates in the future will be at the level experienced in the recent past. And suppose also that in this situation there is an exogenous increase in the quantity of money. The increase in money supply will, as we have seen, create a downward pressure on the rate of interest. But since a majority of speculators expect the rate of interest to be back at its former level in the near future they will readily sell bonds as the current rate of interest falls so as to avoid the future capital loss that will be incurred when interest rates rise again. Such ready sales of bonds will in fact prevent the rate of interest from falling far. In effect, a large part of the substitution of money for bonds will be made by bear speculators who are readily induced to hoard more money by even a slight fall in long-term interest rates. Keynes thought that this would be the more likely to occur the lower is the level of current interest rates. One reason for this is that, when the opportunity cost of holding money is already low, even a very slight reduction in the compensation for holding assets of uncertain capital value may induce a massive increase in the preference for holding money. The second reason is that the lower is the current rate of interest in relation to the generally experienced norm, the more unanimous is likely to be the market expectation that any further fall in the rate of interest will be reversed in the near future.

What is the significance of the inflexibility of long-term rates of interest? In the first place it rules out of court (at least in the short run) the classical contention that the function of the rate of interest is to move sufficiently to balance changes in investment demand with changes in planned saving so as to preserve stability of aggregate demand. In the second place it implies that it is difficult for the authorities to influence economic activity by means of monetary expansion or contraction. Suppose, for example, that the authorities wish to counter the effects of a decline in investment expectations through monetary expansion induced by open market purchases. If there is a strong market belief that interest rates in the future will be at much the same level as in the recent past, the purchase of bonds by banks may cause scarcely any reduction in the current rate of interest because such purchases will be matched by the bond sales of bear speculators who prefer to hoard money. No doubt if additional money were created on a sufficiently massive scale the influence of speculative hoarding could be overcome and the rate of interest reduced. But Keynes had little faith that the authorities would be prepared to be so adventurous.

But it is important to keep this matter in proportion. Although Keynes thought that the rigidity of expectations about the future norm of long-term interest rates would gravely restrict their flexibility he did not imply that such expectations never change. Past experience is not the only influence on expectations. Monetary expansion or contraction affects short-term rates of interest and a change in short rates maintained over a sufficiently long period will begin to affect market expectations about the future norm of long rates. The authorities can influence expectations by clear statements on the future direction of monetary policy. The market must also take account of the prospective future demand for funds. For example, if the market takes a very optimistic view of future investment conditions it will anticipate a larger issue of bonds and equities and, in consequence, is likely to expect a higher future norm for long-term rates. Keynes did not assume, therefore, that long-term rates of interest are rigid. But he did believe that their inflexibility is sufficient to impair the functioning of the economic system and to hinder changes in the quantity of money from exerting a significant influence on economic activity, in the short run at least.

8.22 *The Interest Inelasticity of Investment*

We saw earlier in this section that the extent to which changes in the money supply affect aggregate demand depends not only on the degree of response of long-term rates of interest but also on the responsiveness of expenditure to such changes in interest rates as do occur. Many Keynesian disciples accepted Keynes' belief in the inflexibility of long-term rates of interest and assumed, in addition, that neither investment nor consumption would respond significantly even if there were changes in interest rates. The implication of such a combination of assumptions is that the money supply 'does not matter'.

The interest-inelasticity of consumption was frequently regarded as self-evident. Belief in the interest-inelasticity of investment was based partly on the rather negative verdict obtained from sample surveys of business opinion on the influence of the rate of interest on investment decisions. It was also held to be justified by two theoretical arguments. In the first place it was contended that bonds and capital goods are highly imperfect substitutes because capital goods, generally speaking, carry a degree of riskiness of an entirely different order from that of bonds. For this reason a moderate change in the yield on bonds will have little influence on the required yield on capital goods. Putting this another way, one can argue that, because bonds and capital goods are imperfect substitutes, a change in the bond yield will have little influence on the rate of interest conventionally employed to calculate the present value of capital goods. If changes in the long-term rate of interest on bonds do not affect the value of capital goods significantly they will not affect the demand for such goods. In the second place, it was argued, the typical industrial capital good has a fairly short life (e.g. 5 years or less). For obvious arithmetic reasons the influence of compound interest is proportionately greater over a longer period than over a shorter period. A change in the rate of discount employed to calculate present value, therefore, will have proportionately less effect on the value of capital assets with fairly short life than on the value of those with long life. Housing and public utility investment may be affected significantly but the mass of industrial investment in plant and machinery and stocks may be very little affected by a moderate change in the appropriate rate of discount. If it is accepted that a moderate change in the bond yield has little effect on the appropriate rate of discount for calculating present value, and if a moderate change in the appropriate rate of discount leaves the mass of industrial investment unaffected, it follows that changes in the long-term bond yield will have little influence on aggregate real investment.

8.23 *The Misinterpretation of Liquidity Preference*

Leijonhufvud takes the view that the first of these two theoretical arguments is based on a misinterpretation of Keynes' theory of liquidity preference. Keynes expressed the theory in terms of a choice between money and bonds. This has generally been interpreted literally. The significant rate of interest has been taken to be the yield on long-term government bonds, assumed to be determined on the one hand by the state of preference as between holding money (conventionally defined) and long-term government bonds, and the relative supply of each on the other hand. But in fact, argues Leijonhufvud, Keynes was prepared to define money very loosely. It could include all short-term financial assets. He also regarded long-term bonds, equities, and capital goods as very close substitutes so that bonds were used to represent all illiquid assets. Looked at from this broader point of view, liquidity preference is the state of preference between holding liquid assets in general and illiquid assets, including bonds, equities, capital goods, land, and buildings. And the significance of the long-term rate of interest to Keynes is that it represents, inversely, the demand price of all illiquid assets. On this interpretation an increase in liquidity preference, unmatched by an increase in the supply of liquid assets, will cause a fall in the prices of all illiquid assets, including the demand price of capital goods as well as the price of long-term bonds. Similarly, given the state of liquidity preference, an increase in the supply of money (including short-term financial assets) will induce greater demand for all types of illiquid assets. On this interpretation of liquidity preference, therefore, a change in the quantity of money can have a direct effect on real investment. It is *not* a question of investment being influenced only indirectly through a change in the bond rate of interest.

If this interpretation is accepted one must regard Keynes' concern regarding the inflexibility of long-term rates of interest as applying equally to the acceptable yield, or required yield, on other capital assets, including capital goods. The rigidity of expectations about the future norm of yields must be interpreted as applying also to the rate of return on capital. The problem, then, does not arise from the insensitivity of investment to changes in the bond yield. The problem is that, because of the rigidity of expectations, long-term yields, including the acceptable rate of return on capital, tend to be too inflexible. The conventional rate of discount employed to calculate present values may therefore be insensitive to changes in the quantity of money.

The broader interpretation of liquidity preference also adds weight to the importance that Keynes attached to the influence of the long-term rate of interest on consumption. Keynes considered two effects of a change in the rate of interest on consumption. A fall in the rate of interest reduces the marginal reward for saving and may therefore increase the preference for present consumption over future consumption. A fall in the rate of interest also implies a rise in the value of bonds in relation to the price of consumer goods, and this 'windfall' effect makes bond-holders feel wealthier and therefore less inclined to save out of current income. Keynes attached much less importance to the former effect than to the latter, but thought that the two influences in combination may cause a significant shift in the consumption function. If a fall in the long-term rate of interest is taken to mean a rise in the price of all illiquid assets, including equities, capital goods, land, and buildings in relation to the price of consumer goods, the importance that Keynes attached to the 'windfall effect' becomes much more understandable.

8.24 *Why Keynes Rejected the Quantity Theory*

There is no justification whatever for the belief that Keynes regarded money as unimportant. He chose to reject the quantity theory approach, not because he thought money supply does not matter, but because that approach ignores the behaviour of relative prices. The quantity theory analyses the determinants and causes of change in national income in terms of the demand for and supply of money. An excess demand for money, for example, implies an excess supply of commodities in general, and therefore a general decline in the level of prices and/or of output. The behaviour of relative prices is not an integral part of the theory. But to Keynes the relationship between the prices of capital goods on the one hand, and wage rates and consumer goods prices on the other hand, is fundamental. Investment depends on the relationship between the demand price of capital goods and their cost, the latter being strongly influenced by the level of wage rates. The 'windfall' effect on consumption depends on the relationship between the value of capital assets and consumer goods prices, and this effect was regarded by Keynes as a major influence on the consumption function. Since it determines investment and has an important effect on the consumption function, this price relationship, in Keynes' view, is the major influence on income and employment in the short run. The basic cause of large-scale unemployment, he thought, is that the general level of longer-term asset prices is too low relative to wage rates and consumer goods prices. Keynes rejected deflation as a remedy for unemployment partly because a balanced reduction in the prices of capital goods, of consumer goods, and of wage rates would leave the fundamental problem unsolved. Even if deflation could succeed in reducing wage rates relative to the prices of capital goods, the policy should be rejected because the inflexibility of wage rates would make deflation a difficult and socially costly operation. The proper solution, in his view, is to raise the value of capital assets by way of monetary expansion. His doubts as to the success of monetary policy in rescuing an economy from depression arose from his fear that the authorities would be unwilling to take sufficiently drastic action to overcome the strength of the speculative motive or to act quickly enough to prevent the multiplier contraction setting in.

SUGGESTED READING

A. Leijonhufvud, *On Keynesian Economics and the Economics of Keynes* (Oxford, 1968), particularly ch. i.

D. Dillard, *The Economics of J. M. Keynes* (Crosby Lockwood, 1948).

A. D. Bain, *The Control of the Money Supply* (Penguin, 1970), ch. iii.

H. G. Johnson, *Essays in Monetary Economics* (Allen & Unwin, 1967), part i.

L. S. Ritter, 'The Role of Money in Keynesian Theory', *Banking and Monetary Studies* (Irwin, 1963).

R. F. Harrod, *Money* (Macmillan, 1969), ch. vii.

Sir J. Hicks, *Critical Essays in Monetary Theory* (Oxford, 1967), chs. vii, viii, ix.

W. T. Newlyn, *Theory of Money*, 2nd ed. (Oxford, 1971), chs. iii, iv, v.

D. R. Croome and H. G. Johnson, *Money in Britain 1959–1969* (Oxford, 1970), part iii.

9 The Monetarist View

9.1 THE DEMAND FOR MONEY

A notable feature of monetary economics since the 1950s has been the revival of belief in the importance of the money supply. This revival has been dominated by the writings of Milton Friedman. The traditional quantity theory stressed the causative role of changes in the stock of money in determining changes in the general level of prices. The theory fell into disrepute, particularly following the Keynesian revolution, because it was abundantly apparent in the inter-war years that there was no stable relationship between changes in money supply and changes in the price level, at least over short periods of time. Friedman avoided a direct confrontation with this criticism by defining the quantity theory of money as a theory of the demand for money. He maintained that there is clear evidence of a stable demand function for money, that is a stable relationship between the quantity of money in real terms that the community wishes to hold and a limited number of independent variables.

The monetarist view is that money enables people to separate the acts of purchase and sale and, as an asset, is a temporary abode of purchasing power. The demand for money is therefore a demand to hold a certain volume of purchasing power. This means that transactors are concerned with real money balances. The nominal amount of money that people want to hold, given the demand for real money balances, will simply vary proportionately with the general price level. If, for example, the general price level were to double, people would want to hold double the nominal amount of money in order to hold the same purchasing power over goods and services.

How much purchasing power will transactors want to hold? Money is one way of holding wealth, so the demand for money is influenced by the same factors as influence the demand for other forms of wealth. These can be summarized as the total wealth to be held, the relative cost of holding each asset in terms of the yields foregone on alternative assets, and the tastes and preferences of individual wealth-owners. Taking tastes and preferences as given, the demand for any asset will vary directly with changes in total wealth and inversely with changes in the cost of holding that asset.

Friedman has argued that wealth includes all sources of income, including the productive capacity of human beings. The total stock of wealth must therefore include human wealth. In practice, even where statistics of tangible and financial wealth exist, there are no statistics of human wealth, but income can be used as a proxy because the value of the stock of wealth, including human wealth, is simply the discounted value of the flows of all incomes derived from that stock. The relevant income however is not the measured income of national income statistics because, among other deficiencies, measured income suffers from transitory fluctuations. A longer-term concept of income is required, which Friedman terms *permanent income*. This can be thought of as the weighted average of current and past values of income. The demand for real money balances is related to the real value of wealth or permanent income (i.e. after allowing for changes in the price level), and the evidence shows that over long periods of time real money balances have grown with real wealth or permanent income, though generally rather faster. It is inferred from this that money is something of a luxury asset, in that a rise in real wealth *per capita* is associated with a more than proportionate increase in the demand for real money balances.

The alternative forms of wealth can be broadly classified as money, bonds, equities, physical goods, and human wealth, on each of which there is a yield. In the case of money the yield can only be measured in terms of convenience and security, and of course the real yield of a nominal unit of money will vary inversely with the price level. A bond is a claim to an income stream of constant nominal amount. The nominal yield varies inversely with the market price of the bond and the real yield inversely with the general price level. An equity is a claim to a *pro rata* share of profit and since profit tends to vary directly with the general price level an equity can be regarded as a claim to an income stream of real amount. The real yield on equities will vary inversely with their market price. Physical goods can be regarded as providing a real yield akin to that of equities. Human wealth is not in the ordinary sense marketable; it is difficult therefore to envisage a comparable yield, though substitution of human capital for other assets is possible, for example by exchanging money or other assets for education and training.

The cost of holding money is the yield foregone on alternative wealth forms compared with the implicit yield on money. A rise in the yields on alternative assets will cause a contraction in the demand for money, and conversely. The monetarists claim that a change in yields on alternative wealth forms, for example in interest rates, has a systematic but rather small effect on the demand for money. The cost of holding money is also affected by the expected rate of change in commodity prices. An expectation that commodity prices will rise, say at 5 per cent per annum, means that it costs 5 per cent per annum to hold money rather than assets such as equities or physical goods, the nominal value of which tends to keep pace with the general price level. This factor has no discernible effect when inflation is moderate but can be of major importance when inflation is rapid and long continued.

In summary, the demand for real money balances is a function of the real value of permanent income, of the yields on alternative assets, and of the expected rate of price change. After allowing for change in real wealth *per capita*, and in the cost of holding money, monetarists claim that the ratio of real money to real permanent income has experienced only minor fluctuations. In other words they maintain that there is a stable relationship between the demand for real money balances, real income, and the cost of holding money.

If the community seeks to maintain a stable ratio between real money balances and real income, subject only to systematic and comparatively minor variations in accordance with changes in real wealth *per capita* and in the cost of holding money, then it follows also that there will be a relatively stable ratio between the nominal quantity of money and the nominal value of income. In other words the income velocity of money will be relatively stable. But it is important to emphasize that monetarists do not claim that income velocity is constant. They claim that fluctuations in income velocity occur in a reasonably predictable and systematic way, and that such fluctuations are relatively minor except during rapid and prolonged inflation.

It is conceded that over short periods of time the relationship between change in money supply and changes in money income and in the price level has not always been stable. But there are several factors which can explain short-term instability. In the first place temporary cyclical disturbances can occur which, at the time, may dwarf monetary influences. In any case the stable relationship is between money and longer-term income (permanent income). The relationship between money and measured income is bound to be unstable whenever there are transitory fluctuations. In the second place, over short periods of time, changes in money supply can be the consequence as well as the cause of changes in expenditure.

Finally there is a variable time lag between changes in money and the resulting changes in money income which, in the U.S.A., has been anything between six months and two years, so that over a period of say a year the effects of a change in money supply may sometimes have been fully manifested and sometimes hardly manifested at all.

9.2 THE CAUSATIVE ROLE OF MONEY

The existence of a stable relationship between the quantity of money and the value of income implies nothing about the direction of causation. Money may determine income, income may determine money, or some third factor may determine both. Generally speaking, if the supply of money normally responds to changes in the demand, the role of money may be merely passive; but if the supply is determined independently of the demand for money, this is *prima facie* evidence that money plays a causative role in maintaining the stable ratio between money and money income. Monetarists do not deny that there are influences running from income to money supply but they claim that money also exerts an important independent influence and is a vital determinant of money income. They maintain that there is abundant evidence in history of the supply of money being influenced by factors independent of the demand for money. At times such factors have been the conditions of supply of gold or silver, and at times the deliberate policy measures of the monetary authorities. Moreover there have been no cases in history where a major change in the money supply has not been accompanied by a major change in the value of income and in the price level. Since this relationship has been maintained over many centuries and in widely different conditions, and since the changes in the quantity of money have almost invariably preceded, it is reasonable to conclude, they argue, that changes in money supply have played a predominantly causative role.

The influence of the monetarist school rests in part, of course, on the intellectual appeal of their theory, but perhaps it is mainly due to the vast amount of research and statistical testing which has been undertaken. This is claimed to provide overwhelming evidence that changes in money supply have been the dominant cause of economic disturbance and that the behaviour of the money supply is a reasonably reliable indicator of changes in expenditure and in the price level. Indeed it is claimed that the statistical evidence shows the relationship between changes in money and changes in consumer expenditure and income to be much more stable than the Keynesian relationship between changes in autonomous expenditure and changes in consumption and income. In other words it is claimed that the demand function for money is more stable than the Keynesian consumption function, and that the *money multiplier* is more consistent than the autonomous expenditure multiplier. In short, that the monetarist approach is analytically superior to the Keynesian approach.

This research and statistical work has stimulated similar study by other economists, and some of the monetarists' conclusions have been challenged. For example, the contention that money supply is a more important and reliable determinant of income than Keynesian autonomous expenditure has been challenged on the grounds of faulty methodology. With different methods and a more complex model opposite results have been claimed. In general, however, research has so far shown that there is a more stable relationship between money and permanent income or wealth than between money and measured income. Most research has shown that the long-term bond yield has a significant and consistent influence on the demand for money, but that the demand is also systematically influenced by short-term interest rates, equity yields, and the rate of inflation. There is also evidence that the demand for money has risen faster than wealth over long periods of time.

No mention has been made so far of how money is defined. Friedman has chosen to define money as currency in circulation plus total deposits with commercial banks. Some other research workers have used the narrower definition of currency plus demand deposits. The evidence has not pointed conclusively to the superiority of either definition. The demand functions for money defined in either way have proved to be relatively stable. It is worth mentioning that recent work in the Bank of England has indicated some superiority for the narrower definition.

9.3 THE MONETARIST VIEW OF MONETARY POLICY

Friedman's analysis of the role of monetary policy has influenced monetary thinking considerably. His contention is that monetary policy cannot be used effectively to control interest rates or unemployment, nor can it be used effectively for fine tuning of the economy. Its role, he maintains, should be to provide a stable background for economic growth.

Monetary authorities can change the level of interest rates, but only temporarily in an economy at all close to full employment, and the end result may be the opposite of what was intended. Monetary expansion, via open market purchases, is likely to cause a fall in bond yields initially, but this will tend to be reversed by the forces set in motion. The reduction in interest rates is likely to stimulate borrowing, and a greater supply of bonds. The increase in the money supply will, by stimulating expenditure, cause either a rise in real income and therefore an increase in the demand for real money balances, or a rise in the price level which will reduce the supply of real money balances, or both. These developments, in combination, are likely to pull rates of interest towards their former level probably within a year or two. Indeed rates may be pushed above the initial level. This will occur if a rise in prices evokes fears of greater inflation; borrowers will then be willing to pay higher interest rates and lenders will demand higher rates to compensate for the anticipated rise in prices. In other words, fears of inflation must cause the nominal rate of interest to rise if the real rate of interest is to be maintained at the former level. The full effect of inflationary expectations on interest rates is slow to develop and equally slow to disappear. Once the effect is established the authorities will be obliged to make even larger open market purchases in the effort to keep interest rates down. A vicious circle will then develop. Friedman maintains that this explains why high and rising interest rates are associated with rapid growth in the money supply. Low interest rates, on the other hand, are a sign that money has been tight. Paradoxically, from a Keynesian point of view, the authorities can only ensure low interest rates through a deflationary policy. Interest rates could, in theory, be pegged at the equilibrium level, but the authorities have no means of knowing what this level is, particularly since it is by no means constant. An attempt to peg rates at any other level is doomed to failure. The rate of interest is therefore a poor criterion for monetary policy.

The level of unemployment is an equally impracticable target for monetary policy. One can perhaps envisage an equilibrium level of unemployment reflecting that demand for labour which would induce a growth of wage rates consistent with the growth of productivity. But if the authorities attempt to peg the level of unemployment at other than the equilibrium level, they will be doomed to failure. An attempt to reduce unemployment by monetary expansion will succeed initially to the extent that real wages are lowered, that is to the extent that the prices of output rise in advance of nominal wage rates. But this reduction can only be temporary. In due course labour will demand a rise in nominal wage rates to restore their real wages, and the stimulus to higher employment will disappear. Moreover if the policy results in commodity prices rising over a sufficiently long period, labour will come to expect the price rise to continue in the future. Wage demands will increasingly anticipate future price inflation. To maintain a lower level of unemployment in these circumstances will require expansion of the money supply at an accelerating rate to keep commodity price inflation ahead of wage inflation. This policy too establishes a vicious circle. A corollary of this is that once a general expectation of rising prices becomes established, higher and higher levels of unemployment will be required to keep the rise in wage rates in line with the growth of productivity. Friedman surmises that the beneficial effects on employment of monetary expansion may last from two to five years. Thereafter the effect begins to be reversed unless inflation is allowed to accelerate continuously.

Neither the level of interest rates nor the level of unemployment are suitable criteria for monetary policy because the authorities cannot control either for more than limited periods. The proper policy of the authorities is to control the money supply, since this is the only magnitude that they can control. But this control cannot be used effectively to offset cyclical disturbance or for fine tuning of the economy. This is because of the lag in time, both long and variable, between a change in money supply and the resulting effects on expenditure, and the further lag before the authorities are able to diagnose the policy required. In consequence, counter-cyclical monetary policy is as likely to intensify as to reduce fluctuation. The diagnosis lag often means that policy changes are made too late, while the effect lag often means that a greater monetary change is made than is required. An increase in money supply designed to counter a recession, for example, may be made too late to affect the recession significantly, and the authorities may be induced to increase the money supply more than is required anyway in the attempt to hasten the stimulus to expenditure. The policy may serve merely to intensify the subsequent cyclical upswing. Monetary restriction is also an unsatisfactory method of countering a sudden inflationary pressure because it curbs output long before it affects the price level. Monetary restriction is therefore likely to impose prolonged recession before price inflation is checked.

The proper objectives of monetary policy are to provide a stable background for economic growth and to prevent money being a source of disturbance. For these purposes the ideal policy is a steady and moderate rate of growth of money supply, just sufficient to finance the growth of output with a stable price level, say between

3 and 5 per cent per annum. Short of this ideal, steadiness in monetary growth should be given high priority and, at the very least, wide swings should be avoided. A policy which succeeds in achieving a stable internal price level cannot at the same time permit price level adjustment to correct a balance of payments disequilibrium, arising for example from differing national rates of growth of productivity. A policy of steady money growth should therefore be combined with a policy of flexible exchange rates.

9.4 THE TRANSMISSION MECHANISM

Perhaps the two most frequent criticisms of the monetarist view are first that the monetarist school fails to explain adequately how changes in money supply cause changes in economic activity, and secondly, that changes in money supply are, in practice, more often the consequence than the cause of changes in expenditure.

Recent writings have helped to meet the first criticism, and an article in the Bank of England Quarterly Bulletin of June 1970 compares in an illuminating manner the transmission mechanism implicit in the Keynesian school of thought with that of the monetarists. Both approaches can be regarded as assuming that a change in the quantity of money exerts its influence through the disturbance to the equilibrium of portfolios. Wealth-owners tend to distribute their wealth between various assets such that the marginal advantage of each is equal, and money balances are adjusted to ensure that the marginal advantage of money, measured in convenience and security, is equal to the marginal advantage of other assets held. In other words, wealth-owners seek to equate the marginal advantage of money to its marginal cost, in terms of the yields on assets foregone. When money holdings are disturbed the main weight of adjustment falls on those assets which are regarded as close substitutes for money. The B.E.Q.B. article argues that the major distinction between the Keynesian and the monetarist views lies in their respective beliefs about the closeness of substitution of other assets for money. This distinction can be usefully illustrated by a brief sketch of what may be regarded as typical explanations of the transmission mechanism of each school of thought.

9.41 *The Keynesian Mechanism*

The typical Keynesian belief (which must be distinguished from what Keynes himself might have believed) is that only financial assets, and short-term financial assets in particular, are close substitutes for money. When transactors find themselves holding more money than they wish, the immediate and main adjustment of portfolios takes the form of the purchase of liquid financial assets. Such purchases raise the price and lower the yield on short-term financial assets. This, in turn, causes some substitution of less liquid financial assets. But as the substitution proceeds along the liquidity spectrum the extent and predictability of the effects on asset prices and yields diminish. Expenditure on output is affected to the extent that the change in financial asset yields, particularly at the long end of the spectrum, causes a divergence between the cost of borrowing and the return on real capital assets. The change in financial asset yields can therefore cause a change in business investment and, via multiplier repercussions, in consumer expenditure as well. In addition, because of rigidities in certain short-term interest rates, the attempt to substitute short-term assets causes, not a fall in the yield on such assets, but a greater availability of finance from intermediaries. This permits expenditure on output which otherwise would not have occurred. Finally the rise in the price of financial assets, by making wealth-owners feel wealthier, may induce less saving out of current income. With the exception of the availability of finance effect, one can say that a change in the quantity of money influences expenditure only as a consequence of changes in yields on financial assets. Many Keynesians have held that moderate changes in the quantity of money are unlikely to affect expenditure significantly. In the first place short-term financial asset yields will be very little affected because these assets are such close substitutes for money. A slight rise in yields readily induces transactors to hold smaller money balances and a slight fall in yields readily induces them to hold larger money balances. In the second place many Keynesians have believed that investment and consumption are insensitive to moderate changes in yields. There is therefore a double reason for expecting the influence of moderate changes in money on expenditure to be slight. It is agreed that large changes in the quantity of money are likely to have a significant effect on interest rates, but the effect at the longer end of the spectrum is also unpredictable since the behaviour of long-term rates is dominated by expectations about the future level of rates. Even very large changes in money supply cannot therefore be relied upon to produce a reasonably predictable expenditure response. In consequence monetary policy is thought to be more reliable and effective if used to control the level of interest rates rather than the money supply.

9.42 The Monetarist Mechanism

The typical monetarist does not regard any particular group of financial assets as an especially close substitute for money. The unique feature of money is that it is a substitute, more-or-less equally, for all other assets, financial and real. Since no one asset is a closer substitute for money than any other, the elasticity of substitution between money and any other asset will be fairly low. It follows from this that transactors are likely to react to the receipt of a larger quantity of money by purchasing more assets of all types, including capital goods and consumer durables. The effect of a change in the money supply is therefore widely diffused. Open market purchases must, of course, have an impact effect on the yields of the relevant financial assets to induce holders to sell. A Keynesian would argue that the fall in yields makes wealth-owners content to hold larger money balances. But, argues the monetarist, the fact that transactors are induced to sell short-term (or other) financial assets by the offer of an attractive price does not imply that they want to hold more money indefinitely. Larger balances are held simply as a transitional step in the rearrangement of portfolios. Financial assets are not sufficiently close substitutes for money for transactors to be induced to hold more money indefinitely by the fall in interest rates. Non-monetary assets, on the other hand, are regarded as fairly close substitutes for each other, so that the main effect of the fall in short rates will be to induce a substitution of other non-monetary assets (real and financial) for short-term financial assets, while the money balances, though changing hands, remain excessive. And as long as money balances are felt to be excessive there will be a widely diffused and continuing attempt to substitute real and financial assets as the redundant balances spread through the economy. Throughout this process the demand for real assets rises, not only because of direct substitution of money for these assets, but also because as prices of financial assets are bid up and become relatively expensive, real assets become a preferable substitute. Prices of existing real assets therefore rise and, as these in turn become expensive relative to newly produced assets, demand for current output rises. Equilibrium will only be restored when demand for real money balances is once more equal to the supply. Either the general price level must rise to reduce sufficiently the supply of real money balances, or real income must rise to increase sufficiently the demand for real money balances, or some combination of both. By the time equilibrium is restored interest rates will be back to, or close to, their former level as a consequence of the decline in the supply of real money balances (due to the rise in the price level), the increase in the demand for real money balances (from any resulting increase in real permanent income), increased borrowing (because of greater demand for real capital assets), and, perhaps, greater fear of inflation.

9.43 *The Mechanisms Compared*

Both schools of thought would agree that a change in the money supply sets in motion a train of disturbance and that equilibrium will not be restored until demand for and supply of money are once more equal. The essence of the Keynesian case is that demand for money is re-equated to supply mainly by a change in the rate of interest and only to a limited extent by induced changes in the value of income. The essence of the monetarist case is that the demand for money is not very significantly affected by changes in the rate of interest (which are not in any case permanent), so that adjustment of demand for money depends mainly on changes in the value of income resulting from expenditure repercussions. An extreme Keynesian expects an increase in money supply to be accompanied by a fall in interest rates, a fall in the income velocity of money, and not very much change in the value of income. An extreme monetarist expects interest rates and income velocity to be affected very little, and the value of expenditure to increase more-or-less proportionately with money supply. The evidence does not provide conclusive proof of either point of view. The ratio of money to the value of income has tended to vary inversely with interest rates, indicating that demand for money is affected significantly by the rate of interest. On the other hand, the relationship between income velocity and the rate of interest is not significant enough to justify the more extreme Keynesian view.

9.5 ARE CHANGES IN MONEY SUPPLY EXOGENEOUS OR ENDOGENEOUS?

Over long periods of time the rates of growth of money supply and the value of national income have tended to be much the same. But correlation is not, in itself, proof of causation. As Professor Kaldor pointed out in Lloyds Bank Review of July 1970 there is close correlation between the note issue and consumer expenditure, but few would suggest that the rise in the note issue at Christmas is the cause of additional expenditure at such time. It is clearly a very important question whether money is the cause of change in income, or vice versa, or whether some common factor determines both.

As we have seen, monetarists believe that, in general, the supply of money is determined independent of demand and that money plays a predominantly causal role. This belief is based on historical research, on statistical testing, and on the fact that monetary changes precede income changes. But in modern times it is difficult to accept the view that money is determined exogeneously. In the United Kingdom the authorities have followed fairly consistently a policy of limiting interest rate fluctuation so as to facilitate management of the national debt, and have also sought to preserve a high level of employment. Both policies tend to make the money supply the consequence rather than the cause of changes in money income. An increase in government expenditure or an improvement in the balance of payments will expand money income and will also increase the supply of money if, in order to preserve interest rate stability, the authorities are unwilling to sell more public sector debt. Increased private sector expenditure also results in a larger money supply if the authorities are reluctant to allow interest rates to rise. Cost inflation involves monetary expansion as long as the authorities are determined to maintain a high level of employment. Even in former days, when interest rate stabilization and full employment scarcely figured as policy objectives, it is doubtful whether changes in the money supply were exogeneous in any true sense. Under the gold standard, for example, the state of the balance of payments was an important determinant of both money income and money supply. Finally, it is doubtful whether in the very long run the authorities have the power to control the stock of money in an independent fashion. One of the lessons of history is that where, for one reason or another, the existing means of payment have proved inadequate for the spending needs of the community, people have invented new means of settling debts. Money is not a unique substance, the supply of which the authorities have power to control at will. The more one form of money is restricted the more will other forms emerge. Control of the money supply in the long run is an illusion. Professor Kaldor suggests that the comparative stability of income velocity has in fact been due to the instability of the money supply. A relatively stable ratio has been maintained between the stock of money and the value of income precisely because the supply of money has normally been adjusted to changes in money incomes. One reason why new forms of money have not developed to any marked extent in recent times is because the flexibility in the supply of existing forms has rendered such development unnecessary.

The argument of the critics is, in brief, that the supply of money is not exogeneous but is determined primarily by the level of expenditure. The relative stability of the ratio between the stock of conventional forms of money and the value of money income has been due to the fact that the authorities, in pursuit of policies such as interest rate stabilization and full employment, have allowed the supply of conventional forms of money to adjust to changes in money income. Even had the authorities severely restricted the stock of conventional forms of money their policy would have been defeated in the long run by the emergence of new forms of money. Money in a wider sense would adjust to expenditure despite the control of conventional forms.

This argument, however, may be regarded as rather extreme. No doubt attempts to influence economic activity by severe restriction of existing forms of money will be defeated in the very long run by the emergence of alternative forms. But this does not mean that control of the money supply is entirely ineffectual in the shorter run. It takes time for new forms of money to emerge fully, and it is particularly difficult to develop satisfactory and efficient substitutes for currency. In the meantime control of the quantity of existing forms of money may exert a significant influence on economic activity. As to whether the comparative stability of income velocity has been due to money causing changes in money income, or to money income causing changes in money supply, it is not unreasonable to suggest that it has been partly one and partly the other. It is difficult to accept the extreme monetarist view that money supply has played a mainly independent and causative role because we know from experience, particularly in modern times, that changes in money supply have often been the residual consequence of other policies, such as interest rate stabilization and full employment. At the same time, even if changes in money supply are mainly endogeneous this does not exclude the possibility, or even probability, that changes in money supply have a feed-back effect on expenditure and money income.

That changes in money supply generally precede changes in money income may be regarded as *prima facie* evidence that money plays the causative role, on the grounds that, if income were the cause of change in money supply, income changes should normally precede changes in money. But this is too simple a view. It is not so much the case that income causes changes in money as that a third factor, such as government expenditure or the balance of payments, causes a change in both. In any case it takes time for a change in income to be fully realized. A disturbance to income initiated, for example, by an increase in government expenditure financed by borrowing from the banking system, will not be completed until there has been time for the multiplier repercussions on consumption to run their course; whereas the rise in the money supply occurs at the time of the government expenditure.

Research in the Bank of England has shown evidence of a double lead of changes in money over changes in income; one lead is of two to three months, and the other of four to five quarters. The shorter of these leads is not good evidence of a causative role. It may merely indicate that money is normally accumulated in advance of expenditure, the authorities accommodating the demand for finance to avoid upward pressure on interest rates. Moreover one would not expect money to exert a causative influence on expenditure in a period as short as two to three months. But the longer lead of four to five quarters is more suggestive of a causal role. The existence of these two leads lends some support to the view that there is a two-way relationship between money and income. The short lead may reflect the fact that changes in both money and income are induced by a third factor; and the longer lead that the change in money supply has a feed-back effect on money income. In general, however, statistical evidence does not provide conclusive proof that money plays an exogeneous or an endogeneous role.

9.6 THE NOMINAL RATE AND THE REAL RATE OF INTEREST

It has been said that Friedman's demand function for money is only an elaboration of Keynes' theory of liquidity preference. As we saw earlier, in Friedman's version the demand for money is a function of permanent income, the cost of holding money, and the tastes and preferences of wealth-owners. In Keynesian theory the demand for money is a function of the current level of income, the current rate of interest, and the pattern of expectations about future interest rates. With both versions interpreted in real terms, the difference between them is perhaps not very great, especially as Friedman allows for expectations in his 'tastes and preferences'. But monetarists have been much more concerned than Keynesians with the influence of price change and have stressed much more the importance of analysis in real terms. Real money balances, real permanent income, real yields and interest rates have all been accented. Keynes himself was concerned with the real rate of interest, but the liquidity preference theory was formulated at a time of economic depression so that the problems of price inflation and the distinction between the real and the nominal rate of interest received no emphasis. In consequence Keynesians have tended to regard the demand for money as a function of the nominal rate of interest despite the development of continuous inflation.

A theory formulated in terms of the nominal rate of interest is seriously defective if applied to an economy suffering from inflation. Transactors have to take account not only of the nominal rate of interest but also of the prospective rate of inflation since it is the real rate of interest which is relevant to expenditure decisions. If the current rate is 10 per cent but prices are expected to rise at the rate of 5 per cent per annum, then the real rate of interest to a borrower is halved. The apparent insensitivity of expenditure to changes in nominal interest rates may be due to the fact that inflationary expectations make the change in the real rate of interest very much smaller than the change in the nominal rate. Indeed the nominal rate and the real rate of interest may, at times, move in opposite directions. For example, if fears of inflation intensify, wealth-owners tend to sell gilt-edged securities. Market forces would cause the nominal rate of interest to rise sufficiently to compensate for the expected rate of inflation, leaving the real rate of interest unchanged; but the authorities may choose to support the market, allowing only a moderate rise in the nominal rate of interest. Since this rise is insufficient to compensate for the expected rate of inflation, the real rate of interest will fall.

The nominal rate of interest is therefore a very unsatisfactory indicator of monetary conditions when commodity prices are changing. A rise in the nominal rate of interest may persuade the authorities that deflationary pressure is being exerted whereas in practice the real rate may not have risen or may even have fallen, encouraging greater borrowing and expenditure. A major difficulty is that although the authorities can observe the behaviour of the nominal rate of interest in the market they cannot judge the behaviour of the real rate. Views about future inflation vary from group to group and from time to time. This is of course a major reason why monetarists condemn the use of the market rate of interest as the criterion of monetary policy, and why they prefer the rate of growth of money supply to be the monetary objective.

9.7 CONCLUSIONS

The tentative conclusion is that the truth lies neither with the more extreme Keynesian view nor with the more extreme monetarist view, but somewhere between the two. It is evident that changes in money supply are frequently the consequence of expenditure decisions; but at the same time changes in money supply, whether exogeneous or endogeneous, are likely to have a feed-back effect on expenditure. An increase in the money supply, however caused, disturbs the equilibrium of portfolios. Rates of return on financial assets, including the imputed yield on money, are lowered in relation to the rates of return on tangible assets (including the imputed yields on durable consumer goods), and in consequence greater expenditure on current output is encouraged. In a general sense it is through changes in relative rates of return, including imputed returns, that change in money supply exerts an influence on expenditure.

The monetarist criticism of the use of market rates of interest as a criterion for monetary policy is sound, and the rate of growth of money supply is likely to prove the better criterion. But although a moderate rate of growth of the quantity of money may be a good index of stable conditions, control of the money supply is not an all-powerful tool of economic management. As we have seen, severe restriction of money can, in the longer term, be defeated by the emergence of new forms of money. But even in the shorter run severe control of money supply is unlikely to be practicable. As A. B. Cramp pointed out in Lloyds Bank Review of October 1970 a central bank not only has a duty to exercise some control over money supply, but it has also a duty to act as lender of last resort. The central bank must maintain confidence in the liquidity of the entire financial system so that, when markets are under pressure, the central bank must be ready to lend cash, if necessary without limit, though if necessary at higher cost. Since financial markets are likely to be most under strain when demand for funds is excessive, argues Cramp, a conflict of duty is bound to arise. Priority given to the strict control of money supply might well result in the bankruptcy of financial intermediaries and in a wholesale collapse of confidence. The stability of the financial system is therefore not compatible with really strict control of the quantity of money. Nevertheless the supply of money does matter, and reasonably flexible control of the rate of growth of money should have a place in the armoury of the authorities. This control is likely to be more practicable and effective if operated in conjunction with appropriate fiscal policy.

SUGGESTED READING

M. Friedman, 'The Quantity Theory of Money – a Restatement', *Studies in the Quantity Theory of Money* (Chicago University Press, 1956).

A. D. Bain, *The Control of The Money Supply* (Penguin, 1970), ch. iii.

H. G. Johnson, *Essays in Monetary Economics* (Allen & Unwin, 1967), part i.

M. Friedman, 'The Role of Monetary Policy', *American Economic Review*, Mar. 1968.

A. A. Walters, 'Money in Boom and Slump', *Hobart Paper*.

'The Importance of Money', *Bank of England Quarterly Bulletin*, Jun. 1970.

A. Schwartz, 'Why Money Matters', *Lloyds Bank Review*, Oct. 1969.

D. R. Croome and H. G. Johnson, *Money in Britain 1959–1969* (Oxford, 1970), part iii.

N. Kaldor, 'The New Monetarism', *Lloyds Bank Review*, Jul. 1970.

A. B. Cramp, 'Does Money Matter?', *Lloyds Bank Review*, Oct. 1970.

M. J. Artis and A. R. Nobay, 'Two Aspects of the Monetary Debate', *National Institute Economic Review*, Aug. 1969.

10 Monetary Policy

10.1 THE NATURE OF MONETARY POLICY TECHNIQUES

Many types of technique are employed by governments and monetary authorities to influence economic conditions or to achieve economic objectives. They include changes in money supply and in interest rates, budgetary changes, various types of incomes policy, and controls on prices, expenditure, lending, and borrowing. It is not easy to define precisely those techniques which should be labelled monetary because there is no clear-cut dividing line between different economic measures. However one may loosely describe monetary policy as one which aims to influence economic activity by variation in money supply, in the availability of credit, or in interest rates. Within this broad definition, techniques such as open market operations or changes in Bank rate are unquestionably monetary. But changes in the level of taxation or in the level of government expenditure have repercussions on interest rates and on the money supply; and so too may an incomes policy. Controls on the terms of hire purchase contracts and on bank lending also affect the availability of credit. Where, therefore, does one draw the line? Indeed one has little choice but to be arbitrary, and, in this chapter, discussion is centred on Bank rate policy, debt policy, and certain controls on lending and borrowing.

Consideration of the effectiveness of monetary policy is also complicated by the variety of objectives to which techniques are directed. The Radcliffe Report stressed five major objectives: high and stable employment, reasonable stability of prices, steady economic growth, a contribution to overseas economic development, and a strengthening of foreign exchange reserves. But clearly this list is not exhaustive and, in practice, the authorities over many years also gave high priority to managing the national debt so as to minimize its cost to the government and disturbance to internal conditions. Experience has shown that these various objectives are seldom compatible so that success with some may be at the expense of failure in others.

10.2 BANK RATE POLICY

The Radcliffe Report stated that Bank rate may be 'strictly defined as the minimum rate at which the Bank of England stands ready to lend at last resort to a discount house which has the privilege of access to the Discount Office of the Bank, either by rediscounting bills of approved quality or by lending against the security of such bills or of short-dated government securities'.* In effect, Bank rate is the price of last resort lending to the banking system, because the discount houses act, for this purpose, as a buffer between the banks and the Bank of England. If banks need to replenish cash they call in short loans from the discount market, and when the banks in aggregate do this the discount houses are obliged to acquire the cash from the Bank of England. It is vital that there should be a source of last resort cash since the banking system depends on the maintenance of complete confidence in the encashability of deposits. The whole credit structure would be threatened if banks were really vulnerable to cash withdrawals. Cash reserves protect banks only against minor withdrawals and it is the last resort lending of the central bank which underpins the banking system.

If banks were able to obtain cash from the central bank without limit or impediment the latter would have no control over the money supply. Access to last resort cash must therefore be restricted in some way. The Bank of England does this through the 'penal' terms which it dictates with respect to the interest payable and the period of the loan, and also through the collateral security demanded. As the Radcliffe Report neatly put it 'Borrowing from the Bank of England is kept at the minimum by reason of the fact that the terms are severe by comparison with the terms on which money can normally be borrowed from day to day in the market (i.e. they are "penal" terms). Loans are usually for a minimum period of seven days (whereas all the other marginal money which the discount houses borrow is from day to day), and at Bank rate (whereas day-to-day money rates in the market are normally anything from 1 to $1\frac{3}{4}$ per cent below Bank rate).'† Moreover Bank rate can be changed by the Court of Directors of the Bank of England provided this has the approval of the Chancellor of the Exchequer.

Since publication of the Radcliffe Report there have been some modifications in the terms of last resort lending. Early in 1963 the

---

* Radcliffe Report, Cmnd. 827, para. 358.
† Cmnd. 827, para. 359.

Bank of England announced that it might sometimes charge above Bank rate for advances to the discount market, and in September 1966 the Bank announced that it might on occasions lend overnight, rather than for the minimum of seven days and might on such occasions lend at a rate below Bank rate. Considerable flexibility is therefore now possible in the use of Bank rate policy.

Of course the Bank does not have to use the Bank rate procedure to provide additional cash. The Bank of England operator in the discount market may intimate to the discount houses or to the banks that they can tide over temporary stringencies by bringing Treasury bills to him and that he will buy the bills at current market rate. Similarly the operator may be ready to sell bills at the ruling market rate to mop up gluts of cash. This 'back door' technique is used when the Bank wishes to remove shortages or surfeits of cash without disturbing market rates.

In principle Bank rate can be used for either of two monetary purposes: as an essential instrument in controlling the money supply, or as a means of influencing the level and structure of interest rates. As regards the former, we saw in Chapter 4 that the Bank of England can contract the money supply, via open market sales, provided that it lends only at Bank rate and provided that Bank rate is maintained at a 'penal' level, that is above day-to-day money rates in the market. We saw that because borrowing at Bank rate involves the discount houses in losses there can be no equilibrium so long as the market remains in debt to the Bank of England, and that the attempts of the market to get out of debt cause bank deposits to continue falling until they become consistent with the reduced reserve base. But we also saw that bank deposits decline because bank customers are persuaded to absorb the sales of securities by the Bank of England, the discount market, or by the deposit banks, and that for the purposes of this persuasion interest rates may have to rise very significantly. It follows therefore that to achieve the reduction in the money supply the authorities must be prepared to raise Bank rate to whatever level is required to maintain the 'penal' relationship to market rates of interest. Even if policy has the much more modest objective of maintaining a stable money supply, wide swings in Bank rate are likely to be necessary. When the pressure of demand for finance increases, market rates of interest are bound to rise, so that to prevent an expansion in the reserve base (via borrowing from the Bank of England) Bank rate must be raised to maintain its 'penal' differential. In the past, as we have seen in earlier chapters, the authorities have been unwilling to accept the degree of interest rate fluctuation believed to be inherent in a single-minded policy of controlling the quantity of money. Bank rate policy has therefore been used mainly for the second purpose, of influencing the level and structure of interest rates.

The Bank of England can induce modest changes in short-term market rates without actually altering Bank rate through the exercise of its choice of lending to the market either at Bank rate or at current market rates. But the Bank can only exercise this choice if the market is obliged to borrow. To ensure this the Bank of England generally arranges for the weekly issue of Treasury bills to exceed marginally the government's needs. By borrowing more than the government is currently dispensing in payments, the Bank keeps the market short of cash and can choose to relieve the shortage either by lending at current market rates or at Bank rate. By lending (or buying bills) at current market rates the Bank leaves interest rates undisturbed, but by lending at Bank rate the Bank obliges the discount houses to raise their market rates in order to retain their profit margin. In practice the Bank generally uses this technique to indicate its views on Treasury bill rates. By lending at Bank rate the Bank indicates that bill rates should rise or cease to fall, and provided that the market reacts appropriately, sufficient cash is generally provided to enable the discount houses to get out of debt to the Bank of England.

An actual change in Bank rate has a much more significant effect on interest rates and tends to lever the whole interest rate structure in the same direction. It may even affect interest rates in other countries. The previous practice of the deposit banks (which as we see in Section 10.6 has now ceased) of tying the rates they charged and offered to Bank rate used to ensure that a change in Bank rate had a direct parallel effect on these rates. As a consequence there was a change of a similar amount in short-term market rates of interest because short-term assets, such as bills, are close substitutes for bank advances and time deposits. Without this direct link the influence of a change in Bank rate may be rather weaker in the future. Nevertheless the Bank of England can always induce a rise in short-term rates of interest by raising Bank rate while at the same time forcing the market to borrow from the Bank. The longer-term market in bonds and equities is then also affected. A rise in short-term rates of interest induces some borrowers to shift to the long-term market and some lenders to shift to the short-term market so that, with more borrowing and less lending, long-term rates are pushed up. But the extent of this sympathetic rise in long-term yields is strongly influenced by the pattern of market expectations of the duration of the change in Bank rate. Speculators who anticipate that Bank rate will be reduced again in the near future also expect that bond yields etc. will come down again (i.e. that bond prices will rise), and if the current bond yield rises now (i.e. current bond price falls now) such speculators tend to buy long-term assets so as to make a capital profit in the future. If these expectations predominate in the market the volume of speculative purchases will, in effect, prevent any significant fall in bond prices at the time that Bank rate is raised. In these circumstances long-term rates may scarcely rise at all. While, therefore, a change in Bank rate is likely to cause a change in all short rates by a similar amount, the extent of the change in longer-term yields is unpredictable. Generally changes in long-term rates are much less than the change in Bank rate, which implies that the market usually expects the change in Bank rate to be reversed in the not too distant future.

The predominant use of Bank rate has always been to influence the foreign exchange situation and, under the gold standard, it was the traditional weapon of defence of the Bank of England against a drain on its gold reserve. The rate was raised to attract gold, or prevent a loss, and lowered when it was unnecessary to attract gold or when Bank rate was out of touch with the market. A high Bank rate also enabled the Bank of England to lend generously at home at a time of crisis without fear of a simultaneous loss of gold abroad. The rise in short-term rates, induced by a rise in Bank rate, encouraged a gold inflow (or discouraged an outflow) in two ways. In the first place some dealers and traders in the international bill market were induced to discount bills in foreign centres since London had become a relatively more expensive centre in which to borrow. But as London was the leading market for bills there was always a large inflow of funds to meet bills previously discounted, so that any significant reduction in the current discounting of foreign bills could be relied upon to produce a net payments surplus and an inflow of gold. In the second place, a rise in short-term rates in London in relation to rates in other centres could also be relied upon to induce a transfer of liquid funds from foreign centres for investment in London, or to discourage the withdrawal of liquid funds from London. To the extent that the long-term market was affected by the rise in Bank rate the foreign exchange situation was also strengthened by a reduction in British long-term lending abroad.

Nowadays none of these effects has the same force. The international bill of exchange has been replaced substantially by alternative methods of debt settlement and short-term credit, and London no longer holds a predominant place in the capital markets of the world. Transfers of liquid funds (hot money) from one centre to another in response to short-term interest rate differentials still occur on a massive scale, but their effect on exchange reserves is no longer the same because there is much less confidence in the stability of exchange rates. Short-term funds transferred to London are often covered by forward sale to remove the risk of loss should the exchange rate change during the period of investment. Any gain in 'spot' transactions may therefore be offset by an increase in forward liabilities. But though weakened in effectiveness Bank rate is still used primarily to influence the foreign exchange situation. A rise in Bank rate is generally intended to encourage an inflow of foreign funds, or to discourage an outflow, and a reduction in Bank rate for the opposite purposes. Changes in Bank rate are also intended sometimes to have a psychological effect in foreign markets. A sharp rise, for example, may be designed to indicate firmness of purpose in maintaining the value of the currency in the hope that this will strengthen confidence in sterling.

Bank rate policy may also have repercussions on internal activity. Under the previous arrangements, in which the rate of interest on bank deposit accounts was tied to Bank rate, the technique of drawing the Treasury bill rate closer to Bank rate (i.e. when the Bank relieves cash shortage by lending predominantly at Bank rate) tended to reduce banking liquidity. This was because a rise in the Treasury bill rate relative to the bank deposit rate encouraged transfer of funds from deposit accounts into Treasury bills so reducing either bank cash reserves or the supply of bills available to the banks. An actual change in Bank rate is also bound to have some effect on internal activity. It used to be thought that the resulting change in short-term rates would, by affecting the profitability of holding stocks, exert a strong influence on economic activity. Prevailing opinion, however, is sceptical of this and regards long-term rates as being the more important influence on expenditure. But since the effect of changes in Bank rate on long-term yields is unpredictable, so too is the effect on economic activity. Of greater importance, perhaps, is the effect on business expectations and on confidence. Business investment in plant, machinery, and inventories is strongly influenced by prospective market conditions and by the availability of finance. If a sharp rise in Bank rate is widely interpreted as signalling the advent of difficult and uncertain conditions, not only will market prospects appear more gloomy but the supply of finance may dry up from lack of confidence. In these circumstances a rise in Bank rate may cause a significant reduction in business investment. Similarly a fall in Bank rate may be interpreted as a 'green light', encouraging optimism and stimulating confidence. Unfortunately Bank rate cannot be relied upon to produce a consistent psychological response and, except as incidental to the control of money supply, Bank rate policy is unlikely to prove a successful regulator of internal economic activity.

10.3 DEBT POLICY

The management of the national debt is bound to have repercussions on the money supply and on the level and structure of interest rates. Debt management can therefore be used as a major technique of monetary policy. Changes in the total debt are due to changes in the relationship between aggregate government expenditure and aggregate government revenue from taxation and other current receipts in consequence of budgetary decisions. Budgetary policy has direct effects on flows of income and generally plays a prominent part in overall demand management. A reduction in the rate of government expenditure or an increase in taxation, for example, has a direct disinflationary effect on national income and expenditure. But we are concerned with monetary repercussions, and these depend on the *form of change* in the total debt. At one extreme, for example, net additional government borrowing may be financed entirely by sales of marketable securities to the non-bank private sector and, *ceteris paribus*, interest rates must rise to whatever level is necessary to induce such purchases, leaving the money supply unaffected. At the other extreme the authorities, by an appropriate expansion of banking liquidity, may persuade the banking system to take up the additional debt so that, *ceteris paribus*, the money supply increases by the same amount and interest rates are not directly affected. Obviously there can be a compromise, the increase in national debt being accompanied by some rise in interest rates and some increase in the money supply. Similarly, when budgetary policy permits a reduction in the total debt, the authorities can choose between exerting a downward pressure on the money supply or on the level of interest rates. It is evident that the more of any additional debt that is financed by an increase in the money supply the more expansionary or inflationary is the effect. And the more reduction in total debt takes the form of a decrease in the money supply the more deflationary is the effect. The reader is reminded of the discussion of this subject in Chapters 4 and 5.

Monetary repercussions spring also from changes in the structure of the existing debt; indeed this is the normal way in which debt policy is used for monetary purposes. This type of policy consists of persuading the private sector to substitute one form of debt for another. Substitution between cash and marketable securities is usually known as open market operations, and substitution between short-term and longer-term securities as unfunding or funding operations. In practice the two types of operations are not always distinguishable. For example the Bank of England may sell Treasury bills on the open market and use the cash proceeds to purchase longer-term securities in the market so that, in effect, two separate open market operations constitute, in combination, an unfunding operation.

Simplified examples of open market and funding operations, often found in elementary textbooks, may give the impression that these operations are normally isolated interventions designed to produce some specific change in the quantity of money or in interest rates. This is far from the case in reality. The financing of two world wars created a huge national debt, portions of which mature more-or-less continuously (currently at the rate of around £1,500 million a year); and, generally speaking, repayment of maturing debt has to be financed by new issue of debt. New debt is also needed to finance the capital requirements of the social services and of the nationalized industries. Issues for these various purposes are frequently too large for the market to absorb wholly at the date of issue, and the residue has to be taken up by the Issue Department of the Bank of England acting as underwriter. The Bank broker subsequently sells this residue over the ensuing months as opportunity occurs. The Bank broker has frequently been a buyer, for example, to absorb bonds approaching maturity so as to reduce the task of repayment, or to absorb large private sector sales of securities so as to soften the impact on interest rates. The Bank also operates in the capital market to minimize disturbances arising from seasonal variations in the relationship between the flows of tax revenue and government expenditure, and in the process of stabilizing the foreign exchange rate. In one way or another, therefore, the Bank operations in the capital market are fairly continuous and it is through the conduct of these continuous operations that monetary conditions are affected. The Bank exerts a funding influence by concentrating more of its sales at the longer end of the spectrum and more of its purchases at the shorter end. This affects the term structure of interest rates, partly by the change in the proportions of maturities that the private sector is required to hold, and partly in consequence of resulting changes in expectations about the future level of interest rates. It may indeed raise the present average level of rates by making the outstanding debt less liquid in aggregate. The Bank exerts an open market sale influence by selling securities of greater aggregate value than it is currently buying. This squeezes banking liquidity and exerts a downward pressure on the money supply and an upward pressure on interest rates in the manner described in earlier chapters.

10.4 SPECIAL DEPOSITS

In April 1960 a new debt policy technique was introduced known as 'Special Deposits'. The discussion of this technique which follows relates mostly to the system which has operated until 1971. In September of that year the Bank of England introduced some changes as part of the revision of the operation of monetary policy and these are described in Section 10.6.

A call for Special Deposits is made at a normal Thursday morning meeting of the Court and has taken the form of an instruction to the deposit banks to transfer part of their cash to a Special Deposit at the Bank of England. Since the banks are not permitted to draw on Special Deposits these constitute illiquid assets, which are repaid only at the discretion of the Bank of England. Interest is earned at the current Treasury bill rate. The amount of the call is expressed as a percentage of gross deposits, the calls on the Scottish banks having been half the percentage applied to the clearing banks. Special Deposits outstanding of the latter banks have varied generally between 1 and 3 per cent of gross deposits, though on occasions repayments by the Bank of England have reduced Special Deposits to zero.

Funds received from a call for Special Deposits provide additional finance to the government so that, *ceteris paribus*, borrowing by way of Treasury bill issue is reduced. The net repayment of Treasury bills restores bank cash, and in effect Special Deposits replace Treasury bills (or call loans) in the banks' asset structure. A call for Special Deposits could therefore be regarded as a technique for squeezing banking liquidity by reducing the supply of Treasury bills and as an alternative to a funding operation. In Chapter 4 we saw that a funding operation was unlikely to exert very significant pressure on banking liquidity since banks could easily acquire other liquid assets to replace Treasury bills, unless bank cash reserves were also reduced. No more success therefore could be expected to follow a call for

Special Deposits unless the call reduced cash reserves (for example, if the repayment of Treasury bills were less than the call for Special Deposits). What, then, was the purpose of the Special Deposit technique?

The introduction of the technique may well have been due in part to the difficulties that the authorities were experiencing at the time, in placing a rising volume of debt in a market which was increasingly disillusioned with fixed interest securities. A funding operation requires the Bank of England to sell additional long-term securities but, since a call for Special Deposits avoids this, it may appear to be a more attractive alternative for reducing the Treasury bill issue at a time when the gilt-edged market is in a difficult state. But a call for Special Deposits does not necessarily obviate downward pressure on gilt-edged prices. Left to themselves, banks are more likely to react by selling bonds to restore liquidity than by reducing advances. The authorities were clearly well aware of this and on a number of occasions the call for Special Deposits was accompanied by a 'request' that the banks should respond by reduction in advances rather than sales of gilt-edged. A cynic might conclude that a call for Special Deposits, accompanied by a request for reduction in advances, was simply a device to enable the public sector to get a larger share of market funds at no higher cost and at the expense of the private sector. Perhaps the most that can be said for the technique, as used until 1971, is that it was easier to operate than open market sales when the gilt-edged market was disorderly; it had a more direct and predictable effect on banking liquidity; and a greater psychological impact on market expectations.

The astonishing expansion of overseas banks and accepting houses since the 1950s has intensified the difficulty of credit control. Unlike the deposit banks, these intermediaries have had very diverse and flexible asset structures and liquidity conventions, making it difficult for the Bank of England to establish a simple and general technique of control. A *cash deposits* scheme applicable to these banks was developed (though never operated) along the lines of Special Deposits, the main differences being that the Bank of England reserved the right to pay interest at less than Treasury bill rate and, if necessary, to treat individual banks differently. The purpose was to give the Bank of England a means of persuading these banks to heed official requests. The scheme is abandoned in the new proposals for credit control.

10.5 CONTROLS ON LENDING

Deposit banks have been subjected to official requests and recommendations for many years. In principle this is a matter of voluntary co-operation but, in practice, requests and recommendations are regarded as controls since, under the Bank of England Act of 1946, the Bank 'may, if so authorized by the Treasury, issue directions to any banker for the purpose of securing that effect is given to any such request or recommendation'.

Controls on lending have taken two forms. Directional or qualitative controls, which date back to 1939, relate to lending priorities. Banks have been asked periodically to restrain certain types of lending, such as to personal or professional borrowers, to finance companies, or for speculative purposes, and to give priority to other types, for example to assist exports or save imports. This has influenced the direction rather than the total of lending. The second form related to the aggregate volume of lending. This quantitative control was first used in July 1955 when banks were asked to make a significant reduction in total advances by the end of the year. The terms of requests varied from time to time, sometimes being no more than a mild request to reduce the rate of growth of lending, at other times consisting of a definite ceiling to the increase in advances. Between 1964 and 1971 specific ceilings were in force most of the time and controls were extended to include bill purchases and acceptances and to embrace all types of banks and finance houses. The Bank of England also asked institutions such as insurance companies, pension funds, building societies, the I.C.F.C., and the F.C.I., to bear its objectives closely in mind.

Lending controls were extremely unpopular with the banks because they were thought to damage banker-customer relationships and to cause loss of business to other intermediaries. There is little doubt that the controls did contribute to the relative decline of the deposit banks. Frustrated borrowers turned to other intermediaries which, on the basis of the inflated demand for loans, were able to bid successfully for larger deposits. More serious, from a general point of view, was the damage to the efficiency of banks and other intermediaries from the blunting of competition. With an arbitrary ceiling on lending there was little incentive for a bank to seek new custom, to compete for additional deposits and loans, or to innovate. And there was every incentive to perpetuate collective agreements on borrowing and lending rates. In this state of affairs the less efficient financial institutions have been supported and the more efficient hindered from growing.

If controls on lending are so potentially damaging why did their use play such a major role in British monetary policy? Part of the explanation lies in the influence of the Radcliffe view that the flow of credit is more important than the stock of money and the volume of advances more important than the volume of bank deposits. A more direct reason arose from the reluctance of the authorities to permit interest rate variation since this made them vulnerable to asset switching. Banks are inclined to meet a demand for advances by selling investments provided that holdings of the latter are above the minimum acceptable ratio. If the authorities attempt to keep interest rates stable they are obliged to absorb the gilt-edged sales, so increasing the money supply. In these circumstances the money supply is determined by the demand for advances. Controls on bank lending can be regarded, therefore, as a way of exerting some restraint on the growth of money without abandoning interest rate stabilization.

It can also be argued that controls on lending give the authorities a better grip on the velocity of circulation, particularly if controls are extended to other intermediaries. When banks make room for additional loans by selling investments to the private sector the bonds are likely to be bought by holders of idle bank deposits. In effect, these deposits are transferred via advances to spenders, and move into active circulation. Transfer of idle bank deposits to the ownership of a non-bank intermediary accelerates velocity in much the same way since the intermediary is likely to lend to spenders all or most of the newly acquired deposits. A ceiling on lending by banks and other intermediaries therefore helps to frustrate the acceleration of velocity.

Finally, in the short run at least, a tightening of controls on advances jams up part of the flow of credit, and the sheer difficulty of obtaining finance causes curtailment of expenditure. In the longer run, demand for credit will find means of by-passing controls, and only the higher cost and greater inconvenience of the alternative sources of credit will continue to exert restraint on borrowing and expenditure. Alternatively the authorities may try to prevent the by-passing by continuous extension of the range of controls, at the cost of increasing damage to the efficiency of the financial mechanism.

10.6 THE NEW CREDIT CONTROL ARRANGEMENTS

It seems that the long era of quantitative guide lines and ceilings on lending has at last come to an end. In his 1971 budget speech the

Chancellor announced that the techniques of monetary policy would be made more flexible so as to encourage greater competition and innovation in the banking system. He also envisaged that monetary policy operating through the reserves of banks and other financial institutions would replace quantitative controls on advances. Subsequently the Bank of England issued a consultative document on possible new techniques of monetary policy and, after discussions, agreement was reached on new arrangements for the control of credit to come progressively into effect from 16 September 1971.

Policy along the lines agreed is bound to imply greater flexibility of interest rates. Indeed the Bank of England declared in May 1971 that it no longer feels obliged to maintain the degree of support previously given to the gilt-edged market. The Bank will cease to offer a price, when requested, at which stock would be bought outright (except in the case of stock with a year or less to run) and will purchase stock only at its own discretion and initiative. This means that movements out of gilt-edged, by banks and other institutions, will no longer be eased automatically, even if sales threaten a sharp rise in interest rates. It implies that banking liquidity should become more controllable, and that interest rates will be allowed to reflect market conditions more closely.

The new arrangements for the control of credit can be summarized as follows.

1. The general purpose of the new policy is to combine effective credit control with an enlarged scope for financial competition and innovation. Main reliance will be on changes in interest rates, supported by calls for Special Deposits, on the basis of a uniform reserve ratio across the whole banking system, with parallel arrangements being made for deposit-taking finance houses.
2. The following constraints on financial competition and innovation are abandoned:
    (a) the quantitative lending controls on banks and finance houses (though qualitative lending guidance will continue);
    (b) the discriminatory liquidity requirements which London clearing banks and Scottish banks, but not others, have been required to maintain;
    (c) the collective agreements of the deposit banks on rates paid on deposit and charged, as a minimum, on advances. (These rates have therefore ceased to be linked to Bank rate and are expressed in relation to a 'base rate' determined by each

bank individually in the light of market conditions. Each bank quotes independently for deposits at seven days notice and for term deposits).
3. All banks will hold (day by day) not less than 12½ per cent of their 'eligible liabilities' in certain specified reserve assets.
   (a) This minimum reserve ratio is uniform for all types of banks so as to provide the authorities with a known firm base for the operation of monetary policy.
   (b) Eligible liabilities are sterling deposit liabilities, excluding deposits having an original maturity of over two years, plus any sterling resources obtained by switching foreign currencies into sterling. Interbank transactions and sterling certificates of deposit are included on a net basis, irrespective of term.
   (c) The reserve assets comprise Bankers' Balances at the Bank of England (but not bank till money), United Kingdom Treasury bills, company tax reserve certificates, money at call with the London money market, British government securities with a year or less to run, local authority bills which are eligible for re-discount at the Bank of England, and, up to 2 per cent of eligible liabilities, commercial bills eligible for re-discount at the Bank.
   (d) The common reserve requirement applicable to banks would be inappropriate for the eleven London discount houses and in their case a rather different type of asset control has been agreed. These houses are required to hold a minimum of 50 per cent of their funds in Treasury bills, company tax reserve certificates, local authority bills and bonds, and gilt-edged bonds and local authority stock with no more than five years to run. Although this percentage is in line with previous average practice, the discount houses will in future find it more difficult to run down bond holdings when interest rates are expected to rise. The houses are expected to continue covering the weekly Treasury bill tender but no longer at a collectively agreed rate, and the Bank will continue to act as lender of last resort. The agreement whereby the clearing banks do not tender for bills themselves is to be discussed.
4. All banks will place Special Deposits with the Bank of England as may be called for from time to time in the light of monetary conditions, including the state of bank lending in sterling.
   (a) The amount of Special Deposits called for will normally be calculated with reference to each bank's total eligible liabili-

ties but further consideration will be given to the use of different rates of call relating to overseas deposits. (By such discriminatory use of Special Deposits the authorities could exert some independent influence on euro-currency borrowing and movements of hot money.)

(b) The rate or rates of call will be the same for all banks, and all Special Deposits will bear interest at the Treasury bill rate. This implies the abandonment of the cash deposits scheme.

5. Instalment credit finance houses (other than those recognized as banks) which take deposits and which have eligible liabilities of £5 million or more are required to maintain a minimum reserve assets ratio of 10 per cent, the eligible reserve assets being the same as those for the banks. The eligible liabilities of finance houses will exclude amounts borrowed from banks. Calls for Special Deposits will normally be at the same rate as calls on the banks but could be at a higher rate in certain defined circumstances. Finance houses were given a transitional period of twelve months to build up reserves.

The Governor of the Bank of England has pointed out that the new techniques imply major changes both as regards the monetary variable which the authorities aim to influence and as regards the means of influence. Emphasis will shift from the volume of bank lending to the size of the money supply or domestic credit expansion, and the decision of the Bank to cease acting as an automatic buyer of last resort in the gilt-edged market makes this change of emphasis possible. Rationing of credit will be replaced by a system in which allocation of credit is determined primarily by the price mechanism.

The arrangements mark a historic change for British banking. They sweep away not merely the post-war apparatus of quantitative regulation but also other constraints on competition which have existed for most of this century. Entirely novel, too, is the placing of all types of banks on a common basis and the concept of uniform reserve assets. But it would be unwise to assume that the proposals imply a complete swing over to reliance on control of the money supply. Despite the change in the reserve base of the banking system it is on a type of liquid assets ratio and not on a cash ratio that control is to depend. Indeed a cash ratio requirement appears to have been abandoned* presumably because it would have been

---

* The London clearing banks have agreed to maintain (day-by-day) 1½ per cent of their eligible liabilities in balances at the Bank of England.

impracticable to insist on other types of banks, the liabilities of which are largely fixed term, observing a cash ratio in common with the deposit banks. This is also presumably the reason why till money is not included among reserve assets since the working balance requirements of the various types of banks are so very different. The reader will recall the argument of Chapter 4 that the liquid assets ratio cannot provide a firm fulcrum because the authorities have no real control over bank holdings of liquid assets other than cash. However, in contrast to the requirements of the former liquid assets ratio, the reserve ratio requirements now apply to a range of financial intermediaries far beyond just the London clearing banks. This seems likely to make it more difficult for banks to acquire additional reserve assets to replace those absorbed by open market sales or calls for Special Deposits. The ability of banks to control their own holdings of reserve assets is also reduced by the restriction on the inclusion of commercial bill discounts to 2 per cent of eligible liabilities and by the exclusion of refinanceable export credits and of short loans other than to the money market. On the other hand the inclusion of British government securities of up to a year to run appears to offer considerable opportunities for the banks to acquire additional reserve assets on their own initiative and this may more than offset the influence of the other factors mentioned. It is therefore doubtful whether the new base will provide a firmer fulcrum of control than did the former total liquid assets ratio requirement. In any case the Governor of the Bank of England has made it clear that the mechanism of the reserve ratio and the call for Special Deposits is not intended to achieve a precise multiple contraction or expansion of bank deposits, but to enable the authorities to exert pressure over the liquidity of the whole banking system.

Calls for Special Deposits and open market sales can be used to mop up surplus liquidity and may persuade banks to dispose of assets which are not eligible for the reserve base. Alternatively these measures may drive the banks to compete for additional reserve assets from outside the banking system, thereby lowering yields on such assets, and so reducing bank profitability. By these means, and in the more competitive setting envisaged, in which bank lending and borrowing rates and Bank rate itself are expected to be more flexible, the pressures exerted by Special Deposit calls and open market sales will influence economic activity rather less by tighter rationing of credit and rather more by making all forms of credit more expensive. But this is a long way from complete reliance on firm control of the money supply. If demand for credit were to be restrained by the price of credit alone, very violent fluctuations in interest rates would be necessary, and firm control of the money supply implies that fluctuations are at the mercy not only of every shift in demand for credit but also of every shift in confidence and in expectations regarding future prices and interest rates. Although the Bank's decision to discontinue automatic support of the gilt-edged market puts the Bank in a stronger position to control the money supply and implies greater flexibility of interest rates, it does not mean that the intention is to leave interest rates entirely to the forces of the market. Indeed the Bank has made it clear that it reserves the right to intervene in the market on its own initiative. In any case, in a system of fixed exchange rates, where a growing volume of mobile international funds is highly responsive to interest rate differentials, independent control of the money supply is increasingly difficult.

10.7 STATUTORY CONTROL OF TERMS OF CONSUMER CREDIT

The last monetary technique to be briefly reviewed is that of control of the terms of consumer credit, though this is rather on the fringe of monetary policy. The Report of the Crowther Committee on Consumer Credit (Cmnd. 4596) points out that statutory control of credit terms was first used in Britain in 1943 with the purpose of preventing excessive prices being dressed up as credit charges. In 1952 control of credit terms was used to restrain home demand for metal-using goods and, after a short break with no controls from summer 1954, they were re-introduced in February 1955 with the object of reducing internal demand over the whole field of durable consumer goods. The Radcliffe Report took the view that these controls were legitimate only at times of emergency; nevertheless they remained in force, though with numerous changes, until their complete removal in the mini-budget of July 1971.

Credit for the purchase of durables has been regulated in two ways: by the requirement of a minimum initial deposit and of a maximum repayment period. For example, in the first Control Order to be used as a measure of economic policy (February 1952), the required minimum initial deposit was $33\frac{1}{3}$ per cent and the maximum repayment period 18 months in respect of specified consumer durables. Regulations can be tightened either by an increase in the minimum required deposit or by a shortening of the maximum period of repayment. Either change makes it more difficult for consumers to buy durable goods on credit. In the former case more saving must be accumulated before the article can be acquired. In the latter case the amount of the weekly or monthly payment is increased.

The Crowther Report lists the advantages of terms control for the purposes of economic policy as first, that a tightening of controls produces an effect at once since an Order can come into operation immediately it is announced. Secondly, it is almost the only technique for restraining private sector expenditure that does not affect the cost of living, and therefore wage claims. Thirdly, unlike many other methods of restraint it acts specifically on consumption and not on business investment. But the Report points out that there are serious disadvantages. The evidence shows that a very small proportion of consumer expenditure is on purchases subject to Control Orders, so that even a drastic restriction of credit terms could do no more than reduce consumer expenditure by perhaps 2 per cent. For terms control to play a significant part in economic policy, changes would have to be very sharp and the limited number of industries involved would have good cause to complain at the resulting damage suffered. The effect of a tightening of controls also tends to wear off after a few months, particularly in the case of an increase in the minimum deposit because, once the larger deposit is saved, total periodic payments become smaller. Moreover there is no guarantee that a tightening of controls which reduces expenditure on durables will not simply divert expenditure to other forms of consumption. Two other disadvantages should be mentioned. Artificially induced fluctuations in the demand for a limited number of durables are likely to harm development and productivity in the industries concerned and, in the long run, damage their export potentiality. Finally, all controls encourage avoidance. Alternative forms of credit contract emerge, and if controls are to remain effective their range must be greatly extended at considerable administrative cost.

On balance the Committee concluded that these disadvantages far outweigh any value the controls offer to economic policy, and that consumer credit should be regulated only through general credit policy. As noted above, this advice has now been implemented by the government.

10.8 THE EFFECTIVENESS OF MONETARY POLICY

The extent to which and the manner in which monetary policy influences economic activity have always been matters of controversy. The Radcliffe Committee insisted that the major purpose of monetary measures is to influence the total pressure of demand, and regarded the 'structure of interest rates rather than the supply of money as the centre-piece of the monetary mechanism'.* The Committee justified this view by claiming that the decision to spend depends 'upon liquidity in the broad sense, not upon immediate access to the money',† and that 'spending is not limited by the amount of money in existence; but it is related to the amount of money people think they can get hold of, whether by receipts of income (for instance from sales), by disposal of capital assets or by borrowing'.† This argument implies that the money supply is not, in itself, an important direct influence on spending decisions, and is important only as part of the wider structure of liquidity. The Radcliffe Committee argued that the monetary authorities can influence aggregate demand in two ways. First, by changing interest rates, they influence the incentive to buy capital goods. Secondly, the authorities can change liquidity conditions generally 'so that those wanting money to spend (whether for capital development or other purposes) find it more (or less) difficult to get than it was before'.‡ These *incentive* and *liquidity* effects provide a useful framework for examining the effectiveness of monetary policy.

10.81 *The Interest-incentive Effect*

This effect, familiar in economic literature, was discussed at some length in Chapter 8. The reader is reminded of the theory that the demand for capital goods depends upon a comparison between the cost of borrowing and the expected rate of return on capital goods and that, given the latter, the incentive to acquire capital goods varies inversely with the rate of interest. The reader is also reminded of the belief that investment demand is insensitive to moderate changes in bond yields, based partly on the evidence of sample enquiries, partly on the contention that bonds and capital goods are imperfect substitutes, and partly on the argument that the cost of borrowing only exerts a significant influence on the demand for capital goods of long life. One should also point out that the state of price change expectations may have a crucial influence on the interest-incentive effect because it is the *real* rate of interest rather than the *nominal* rate which matters to borrowers. High rates of tax on income, in circumstances where interest charges can be set against tax, also reduce the impact of interest rate changes. Finally, the influence of the cost of

* Cmnd. 827, para. 397.
† Cmnd. 827, para. 390.
‡ Cmnd. 827, para. 385.

borrowing varies with the extent to which investors are dependent on borrowing for the finance of projects. The high liquidity of companies in the decade after the war may indeed partly account for the indifference shown to the rate of interest in many of the sample enquiries. Since the 1950s the corporate sector has grown more dependent on external finance and more recent investigations indicate a greater sensitivity to the rate of interest. But there is really no such thing as *the* rate of interest. There are many short-term rates of interest, government bond yields spanning the entire maturity spectrum, debenture yields, and equity yields. The general cost of borrowing, therefore, can only be thought of as a sort of weighted average rate of interest, with weights being rather heavier at the longer end. One weakness of monetary policy is that though it can exert a powerful influence on short-term rates, the effect on longer-term bond yields and equities is far less predictable because of the dominating influence, in the short run at least, of market expectations about future interest rates and profits.

The Radcliffe Committee took the view that the interest-incentive effect would be appreciable only where there is a significant change in the general level of interest rates which is expected to be long-lasting (a 'change of gear'). One argument was that those planning capital development frequently employ a conventional rate of discount to estimate the worthwhileness of investment projects. A change of interest *gear* may cause revision of such conventional rates, with profound repercussions on the allocation of resources for investment and on the life of projects. Against this view it has been argued that a change of interest rates which is *not* expected to last long may affect the timing of investment decisions; a rise in rates, for example, causing a postponement of projects. In general, the Radcliffe Committee considered that 'only very limited reliance can be placed'[*] on the interest-incentive effect, though it seems likely that the judgement of the Committee was unduly influenced by the exceptional liquidity of the economy in the decade or so prior to their Report.

A more sophisticated and perhaps more generally applicable version of the interest-incentive effect is the *portfolio* effect. Whereas the simple interest-incentive effect stresses the impact of monetary policy on the relationship between the rate of interest and the rate of return on capital, the portfolio effect is concerned with the much more complex reaction to the disturbance of portfolio equilibrium created by monetary measures. Open market purchases of bonds, for example, create money and tend to lower bond yields, but the bond

[*] Cmnd. 827, para. 397.

seller is seen as a transactor who, though persuaded to sell by the offer of a more attractive price, normally holds the additional money proceeds only while he looks around for a more rewarding investment. In due course he may deposit the proceeds with an intermediary, pay off debts, purchase other securities, or invest in durable goods, and in each case his action disturbs the portfolio equilibrium of other transactors. The effects ripple outwards and, as the yields on financial assets fall, wealth-owners tend to invest in riskier real assets in the search for a satisfactory return. In other words, during the process of the spreading of portfolio adjustment, prices of financial assets rise and become more expensive in relation to the prices of real assets, so that wealth-owners begin to substitute consumer durables, real property, plant and machinery, etc. This process of substitution raises the prices of existing real assets in relation to their cost of production, so stimulating demand for newly produced real assets. The influence of the monetary injection therefore spreads to current production. In summary, one can say that monetary measures, by disturbing the equilibrium of portfolios, set in motion a spreading process of asset substitution which eventually involves real assets and their rate of production.

10.82 *The Liquidity Effect*

It was the liquidity effect that the Radcliffe Committee considered important. No one would deny that measures which affect the liquidity of the economy have repercussions on economic activity. The commonsense view is that if the authorities restrict the supply of credit by, for example, a reduction in the money supply, there will be a rise in the price of credit which will curb the demand of borrowers. But this is the interest-incentive effect in which the Committee had little faith. The liquidity effect, in the eyes of the Committee, is quite different; it is the effect of a rise in the price of credit on the attitude of lenders. As the Report puts it, 'a rise in rates makes some less willing to lend because capital values have fallen, and others because their own interest rate structure is sticky. A fall in rates, on the other hand, strengthens balance sheets and encourages lenders to seek new business.' This is a curious doctrine. The argument is not the simple one that a reduction of credit causes a rise in its price which leads to a contraction of demand; it is that a rise in the price of credit causes reduction in its supply and that this constrains economic activity. Why should the credit market defy the normal economic laws of demand and supply? The Report indicates two reasons for the negative response of lenders: the fall in capital values, and the sticky interest rate structure, both of which require some examination.

The capital value doctrine was popularized in the 1950s, when it was known as the 'Roosa' effect. In brief, it is that a rise in interest rates implies a fall in security prices and that this deters both lending and spending; furthermore, with a large public sector debt widely spread throughout the community, the influence of a change in security values will be widely diffused, so that even a small change in interest rates might have a powerful effect on economic activity. As far as the effect on lending is concerned there seem to be only two logical reasons why a financial intermediary might seek to reduce lending in response to a fall in the market value of securities held. The first rather unconvincing reason is that the intermediary may feel the need to build up liquid reserves, either because the fall in security prices has created greater uncertainty, or because the intermediary tries to maintain a balance between the value of liquid reserves (including securities) and loans. The second reason is that the fall in security values may deter an intermediary from making loans for which funds have to be acquired by selling securities. But this assumes that the capital loss incurred by the intermediary in selling securities is not adequately compensated by higher interest charged on loans. In other words it assumes that the lending rates of the intermediary are sticky, an aspect of the argument to be discussed presently.

Before turning to the sticky rates effect it may be useful to review the possible manner in which changes in the value of securities can affect expenditure more directly. This *windfall* effect, as Keynes called it, was discussed in Chapter 8. In brief, a fall in security prices makes holders of securities feel poorer and less willing to spend, and conversely. There are however two grounds for scepticism. In the first place there is some reason to believe that if a rise in interest rates makes one section of the community poorer, it is just as likely to make other sections richer. In other words a change in interest rates may affect the distribution rather than the total wealth. In the second place holdings of securities are rather unevenly spread among individuals and corporate bodies, and it is probable that the spending decisions of only a small minority of transactors would be affected.

We turn then to the sticky rates argument. An intermediary can increase its lending either when it receives additional deposits in the form of money for which loans are then substituted, or by substituting additional loans for existing assets, including marketable securities. In both cases the lending of an intermediary may be inhibited when market rates of interest rise, or encouraged when market rates fall, if that intermediary's own rates structure cannot be changed quickly or easily. Building societies are a prominent example. These societies are reluctant to alter their rates frequently because of the long-term nature of their lending contracts. When interest rates in general rise building societies therefore lose funds to competing institutions such as the national savings movement, unit trusts, finance companies, etc., and they are forced to restrict their lending unless and until their own interest rates are brought into line. But although building societies are forced to restrict lending, other intermediaries to which the funds now flow are in a position to lend more so that there is no certainty that lending in aggregate is affected. The clearing banks have, in the past at least, provided another example. A bank, the liquidity position of which prevents an expansion of assets in total, can make room for additional loans by selling investments (if holdings are above the safe minimum). But when security prices fall the seller has to accept a capital loss, and this may deter lending if loan rates are prevented from rising sufficiently to compensate for the capital loss. The collective agreements of the clearing banks, whereby minimum loan rates were tied to Bank rate, had just this effect, and a rise in market rates of interest unaccompanied by an equivalent rise in Bank rate did tend to discourage such asset switching. The extent of this deterrent to lending is, however, much modified if banks (or other intermediaries with sticky lending rates) are in a position to dispose of shorter-dated securities, the capital values of which are comparatively stable.

10.9 THE AVAILABILITY OF CREDIT

The discussion of the last section suggests that the importance attributed by the Radcliffe Committee to the liquidity effect may have been exaggerated. Yet, in a wider sense, the stickiness of certain interest rates has an important bearing on the mechanism of monetary policy. If the prices of all types of credit were to respond immediately and fully to any changes in conditions of demand and supply, the availability effect and the price effect would be simply two aspects of the same thing. An analogy may make this clearer. Suppose the price of apples to be perfectly responsive to demand and supply. If, now, some disturbance creates a shortage of apples, the price of apples rises immediately to the level at which demand is equated to the reduced supply. The price incentive effect curbs demand, and the price rise reflects the shortage of apples. Contrast this with an example where apple prices are imperfectly responsive and where prices respond only partially to the shortage of apples. The necessary reduction in demand is therefore only partially attributable to the price rise; the remainder of the reduction in demand results from the unwillingness of people to queue, or from arbitrary rationing by sellers, or because people are just unable to buy apples at all. In this imperfect market one can therefore distinguish the price incentive effect from the availability effect in curbing demand.

The market for credit is far from perfect. For many interest rates, variation is inhibited by custom or the needs of convenience. Indeed a major reason why monetary measures cannot exert their influence wholly or even mainly through the interest-incentive effect is that to do so would require interest rate fluctuations, particularly at the short end of the market, so violent as to be unacceptable to the community. In practice restrictive monetary measures cause interest rates to rise in some markets sufficiently to equate demand with supply. But in other markets such measures cause a rationing of credit or rationing combined with a partial rise in rates. In the past this has been particularly true of bank credit, though it will be less true in the future now that the new proposals are implemented. It is true also of trade credit, of building society credit, and of many other forms of credit. Most borrowers find difficulty in moving from one source of finance to another, so that when monetary measures provoke a rationing of credit in some areas of the market, many would-be-borrowers are compelled to reduce expenditure. Tighter rationing of credit in one part of the market also tends to make other parts of the market more restrictive. If bank advances, for example, become more difficult to obtain, other transactors are quite likely to become less willing to extend credit for fear of endangering their own liquidity. In Keynesian language, credit rationing in any important sector of the market is likely to increase the general precautionary demand for money, and in so doing spread the influence of the credit rationing over a wide field.

Monetary measures, therefore, influence economic activity partly through the price of credit – the interest-incentive or portfolio effect, and partly via a tightening or easing of the rationing of credit in a host of imperfect credit markets. It is not so much that a rise in interest rates causes a restriction of credit by making lenders less willing to lend, as seems to be implied by Radcliffe, as that the inability of interest rates to rise to an equilibrium level forces intermediaries to ration their lending. The effectiveness of any given measure of monetary policy is governed largely by the prevailing degree of liquidity of the economy, including the ratio of money and of short-term debt to national income and to other assets. The less liquid is the economy the greater is the effect likely to be of any given restrictive measures on interest rates and on credit rationing, and the more difficult will it be for transactors to evade credit rationing by resort to other sources of credit. For this reason one can expect monetary policy to be more effective in the future than it was during the years of excessive liquidity after the war.

There is one qualification to this optimism. We live in a world in which nation states are growing less and less independent. With improving communications, growing international trade, and larger international capital movements, it is becoming increasingly difficult for national governments to exercise independent control of domestic interest rates, money supply, and credit in a regime of fixed exchange rates. The attempt to impose a tight monetary policy within one country can be partially undermined by an inflow of funds from abroad, attracted by the very measures which are designed to restrict activity. This difficulty, however, is considerably modified in Britain by the manner in which the operations of the Exchange Equalization Account are conducted. To keep the exchange rate within narrow limits, the E.E.A. prevents a rise in the exchange rate by buying any excess market supply of foreign currency, and prevents a fall in the rate by selling sufficient foreign exchange to match any excess demand in the market. But in the former case the sterling needed to purchase the foreign currency is obtained from sales of Treasury bills and, in the latter case, the sterling acquired from sales of foreign exchange is used to buy Treasury bills. In effect, the E.E.A. exchanges Treasury bills for foreign currency with the result that the internal monetary repercussions of balance of payments surpluses or deficits can be substantially, if not wholly, neutralized. Suppose, for example, that external receipts and payments are in balance except for an inflow of foreign funds, attracted by high interest rates, amounting to say £1 million. To prevent an appreciation of the exchange rate the E.E.A. buys the inflowing foreign currency, paying by cheques on Public Deposits at the Bank of England. Bank deposits and bank cash holdings therefore rise by £1 million. We now have to take account of the effects of the E.E.A. sales of Treasury bills and of the use to which the foreign owned bank deposits are put. At one extreme, if the inflow of funds leads to an additional demand by the non-bank private sector for Treasury bills by the full amount of £1 million, then bank deposits and bank cash holdings will both be reduced to the previous level and, since the additional supply of Treasury bills is matched by an equal additional demand, interest rates remain unaffected. The monetary effects of the inflow of funds are therefore completely neutralized. This extreme case may seem at first glance improbable. Yet funds which are attracted to London by high interest rates are likely to be invested in short-term securities and, directly or indirectly, there is likely to be a greater demand for Treasury bills. In any event, the sales of Treasury bills by the E.E.A. will tend to absorb excess bank cash holdings, so preventing a multiple expansion of deposits. A. B. Cramp, in his book *Monetary Management Principles and Practice*, has pointed out that, though the E.E.A. type technique of operation may enable a country to conduct a disinflationary monetary policy despite an attraction of foreign funds, or a reflationary monetary policy despite an exodus of foreign funds, such movements of funds are bound to affect interest rates in other centres, with repercussions, such as the spiralling of international interest rates, which may be undesirable. Moreover a reflationary monetary policy may be defeated by inadequacy of foreign exchange reserves. Successful monetary policy in the future is likely to require international co-operation unless the system of fixed exchange rates is abandoned. That is a subject for the next chapter.

SUGGESTED READING

Radcliffe Report (H.M.S.O., 1959), chs. vi, vii.
W. T. Newlyn, *Theory of Money*, 2nd ed. (Oxford, 1971), ch. ix.
R. S. Sayers, *Modern Banking*, 7th ed. (Oxford, 1967), chs. v, ix.
A. T. K. Grant, *The Machinery of Finance and the Management of Sterling* (Macmillan, 1967), ch. v.
J. C. R. Dow, *The Management of the British Economy, 1945–1960* (Cambridge, 1964), chs. ix, xi, xii.
H. G. Johnson, *Essays in Monetary Economics* (Allen & Unwin, 1967), part i.
D. R. Croome and H. G. Johnson, *Money in Britain 1959–1969* (Oxford, 1970), part v.
W. Hamovitch (Ed.), *Monetary Policy, The Argument from Keynes' Treatise to Friedman* (Heath, 1966).
A. B. Cramp, *Monetary Management Principles and Practice* (Allen & Unwin, 1971).
A. D. Bain, *The Control of the Money Supply* (Penguin, 1970), chs. v, vi.
Bank of England Quarterly Bulletin, June 1971.

11 International Payments

11.1 INTRODUCTION

No book on financial economics can ignore international payments, least of all a book in which the United Kingdom economy provides the background setting. On the other hand to do proper justice to this subject would require an entire book, and in this Chapter one can only attempt to survey the main aspects and problems of international payments. The reader is referred to the suggested reading at the end for fuller studies of the subject.

Monetary transactions occur between persons and institutions resident in one country and those in other countries in the course of trade and in the exchange of assets. As a generalization one can say that output is traded because differences in the distribution of resources and in historical development create variations in the productive capabilities of different areas. Some goods and services can be produced more cheaply or in preferred qualities in one country rather than another. Those that can be bought abroad more cheaply (allowing for transport costs and tariffs, etc.), or in preferred qualities abroad, tend to be imported. Those that can be produced relatively more cheaply at home tend to be exported. But there is nothing static about the pattern of international trade since productive conditions change constantly; moreover the pattern can be influenced by trade policies such as changes in tariffs and subsidies, by changes in exchange rates, and by domestic economic policy. The residents of one country may acquire assets in another country for many reasons. Such assets may be expected to offer a higher yield, higher rates of interest, or greater prospects of capital appreciation. Foreign assets may be acquired because domestic assets are expected to incur losses as a result of changes in exchange rates or in taxation, etc. Loans may be made or debts incurred by government for political reasons. Credit may be granted to or received from foreigners in the normal course of commodity trade. Finally, monetary authorities may buy or sell international reserve assets in the process of stabilizing the exchange rate.

Nearly all these international transactions involve exchange of currencies. Each country's currency is the only acceptable medium of exchange within that country so that home residents, exporting goods, services, or financial assets, generally require to exchange the receipts of foreign claims for their own currency. Similarly, home residents purchasing commodities or financial assets from abroad may have to purchase the foreign currency with which to settle transactions with foreign residents. This exchange of currencies is conducted in the foreign exchange market, a brief description of which was given in Chapter 2. The reader is reminded that, in a free market, demand and supply are equated by movements in the exchange rate (the price of one currency in terms of another). However, in most countries the monetary authorities, and bank dealers to some extent, intervene on the side of either demand or supply so as to limit severely the range within which the rate has to move to clear the market. When such intervention occurs it implies that exchange rate fluctuations are not sufficient to maintain a continuous balance between normal foreign payments and receipts. This is why a deficit or surplus can occur in the balance of payments.

11.2 THE BALANCE OF PAYMENTS

Balance of payments statistics consist simply of the receipts and payments between a country and the rest of the world over a period of time such as a year or a quarter. In principle receipts and payments must be equal in total because balancing transactions such as changes in indebtedness are included. In practice, however, statistical information is always to some extent inadequate and inaccurate so that an item of errors and omissions is necessary to equate the two sides.

It is conventional to distinguish current and capital transactions. The *current account* includes all transactions in settlement of a flow of goods and services between the country and the rest of the world. Transfers which are normally regarded as income by the recipient such as private remittances, pensions, and certain official grants are also included. Current transactions are commonly sub-classified into *visible trade*, the exports and imports of tangible goods, and *invisible trade* which is essentially receipts and payments for services. Invisible transactions cover such obvious services as tourism, shipping, banking, and insurance. Also included are receipts of interest, dividends, and profits from foreign assets owned by home residents and similar payments to foreign owners of home securities or property. These can be regarded as payments for the services of capital. Finally there is government expenditure abroad which, in a sense, is payment for services rendered to the government.

Capital transactions are all those which are not in settlement of the current inflow or outflow of goods and services. They are transactions which alter the foreign asset holdings of home residents, the foreign ownership of home assets, or the state of indebtedness between the country and the rest of the world. Until 1970 British statistics attempted to distinguish long-term capital flows which were recorded in a *long-term investment* account from the remainder which were classified as *monetary movements*. In principle the former consisted of deliberate or autonomous capital transactions not intended to be reversed in the immediate future, including official loans and repayments, private sector investment abroad, and foreign investment in the United Kingdom. Monetary movements included changes in foreign ownership of bank balances in the United Kingdom, in the home ownership of bank balances abroad, in official foreign exchange reserves, in euro-dollar borrowing, and in short-term credit granted or received. They reflected essentially the short-term changes in indebtedness and in reserves induced by other transactions in the balance of payments.

In 1970 the classification of capital transactions was reorganized. Net drawings from or net repayments to the International Monetary Fund (*see* Section 11.5) or other monetary authorities, and drawings on or additions to official reserves are categorized as *official financing*. Another separate item consists of periodic receipts of Special Drawing Rights (*see* Section 11.6) and gold subscriptions to the International Monetary Fund. All other capital transactions (the former long-term items and the residue of the former monetary movements) are termed *investment and other capital flows*. The change was made because of the increasing difficulty of distinguishing between long-term and short-term capital flows.

Table 11.1 illustrates these balance of payments transactions (*see also* Figure 11.1 on page 245). In interpreting the table one must remember that positive signs imply a receipt of or claim to foreign currency and negative signs imply the use or depletion of foreign currency. This is obvious in the case of the export and import of goods and services, a positive balance indicating a net excess of exports over imports, but is perhaps less obvious in the case of the capital account. The following are examples of positive capital transactions: a loan received from a foreign government, overseas investment in the United Kingdom, import credit received, an increase in foreign-owned bank balances in the United Kingdom,

TABLE 11.1

UNITED KINGDOM BALANCE OF PAYMENTS

1970 (£ million)

Current account	Receipts	Payments	Net balance	
Visible trade	7,885	7,882	+3	
Invisible trade	4,546	3,982	+618	
Total	12,431	11,810	+621	(1)

Investment and other capital flows		
Official long-term	−201	(2)
Overseas investment in U.K. public sector	−21	(3)
Overseas investment in U.K. private sector	+667	(4)
U.K. private investment overseas	−701	(5)
Euro-dollar borrowing in London for investment overseas	+184	(6)
Import credit	+9	(7)
Export credit	−302	(8)
Bank balances (gross) of sterling area countries	+401	(9)
Bank balances (gross) of non-sterling area countries	+97	(10)
Foreign currency transactions of U.K. banks	+295	(11)
Other short-term flows	+112	(12)
Total	+536	(13)

Balancing item	+130	(14)
Total currency flow [items (1) (13) (14)]	+1,287	(16)
Allocation of SDRs	+171	(17)
Gold subscription to IMF	−38	(18)
Total of items (16) (17) (18)	+1,420	(19)

Official financing		
Net transactions with IMF	−134	(20)
Net transactions with other monetary authorities	−1,161	(21)
Drawings on official reserves (+) additions to (−)	−125	(23)
	−1,420	(24)

net borrowing from overseas monetary authorities, and a reduction in gold reserves. The opposite transactions are of course negative. In the *official financing* transactions of 1970 the negative signs indicate repayment of borrowings and additions to reserves. The *balancing item* (14) represents the net errors and omissions referred to previously, and the positive sign in 1970 means that the net actual receipts, whether current or capital, were greater than recorded.

The balance of payments is sometimes described as favourable or unfavourable, in equilibrium or in disequilibrium. Clearly, since receipts and payments are necessarily equal in total, it is the balance of a certain group or groups of transactions to which reference is made. Although in Britain the balance of visible trade receives considerable publicity because of the availability of monthly estimates, there is no inherent reason why trade in tangible goods should be more significant than trade in the invisible services. It is the total current balance which reflects the current earning and expenditure of the nation in its dealings with the rest of the world. A nation with a positive current balance is in the same position as an individual who is earning more than he is spending; the nation is saving in its dealings with the rest of the world and is adding to its stock of foreign assets. Similarly a nation with a negative current balance is financing an excess of expenditure over earnings by running down its stock of foreign assets. The current balance is therefore highly significant. In a very long-run sense equilibrium may be defined as a zero balance on current account because there can be no true equilibrium if a country is indefinitely losing assets to or gaining assets from the rest of the world. Nevertheless it is quite normal and indeed often desirable for some nations to make net investments in other countries over considerable periods of time, and for this reason attempts are made to find alternative criteria of the state of external payments.

Until 1970 the *basic balance* was used in Britain as the main criterion. This is the sum of the current balance and the balance of long-term investments (the sum of items (1) to (5) in Table 11.1) which, after allowing for the balancing item, is also equal to the balance of monetary movements but with the opposite sign. A zero basic balance implies that the surplus on current account is just sufficient to finance the nation's net long-term lending and investing overseas, or that the deficit on current account is just financed by the nation's long-term borrowing. Either way it implies no net change in the short-term indebtedness and reserves of the country. A negative basic balance means that a country is investing and lending abroad more than it can afford to in terms of its surplus earnings on current account, or that it is failing to borrow sufficient on a long-term basis to finance its current account deficit. It measures the extent to which the country is dependent on increasing its short-term indebtedness and/or running down foreign exchange reserves, and therefore the extent to which its international liquidity is reduced. A negative basic balance is regarded as *unfavourable*.

Another way of looking at the problem is to distinguish those payment transactions which are *autonomous* from those which are *induced* or *accommodating*. The former are in principle all transactions which are undertaken deliberately for their own sake. They include all current account transactions and such capital account transactions as inter-government lending and private sector investment, which are undertaken from political or economic motives. The accommodating transactions are in principle the changes in indebtedness and in reserves which are induced by or result from the behaviour of other transactions. In a system of freely flexible exchange rates there would be no reason to make any distinction since all transactions could be regarded as autonomous. It is precisely because rates of exchange are not allowed to move sufficiently to match demand and supply arising from autonomous transactions that accommodating transactions are required to fill the gap. The volume of accommodating transactions therefore measures the gap between autonomous receipts and payments and can be regarded as a measure of disequilibrium in the balance of payments.

The difficulty lies in distinguishing precisely between those transactions which are autonomous and those which are accommodating. The *basic balance* is unsatisfactory in this respect, not only because some so-called long-term capital movements are reversed so quickly as to be indistinguishable from short-term capital movements, but also because changes in short-term indebtedness are often the result of deliberate search for higher rates of interest. It is for these reasons that the British authorities have chosen to select the *total official financing* and its counterpart the *total currency flow* as a measure of disequilibrium. Official financing indicates the amount of accommodating finance in terms of official short-term borrowing, repayments, lending, and/or changes in reserves, that is necessary to fill the gap between all other external receipts and payments.

In conclusion, one can say that the current balance shows whether the nation is increasing or decreasing its net stock of foreign assets, and the balance of official financing or the total currency flow show whether the net state of official short-term indebtedness and reserves is improving or worsening. Of course the quarter or year to which payments statistics relate is an entirely arbitrary period and not necessarily typical or representative. What really matters therefore is the average balance of current account and of the total currency flow over a longish period of time. Moreover, while a zero total currency flow may indicate medium-term equilibrium in normal circumstances, a positive total currency flow is essential so long as repayment of past official borrowing or the building up of reserves is required.

11.3 BALANCE OF PAYMENT PROBLEMS

Disturbances to the balance of payments can occur as a result of shifts in demand, because costs in different areas diverge, because of changes in portfolio preferences, or because of events such as natural disasters. Why do disturbances to international payments create special problems when, apparently, disturbances to payments between regions within a country pass unnoticed? The basic answers to this question are: first, that international payments are generally so much less easily adjustable by market forces than inter-regional payments and tend to create so much disruption that these corrective forces are often deliberately impeded. Secondly, cost divergences are more likely to develop and persist between countries than between regions. To illustrate these differences it is useful to compare the effects of disturbances to the flow of payments between two areas, first where these are assumed to be two regions constituting a country, and then where they represent independent countries.

11.31 *Payments Imbalance between Regions*

Disequilibrium in payments can be corrected by induced flows of assets, changes in relative incomes, or by liquidity pressures. We examine initially how these forces react to a switch of demand from the output of one region, which we call Region A, to the output of the other region, which we call Region B.

This switch in demand implies a larger flow of output from B to A and a smaller flow of output from A to B. It also implies that the receipts of some transactors in A are reduced in relation to their payments and that receipts in B have increased in relation to payments. Initially therefore some transactors in A are running down money balances and some in B are accumulating money. Since the form of money is common to both regions there is no difficulty of transfer and, if there is a nationwide branch banking system, the transfer creates no pressures on banking liquidity. At this stage, then, the net additional flow of output from B to A is offset by a flow of money from A to B; but this is not a stable situation because transactors in A will need to restore liquidity by selling other assets; and those in B, experiencing a rising stock of money, will seek to restore normal portfolio distribution by purchasing other assets. In a financially developed country a large proportion of wealth is held in financial assets, such as bonds, shares, and bills, which are readily exchangeable in a nationwide market; and it is these types of asset that transactors in A and B are most likely to sell and buy respectively in the process of portfolio adjustment. The flow of money which has been offsetting the flow of output is eventually replaced by a flow of these other types of financial asset from A to B. And since the selling pressure in A is balanced by equal buying pressure in B for assets which are reasonably substitutable, this flow of assets is likely to be induced with the minimum disturbance to asset prices. This short-term payments solution also tends to induce a longer-term adjustment. As the stock of wealth falls in Region A residents reduce expenditure, including expenditure on the output of Region B. On the other hand, residents in the latter region, enjoying a rising stock of wealth, increase expenditure, including purchases from Region A. The flow of output therefore tends to be corrected.

The original shift in demand from the output of A to the output of B also has an income effect. Lower demand for Region A output implies lower current income earned in production. This may induce reduction in current expenditure, with further repercussions on income in the familiar multiplier fashion. But some portion of each round of reduction in expenditure will take the form of reduced imports from Region B. In the latter region the opposite occurs. The shift in demand raises the level of income and may induce a multiplier expansion of income and expenditure with imports from Region A rising at each stage. As between regions, the *marginal propensity to import* (the relation between the change in imports and the change in income) is likely to be high so that comparatively small changes in the incomes of the respective regions can correct the flow of output. Moreover a greater effort in sales and productivity may be induced in the region from which demand has shifted permitting correction to the flow of output with less income disturbance. Finally, changes in relative regional incomes are likely to induce a counterchange in the flow of transfer payments. For example, tax payments to the central government fall in Region A as incomes decline, but rise in Region B; so that, assuming the amount and distribution of government expenditure to remain unchanged, there will be a net flow of transfer payments from B to A.

Little need be added to this analysis with respect to disturbances emanating from cost divergences and changes in regional asset preferences. Cost divergences seldom produce a payments problem between regions because the ease of movement of commodities, labour, and capital, and the absence of independent regional monetary policies, generally prevent cost divergences from arising or persisting. Shifts in asset preferences are also easily corrected by market responses. Suppose, for example, that residents in A seek to buy property in B. To raise the money residents in A are likely to sell financial assets, whereas the recipients in B are likely to invest the proceeds in financial assets. In effect property is exchanged for financial assets with the minimum disturbance.

11.32 *Payments Imbalance between Countries*

We have seen that payments disturbances between regions are corrected with minimal difficulty because transactors in the various regions hold a high proportion of marketable financial assets which are in common demand, because the common medium of exchange and the branch banking system (or its equivalent) avoid problems of banking liquidity, because income effects have substantial repercussions on regional trade, and because cost divergences seldom develop. Payment disturbances between countries, on the other hand, face markedly different circumstances. The effectiveness of asset adjustment, in response to a switch in demand for output, is handicapped by the small proportion of financial assets held by transactors which are internationally marketable and in universal demand. The assets which transactors in Country A attempt to sell to restore liquidity are not, in general, the assets which transactors in Country B are attempting to buy to get rid of surplus liquidity, and asset prices therefore fall in A and rise in B; and, if correction is left to market forces, very marked changes in relative asset prices may have to occur before there is a sufficient flow of assets from A to B to finance any continuing net flow of output from B to A.

The main adjustment of payment flows is likely to depend upon a reversal of the flow of output resulting from changes in expenditure in the two countries in consequence of wealth, income, and liquidity effects. Falling asset prices in Country A imply capital losses and rising interest rates, both of which intensify the reduction of income and expenditure directly produced by the loss of sales to Country B. In the meantime the difficulty of inducing a flow of other assets from A to B leaves the finance of payments heavily dependent on a transfer of money. But because the countries have separate currencies and separate banking systems, banks in A are required to buy the net foreign exchange requirements from their central bank, causing cash reserve losses by the commercial banks and exchange reserve losses by the central bank. This continuing squeeze on banking liquidity is likely to depress asset prices and incomes still further. Parallel but opposite repercussions occur in Country B. The picture, then, is one of falling asset prices, income, and expenditure in Country A; and, if wage rates are not easily reduced, employment is more likely to fall in the short run than prices. In Country B asset prices, income, and expenditure are rising, accompanied by higher employment and/or prices. The expenditure repercussions help to reverse the flow of output since imports fall with expenditure in Country A and rise with expenditure in Country B. But, marginal propensities to import of international trade are likely to be considerably smaller than those of regional trade so that much larger changes in income and expenditure are required to produce any given change in import-export relationships. Price reductions in A and price increases in B further assist the reversal of the flow of output. In general, correction of this type of payment imbalance by market forces involves comparatively severe disturbance to the income and employment of the countries concerned.

Shifts in demand for assets between countries are also likely to produce greater payment difficulties than similar shifts between regions. An increased demand for property in Country B from residents in Country A does not easily induce a counter-flow of non-monetary financial assets because, as we have seen, the types of assets which residents are selling to raise the necessary finance generally differ from those that residents in B are buying with the proceeds received. The shift of demand therefore involves changes in relative asset prices and exchange of currency, with repercussions similar to those considered in the previous paragraph.

A particular difficulty in international payments is the tendency for costs to diverge between countries because of differences in bargaining power of labour, in rates of growth of productivity, in monetary and fiscal policies, and in relative attitudes to unemployment and inflation. Moreover it is more difficult for such divergences to be corrected automatically by movement between countries of commodities, labour, and capital. Cost divergences induce shifts of demand away from the country with faster rising costs and in favour of the country with slower rising costs. And the resulting imbalance is particularly difficult to correct because the factors making for faster rising costs soon undo any benefits to the balance of payments derived from the deflationary repercussions previously examined.

11.33 *The Gold Standard*

The international gold standard provided an example of correction of payments imbalance by market forces within a system of fixed exchange rates. When national currencies consisted of specific weights of gold, or were convertible at fixed prices into gold, exchange parities were established between currencies in the ratio of their respective weights or prices of gold. For example, if dollars were convertible into gold at the price of $35 per ounce and the pound at the price of £7 per ounce a *mint* parity of five dollars to one pound would be established. And so long as currencies remained freely convertible and gold freely exportable exchange rate fluctuations were constrained within a band either side of the mint parity set by the costs of importing and exporting gold between the countries concerned. When an excess of payments over receipts drove the exchange rate to the gold export point, in effect it became more profitable to settle international debt by the purchase and shipment of gold abroad rather than to buy foreign exchange at any lower rate, and conversely at the gold import point. Of course the gold standard could only continue in existence provided that corrective forces eventually restored equality between the external receipts and payments of each country at exchange rates within the gold points, because each country had only limited reserves of gold for export. And it was on the induced transfer of assets and on the wealth, income, and liquidity repercussions on current payments that the process of correction depended.

The gold standard worked tolerably well in the half century before the First World War. There were a number of reasons for this among which we should mention the greater flexibility of internal prices at that time and the sensitivity of the London Capital Market to changes in relative asset prices. A British balance of payments deficit, for example, would quickly experience partial correction by a reduced outflow of capital as asset prices fell and interest rates rose in London. But the gold standard collapsed in the inter-war period because the disturbances inherited from the war and emanating from the great depression were too great for market forces to correct without producing intolerable internal repercussions.

Adjustment of external payment disturbances by market forces, in a regime of fixed exchange rates, is bound to involve the countries concerned in some degree of painful deflationary and inflationary experience. Governments in recent times are increasingly concerned with the maintenance of internal stability and are therefore less and less willing to allow free play to these corrective market forces. But if maintenance of internal stability prevents correction of balance of payments disequilibrium we are in a dilemma. It is this dilemma which is the fundamental problem of international payments.

11.4 BALANCE OF PAYMENT POLICIES

Since correction of balance payments disequilibrium by market forces in a system of stable exchange rates involves deflationary and inflationary disturbances which can conflict with aims of preserving stability of employment and prices, the problem is to devise deliberate policy techniques capable of reconciling external and internal equilibrium. There are, in principle, a number of techniques which the government or monetary authorities of a country can employ. On the assumptions that a country is free to use any, that the problem is straightforward and can be clearly diagnosed, that there are adequate reserves to tide over the period of adjustment, and that the reactions of other governments need not be considered, then it is generally possible to devise a combination of policies capable of achieving external and internal equilibrium. A proper survey of this would be very lengthy and all that can be attempted here is a very brief indication of some examples.

Policy techniques are commonly classified as *expenditure adjusting* and *expenditure switching*. The former consist of monetary and fiscal policies. An expansionary policy of either type raises the level of domestic income and has an indirect negative effect on the balance of payments. Thus an increase in the money supply or an increase in the ratio of government expenditure to tax revenue will stimulate income, expenditure, and employment within the country and, in consequence, raise imports. Monetary policy, however, has an additional effect on the balance of payments since a reduction in interest rates tends to induce a capital outflow. Contractionary monetary or fiscal policy depresses internal activity and indirectly improves the balance of payments, contractionary monetary policy tending to improve the capital account as well as the current balance of payments.

Expenditure switching techniques are those which directly induce a switch in the flow of external payments. Their internal impact is generally indirect. First there are techniques which aim to alter the relationship between domestic and foreign prices. Tariffs on imports and subsidies on exports raise foreign commodity prices to home residents and lower prices of domestic goods to foreigners respectively. Exchange rate devaluation, to be examined in more detail presently, has the same effects. An incomes policy may achieve the same result by keeping the rate of increase of domestic prices lower than that of foreign prices. Any of these techniques may succeed (though not necessarily) in improving the current balance of payments by encouraging exports and discouraging imports, thereby indirectly stimulating internal activity. An opposite use of these techniques tends to have a negative impact on the current balance of payments, indirectly depressing internal activity. Other techniques include direct controls on external payments; for example, quotas on imports, exchange control on capital outflow, or, as an extreme measure, exchange control on all types of overseas payments.

A judicious mixture of techniques should, in principle, be capable of correcting any straightforward problem of internal and external balance. For example, for a country which has internal equilibrium but a persistent external deficit, devaluation would help to cure the deficit, and contractionary monetary or fiscal policy would help to prevent the improvement in the external payments from causing internal inflation. For a country suffering from a payments surplus and internal inflation, currency revaluation might be sufficient to cure both problems, and so on. Unfortunately, although it is relatively easy to devise appropriate remedies for imaginary situations, in practice maintenance of internal and external equilibrium is extremely difficult. Many of the expenditure switching techniques are precluded by international agreement, and even if they were not their use might well provoke retaliatory measures by other countries. Economic problems are seldom straightforward and are often attributable to a variety of causes; moreover it is very difficult to judge whether a problem is temporary and self-righting or likely to prove persistent and therefore requiring adjustment. Finally, corrections of imbalance take time, and slow operating techniques may be inappropriate for the cure of a deficit unless a country has sufficient international reserves to tide over.

11.5 THE INTERNATIONAL MONETARY FUND SYSTEM

Bitter dissatisfaction with the operation of the inter-war gold standard and with the chaos which followed its collapse, and the habit of wartime co-operation, led to the Bretton Woods Conference of 1944 at which plans were laid for what was hoped would be a vastly improved system. The main outcome of the Conference was the establishment of the International Monetary Fund and the International Bank for Reconstruction and Development. Those who fashioned the IMF (as it is usually known) envisaged a world system based on co-operation, on stable exchange rates capable of agreed alteration, and on the provision of adequate international liquidity. The main functions of the IMF are considered in this Section in terms of these three objectives.

When a system dependent on adjustment by market forces, such as the gold standard, is replaced by one dependent on national balance of payment policies, international co-operation becomes an acute issue. Without co-operation there is an obvious danger that national policies may conflict. National objectives may be incompatible, policy techniques may be mutually frustrating, and retaliatory action may be encouraged. The experience of the 1930s showed that the end result can be an intensification of external imbalance and mutual impoverishment. The encouragement of co-operation and consultation is therefore the first vital function of the IMF, and is indeed a built-in feature of its structure. The governors of the IMF, who meet annually to discuss major features of policy, consist of a top representative from each member country; the day-to-day business of the Fund is conducted by a board of executive directors who are also representative of member countries; and there is a powerful secretariat drawn from many nations. The IMF has sought with mixed but increasing success to establish a code of international conduct such as the maintenance of free convertibility of currencies, the avoidance of discriminatory arrangements, the maintenance of stable exchange rates, and the avoidance of parity changes without consultation. The regular process of consultation, not only in the IMF, but also in such other bodies as the Organization for Economic Co-operation and Development and the Bank for International Settlements, helps enormously to make national objectives compatible, and the work of the secretariat helps to provide for better understanding of policy techniques and of the process of adjustment.

The second main function of the IMF is to maintain a system of stable yet adjustable exchange rates. Each member country, on joining, is required to declare a par value for its currency in terms of gold or dollars and to keep exchange rates within 1 per cent either side of this parity. In Britain, for example, the Exchange Equalization Account maintains a stock of key foreign currencies or of gold which can be converted into foreign currencies, and of sterling. The E.E.A. prevents downward movements of the value of sterling from exceeding 1 per cent of parity by selling foreign exchange (and buying sterling) in whatever amount is required to offset the excess market demand for foreign exchange. Upward movements of the exchange rate are prevented from exceeding 1 per cent of parity through offsetting purchases of foreign exchange (and sales of sterling). There is no limit to the ability of the E.E.A. to make offsetting purchases of foreign exchange; but clearly the amount of foreign exchange which the E.E.A. can sell in the market to resist downward movements of the exchange rate is limited by the volume of exchange reserves held and the extent to which additional foreign currency can be borrowed. Depletion of reserves and short-term borrowing is a suitable method of financing a payments imbalance which is temporary or correctable without undue internal disturbance, but unsuitable where the imbalance is persistent and chronic. Indeed it is difficult, if not impossible, for a country with a continuing payments deficit to defend its exchange parity indefinitely. For this reason the regulations of the IMF provide for a change of parity in cases where external payments are in *fundamental disequilibrium*. But changes of parity must be made in consultation with the IMF, and for a change exceeding 10 per cent of the original parity the permission of the IMF is required. A uniform change in all member parities is also permissible where it is desirable to alter the value of gold, for example to remedy a shortage of world gold reserves.

Since, in the IMF scheme of things, changes in exchange rates are envisaged as the appropriate technique for balance of payments adjustment in conditions of fundamental disequilibrium, it may be helpful at this point to sketch briefly the manner and conditions in which devaluation can prove to be corrective. The impact effect of devaluation is to change the price relationships between home and foreign goods and services. Using the devaluation of sterling in November 1967 from $2·80 to $2·40 for illustrative purposes, and ignoring costs of transport, one can say that a home article costing £100 costs $280 abroad at the old rate and $240 at the new rate – a price reduction to foreigners of 14·3 per cent. On the other hand a foreign article costing $100 costs £35·71 at home at the old rate and £41·67 at the new rate – a price rise to home purchasers of 16·7 per cent (the difference in the percentages is due simply to the base or numerator being higher for the former percentage and lower for the latter). It is important to appreciate that this price change is in itself harmful to the balance of payments of the devaluing country. In terms of sterling the home country has to pay 16·7 per cent more for imported goods and services while obtaining the same price for exports, and if the same volume of goods and services are imported and exported as before devaluation, net external payments are clearly worsened. Alternatively viewed in terms of foreign currency, the home country receives 14·3 per cent less per unit of exports while paying the same price in dollars for imports so that, once again, it is clear that the price change is damaging. If devaluation is to improve the balance of payments the country concerned must export a larger volume and/or import a smaller volume than previously. Moreover the changes in volume of exports and imports, in combination (that is the increase in volume of exports plus the decrease or minus the increase in volume of imports), must be more than sufficient to offset the damaging effects of the relative price change. The point of devaluation is that although it increases the initial gap between the value of imports and exports it gives the devaluing country a competitive advantage. Since exports can be sold at a cheaper or more profitable price abroad it is easier to sell more; and since imports are more costly at home it is easier for them to be replaced by import substitutes. The key factor, therefore, is the price responsiveness or price elasticity of foreign demand for home exports and the price elasticity of home demand for imports, though supply elasticities also play a part. As a rough generalization one can say that if one, or other, or both the elasticities of demand are sufficiently high then the percentage changes in the volume of exports and imports in combination will exceed the percentage devaluation so that the balance of payments will improve. In practice elasticities of demand are generally sufficiently high for devaluation to prove beneficial; but there are further considerations. First, it takes a long time, perhaps many months, before the beneficial responses can be fully realized, whereas the adverse effects of devaluation tend to be felt quickly. In the short run, therefore, devaluation may worsen the payments situation. Secondly, successful devaluation implies larger sales of exports and of import substitutes; and for these additional sales to be realized at a time when productive resources are fully extended, sufficient output must be released from other uses. In these circumstances devaluation must be accompanied by sufficient deflation of internal demand. Thirdly, the rise of import costs (implying a corresponding reduction in the real income of home residents) is liable to set in motion or intensify cost inflation, particularly if devaluation is allowed to create a buoyant aggregate demand. All too often the benefit of devaluation has proved to be temporary, the competitive advantage being eroded eventually by the spiral of cost inflation. Nevertheless devaluation, as a method of correcting divergent international cost relationships, is preferable to internal deflation because devaluation realigns prices immediately, whereas deflation can do so only through the wearing down effect of unemployment and low profits. Given the resistance to wage reduction, this is likely to involve a long period of stagnation and social suffering before the required price realignment is achieved. Devaluation, however, is by no means a costless method of adjustment. If, as is likely, it worsens the *terms of trade* (prices of imports rising more than prices of exports), devaluation will lower the real income of home residents; and in any case it causes an arbitrary redistribution of real income with losses concentrated on importers and particularly on those obliged to make payments fixed in terms of foreign currency. Figure

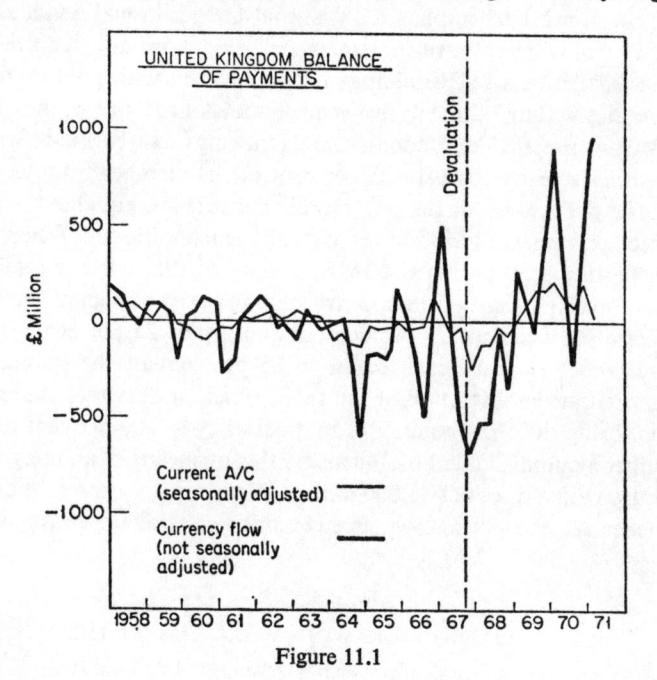

Figure 11.1

11.1 gives some impression of the effect of the 1967 devaluation on the British balance of payments and of the lag in time before the improvement became significant. Of course the changes in the balance of payments were not necessarily due entirely to the devaluation.

After this digression we must return to the IMF to examine briefly that institution's third main function. One of the weaknesses ascribed to the gold standard was the inadequacy and mal-distribution of international gold reserves. A major purpose of the IMF was to help remedy this by the establishment of a stabilization fund to provide supplementary reserves on a temporary basis to assist member countries to ride out temporary difficulties and to carry out adjustments. The fund is subscribed by the members according to quotas, each member's quota being roughly proportionate to its importance in world trade and payments. Three-quarters of the subscription is in the member's own currency (as a balance in favour of the IMF at that member's central bank) and one quarter in gold. The IMF therefore holds a stock of gold and a pool of currencies which are available for members to purchase. A member buying particular currencies from this pool pays in its own currency so that the IMF holdings of that member's currency rise and the holdings of the currencies purchased fall. But it must be emphasized first that the additional finance provided is only temporary, the member being normally required to repurchase excess IMF holdings of its currency with gold or other currencies within a three to five year period. And secondly, the drawings from the IMF are conditional. Drawings can be made within five *tranches* each equal to 25 per cent of the member's quota. The first tranche, known as the *gold tranche* because it is equal to the gold portion of the subscription, is virtually unconditional. When this tranche has been drawn the IMF holding of that currency will be equal to 100 per cent of the country's quota (i.e. the original currency subscription equal to 75 per cent of quota plus 25 per cent). Four more *credit tranches*, each equal to 25 per cent of the quota, are permitted at the discretion of the IMF, which, if drawn to the maximum, bring the IMF holding of that currency to 200 per cent of the member's quota. Table 11.2 illustrates this by means of an imaginary country with a quota of $1,000 million. Not only does access to credit tranches require permission, but countries so drawing must justify

TABLE 11.2

OPERATION OF DRAWING FACILITIES AT IMF

(An imaginary country with a quota of $1,000 million)

	Drawing (25% of quota) $ million	IMF holding of currency $ million	IMF holding as % of quota %
Initial position		750	75
Gold tranche	250	1,000	100
1st credit tranche	250	1,250	125
2nd credit tranche	250	1,500	150
3rd credit tranche	250	1,750	175
4th credit tranche	250	2,000	200

their requirements and indicate (by *letter of intent*) the measures proposed to correct the external imbalance, and the watchfulness of the IMF increases as drawings mount. *Stand-by* credits are also available whereby members can negotiate in advance for drawings for periods of six months or a year, though such drawings are often renewable. The total stabilization fund has increased over the years partly because of the rise in membership (from 39 at the outset in 1945 to well over 100) but mainly because of periodic increases in all quotas. Total quotas in 1971 amounted to $28·491 million as shown in Table 11.3. An important recent development has been the introduction of *Special Drawing Rights*, to be discussed in the next Section.

TABLE 11.3
QUOTAS IN THE INTERNATIONAL MONETARY FUND*

1971	$ million
Total	28,491
United States	6,700
United Kingdom	2,800
W. Germany	1,600
France	1,500
Japan	1,200
Canada	1,100
Italy	1,000
India	940
All other members	11,651

* The individual countries specified in this table are the eight largest quota holders. This group (excluding India) together with the Netherlands, Belgium, and Sweden, form the *Group of Ten* which constitute a kind of inner political power group of the system.

11.6 INTERNATIONAL LIQUIDITY AND PAYMENTS ADJUSTMENT

Within the framework of the IMF system the post-war international economy has functioned remarkably well. Recovery was speedy from the devastation and chaos of war, and thereafter rates of growth of trade and output and levels of employment, in most developed countries, have been unprecedented. Nevertheless there have been increasing criticisms of the Bretton Woods system, particularly with respect to the provision of international liquidity, since, as we have seen, IMF drawing facilities are conditional and temporary; and also with respect to the difficulty and inequity of balance of payments adjustment in the system of fixed exchange rates.

International liquidity is needed by countries for much the same reasons that individuals need money balances. International payments and receipts never synchronize continuously so that, in a system of fixed exchange rates at least, nations must hold adequate stocks of international purchasing power. Liquidity is needed to give nations time: time to diagnose the causes of imbalance, time to ride out those deficits which are temporary, and time to effect correction where this can be achieved without undue internal disturbance. Insufficiency of reserves increases the problems of external disequilibrium and intensifies the burden of adjustment on the deficit countries. Fear of this can provoke a general scramble for liquidity even by countries currently in surplus, and a universal attempt to increase holdings of reserves, unaccompanied by a general increase in the supply of liquidity, implies universal deflation and restriction of output or universal restriction of imports. On the other hand, although adequate liquidity facilitates smooth and gentle adjustment of disequilibriums it may also enable a deficit country to put off adjustment indefinitely. It can be argued therefore that too much liquidity may aggravate payments imbalance by encouraging evasion of corrective action. It might also enable deficit countries to live indefinitely at the partial expense of others, and might stimulate world inflation.

The sufficiency of international liquidity is therefore a delicate question; moreover it is difficult to gauge its appropriate rate of increase. The imbalances between international receipts and payments, the finance of which is a major function of reserves, seem likely to grow in scale along with the value of international trade and capital movements. But it is not at all certain that the need for liquidity rises in the same proportion. Much depends on the susceptibility of the world to cyclical fluctuations, on the state of confidence in trade and in the value of currencies, on the extent to which adjustments are effected by changes in exchange parities, and on the distribution and composition of liquidity.

Table 11.4 indicates the changes that have occurred in recent years in the main types of international liquidity. One should note, however, that there are, in addition, foreign exchange balances held by commercial banks, and reciprocal credit facilities between central banks for agreed amounts and agreed periods of time. The most noticeable feature of the table is the extent to which growth of total liquidity has been dependent on foreign exchange holdings, of which

TABLE 11.4
INTERNATIONAL LIQUIDITY

	1958 $ million	1971 (1st Qr.) $ million	Percentage of total increase 1958–1971 %
Gold held by central banks	38,000	36,900	−3
Unconditional reserves in IMF*	2,600	7,300	+11
SDRs		5,800	+14
Foreign exchange	16,900	48,700	+77
Total	57,500	98,700	+100

* The unconditional reserves in the IMF arise from gold subscriptions to the IMF and from the Fund's use of the respective currencies to finance drawings of others or to purchase gold. In effect these reserves are the amounts in aggregate by which individual currency holdings fall below 100 per cent of quota.

about 60 per cent are United States dollar balances and about 12 per cent sterling. It is not surprising that portions of reserves and working balances should have been held in 'key' currencies such as dollars and sterling because the exceptionally well-developed banking facilities and money, capital, and commodity markets in the United States and Britain make it particularly convenient to conduct credit arrangements, debt settlement, and pricing in these currencies. These are extremely useful currencies to hold. Moreover it can be more profitable to hold reserves in foreign exchange on which interest can be earned than in barren stores of gold. But the enormous growth in central bank holdings of dollars since 1958 has been due to the chronic dollar deficit, attributable in part to numerous earlier devaluations against the dollar, to huge American military expenditure and aid abroad, and the development of America as the most important source of world credit.

Dependence on the deficit for the expansion of international liquidity has been disturbing, partly because this source could dry up suddenly and arbitrarily should the American authorities transform the balance of payments into a surplus by, for example, a drastic curtailment of military expenditure, or by a policy of very high interest rates. Even more worrying has been the susceptibility of this form of international liquidity to the vagaries of confidence. The system has depended not only on a continuing dollar deficit but also on a continuing willingness of central banks to accumulate dollars. But the longer the deficit lasted the lower was the confidence in the dollar and the less the willingness to hold it. The real difficulty lies in the existence of alternative forms in which international reserves can be held. If confidence in one form is undermined there may be a stampede towards alternative forms and, since the reserve country can seldom satisfy fully the demand to convert its currency into gold or into another key currency, a liquidity crisis ensues. Indeed it was just such a crisis in 1968 that led to the establishment of the two-tier gold price (described in Chapter 2) and the virtual suspension of the gold convertibility of the dollar.

The system has also been criticized on the grounds that a reserve country is under no pressure to correct a deficit so long as surplus countries are willing or can be persuaded to accumulate its currency. This gives an inflationary twist to the world economy because while the reserve country does not need to deflate to correct its deficit, the surplus countries are encouraged to expand by the growth which they experience in reserves and money supply. It also means that a reserve country, in continuous deficit, can appear to be enjoying a higher standard of living at the expense of the surplus countries by virtue of its receipts of unrequited imports, and can appear to be acquiring capital assets in other countries on the basis of credit provided automatically by those countries in the process of accumulating the reserve currency. Of course any surplus country has the option of curing its surplus, vis-à-vis the reserve country, either by revaluing its own currency in terms of the key currency or else by investing more in the reserve country. But if all surplus countries were to adopt these solutions this source of additional international liquidity would dry up.

Part of the difficulty with the dollar reserve system in recent years has been the irreconcilability of attitudes in other countries. On the one hand, the long continued dollar deficit and the diminishing gold stock in America increasingly undermined confidence in the dollar. On the other hand, other countries were reluctant to cure the dollar deficit by revaluing their currencies in relation to the dollar, since this would have undermined their competitive advantage in world trade. Whereas the par value of the dollar had been fixed in gold, the par values of most other currencies had been fixed in terms of the dollar, of the gold weight and fineness in effect on 1 July 1944. The dollar, in fact, was the international unit of account. This prevented the United States from initiating a direct change in the parity between the dollar and other currencies without formally changing the value of the dollar in terms of gold. The American authorities were unwilling to do this partly because of internal legal complications, partly because of fear of domestic political reactions, partly because it would be to admit the dollar to be no longer the international unit of account, and partly for a variety of other reasons to be discussed presently. The initiative for altering the external value of the dollar rested, therefore, with all other countries collectively; and to achieve a collectively agreed alteration is clearly difficult.

This was the problem which lay behind President Nixon's decision of mid-August 1971 to declare the dollar inconvertible into gold. This declaration, in itself, scarcely altered the position of the dollar because, as noted above, it had been virtually inconvertible since March 1968. But it was designed to force other countries to face squarely the choice between continuing to accumulate dollars and revaluing their currencies and, in conjunction with the imposition of a temporary 10 per cent import surcharge, to exert pressure in the direction of the latter choice. The immediate reaction of many governments, after an initial closure of foreign exchange markets, was to allow a 'controlled float' for their respective currencies. Market pressures were allowed to push the values of currencies beyond the limit of the 1 per cent above parity, though the authorities intervened in various ways to restrict fluctuations.

On 18 December 1971 agreement was reached by the Group of Ten on the following measures to settle the monetary crisis. First, the United States agreed to lift immediately the 10 per cent import surcharge and the provisions of the job development credit in return for the revaluation of leading currencies against the dollar. Compared with 1 May parities these revaluations were Italy and Sweden 7·6 per cent, Britain and France 8·6 per cent, Belgium and Netherlands 11·6 per cent, West Germany 13·6 per cent, and Japan 16·9 per cent (expressed as devaluations of the dollar the percentages are all smaller because of the reversal of numerator and denominator). Canada decided to continue to float the exchange rate. The revaluations should give the United States a considerable competitive advantage; the corresponding competitive disadvantage to Britain should be offset, in part at least, by the larger revaluations of some other countries. Secondly, when certain trade concessions have been negotiated between U.S.A. and the EEC, Japan, and Canada, Congress will be asked to formally devalue the dollar against gold from $35 to $38 per ounce (a devaluation of 7·9 per cent). While representing a 'prestige' victory for the French and some support to the official value of gold reserves, this devaluation serves mainly to preserve the use of gold as a *numéraire* because the United States has not undertaken, at this stage, to restore the convertibility of the dollar into gold. The new pattern of exchange rates can be expressed in terms of gold, with the parities of Britain and France remaining unchanged, some, such as the mark and yen being revalued. Thirdly, pending longer-term monetary reform, it was agreed that margins of permissible exchange rate fluctuation be widened to $2\frac{1}{4}$ per cent either side of each country's exchange parity. This should reduce the danger of 'one-way' speculation, but the range of possible fluctuation is hardly enough to provide any corrective to trade imbalance.

In general the agreement represents a return to a marginally modified Bretton Woods system; real monetary reform to deal effectively with the problems of international adjustment and liquidity has been left to longer-term discussions through the IMF.

The dollar crisis in fact highlighted the double problem of the IMF system: of how and in what form additional international liquidity is to be provided; and of how payment adjustment is best to be effected. Dissatisfaction with balance of payments adjustment under the IMF system of fixed exchange rates is attributable not only to the difficulty, discussed above, of adjusting the payments imbalance of the reserve country, but also to the tendency for the burden of adjustment to fall disproportionately on any deficit country. So long as exchange rates are fixed, a deficit country (other than the reserve country) is under more obligation to take correction action than a surplus country because the foreign exchange resources of the former are limited. Moreover, although pressure is brought to bear on a country when IMF holdings of its currency rise above the quota, there is no parallel pressure exerted on a country when IMF holdings of its currency fall below the quota. The *scarce currency clause* was designed for this purpose but never operated.

As we have seen, it was envisaged that fundamental disequilibrium would be corrected by agreed changes in par values. This would share the burden of adjustment between deficit and surplus countries and create minimal disturbance to internal activity. But in practice little use had been made of changes in exchange rates. To some extent this may have been due to the exceptionally high rates of growth of trade and output since the 1950s which made it easier for a country to adjust a deficit without recourse to devaluation, since a pause in a country's rate of growth, rather than serious deflation, has often been sufficient to correct an imbalance. The key currency system contributed to the rigidity of exchange rates because of the fear that any change in exchange rates would weaken confidence in reserve currencies. The truth of this was demonstrated by the run on the dollar which followed the sterling devaluation of 1967. Feelings of national prestige also made governments reluctant to devalue; but perhaps the main reason has been the fear that periodic readjustment of exchange rates would encourage speculation and thereby aggravate payment difficulties. The disadvantage of the 'adjustable peg' system is that once a currency appears to be at all weak speculators can gain but cannot lose from selling the currency. One-way speculation can in fact precipitate a devaluation which would not otherwise occur; and in recent years the growth in the volume of mobile short-term capital has enormously increased this danger.

There have been many proposals for reform, some concerned with provision of liquidity, some with easing payment adjustment, and some with both; but space prevents more than a brief glimpse at a few of these proposals. One reform, perhaps pressed more than any other, is official revaluation of gold. A doubling of the dollar price of gold, for example, would double the dollar value of all gold reserves. Revaluation of gold is therefore a method of increasing international liquidity by the stroke of a pen, so to speak. Moreover the higher price would encourage a higher rate of production of gold. Some supporters of this proposal also advocate a return to the true gold standard on the grounds that the greater discipline imposed on national governments would safeguard the value of money. This solution, up to the date of writing, has been firmly rejected, particularly by the American authorities. It is easy to see that any serious suggestion of gold revaluation would undermine the key currency system. Indeed it might well bring to an end the use of dollars and sterling as international reserves, and a very large increase in the price of gold might then be necessary to compensate for the loss of these other forms of international liquidity. A major disadvantage of the gold solution is the inequitable re-distribution of wealth that revaluation would produce. Gold holdings are very unevenly spread. Gold producers, gold hoarders, and those central banks which have chosen to hold a high proportion of reserves in gold would all gain; those holding currencies would all lose. Another disadvantage is that once gold revaluation had been accepted as the main method of increasing liquidity, speculative gold hoarding would be encouraged. This could deprive the world of considerable amounts of liquidity and could provoke further revaluation in a vicious circle. A more general objection is to the reliance on a system that is not only anachronistic, but also susceptible to the vagaries of hoarding and gold production. But despite all these arguments it may be that the rise in the free market price of gold and the dollar crisis will eventually force the world to choose between official revaluation and the abandonment of gold as a form of international money.

An alternative solution which, it is claimed, would not only obviate the problem of international liquidity but would also provide a more equitable and effective method of balance of payments adjustment, is that of flexible or floating exchange rates. If the market is perfectly free to adjust prices of currencies in accordance with the pressure of demand and supply arising from trade and capital transfers there is no need for central banks to accumulate or even hold international reserves. No problems of imbalance arise from exchange rates being fixed at the wrong level; indeed no external disequilibrium can develop at all. Disturbances to the balance of payments from shifts in demand, and divergences of international costs, etc., are corrected automatically by movements of exchange rates; moreover the burden of adjustment is spread between all the countries involved. No government need restrict internal demand, imports, or capital exports for the sake of correcting external disequilibrium, and each government is free to conduct independent domestic policies. In general it is claimed that only with flexible exchange rates can full employment, freedom of trade, and payments equilibrium be made compatible. Despite these attractive arguments proposals to establish universal flexible exchange rates have been firmly resisted. The main objections are that the additional uncertainty of continuously varying exchange rates would seriously curb international trade and investment; that elasticities of demand for imports are not high enough to prevent wide fluctuations of rates in response to disturbances; that exchange speculation would be encouraged which would intensify fluctuations, to the extent that speculators' judgements are faulty; that international cooperation would be discouraged; and, perhaps most damning of all, that the one remaining discipline restraining national governments from all-too-easy inflationary policies would be removed. Supporters of flexible exchange rates argue that these fears are greatly exaggerated and that the real resistance to the proposals comes from conservatism.

Some alternative compromise solutions have been widely discussed. The 'crawling peg' proposal would retain the narrow margin of fluctuations either side of parity but the parity itself would be altered frequently and by small amounts, the actual change being based on the average behaviour of rates in the immediate past. It is claimed that the gradual changes in parities would ease the correction of fundamental disequilibrium with the minimum of additional uncertainty or of encouragement to speculation. Another compromise which, at the time of writing, is finding favour is the widening of the permitted margin of fluctuation from 1 per cent to say 3 or 5 per cent. This would not help correction of long-term disequilibrium but might assist a country to ride out temporary disequilibrium, and reduce the need for reserves. It might also mitigate the danger of one-way speculation by increasing the size of potential speculative losses. Opponents of this scheme argue that uncertainty would be increased without any real assurance that speculation would be reduced or balance of payments adjustment eased. The case for and against greater flexibility thus remains unresolved, though the experience of controlled floating rates, following the dollar crisis of August 1971, may well have strengthened the arguments in favour of flexibility. But even if the case for flexible exchange rates is accepted in principle there must be some lower limit to the area to which the system relates. Whatever advantages might accrue to individual villages, towns, or counties, etc., from having separate currencies and floating exchange rates, would surely be more than offset by the additional inconvenience and uncertainty. An interesting question, therefore, is what factors would determine the point at which separate currencies and flexible rates become positively beneficial?

The final type of reform to be considered is that of the planned creation of international liquidity. Many ingenious schemes have been designed, such as the *Triffin Plan* and the *Stamp Plan*, in which the creation and distribution of additional liquidity would be conducted on a rational basis, according to world needs. Unfortunately space precludes a review of such schemes. They have led however to a positive, though at present modest, reform in this direction by the IMF, through the introduction in January 1970 of *Special Drawing Rights*, sometimes known as 'paper gold'. SDRs differ from ordinary IMF drawing rights in two vital respects: their use is largely unconditional, and most of the SDRs created constitute a permanent addition to liquidity. Thus for the first time additional international money, which can be regarded as 'owned' reserves, has been created in accordance with international needs.

SDRs consist of book entries in a new special drawing account with the IMF, each member country being allocated a share of the total SDRs created, in proportion to its quota in the IMF. Member countries are not intended to use their allocation of SDRs to change the composition of their reserves (SDRs are not convertible into gold for example). But a central bank can use them to settle a debt directly with another central bank (or the IMF) or to acquire foreign currencies so as to finance a deficit. In the latter case the IMF specifies the country or countries which are to provide the currencies in exchange for a transfer of SDRs to them. A country so designated is obliged to accept SDRs in exchange for its currency up to the point at which its total holdings of SDRs reach three times the initial allocation, though the country is free to take more if it chooses. A country which allows the daily average of its SDR holdings over any five year period to fall below 30 per cent of its initial allocation is obliged to buy back the deficient SDRs from other members. In effect therefore only 70 per cent of an allocation of SDRs constitutes a permanent addition to international liquidity.

The initial allocation of SDRs on 1 January 1970 amounted approximately to $9,500 million over a three-year period, about $3,500 million being for 1970 and $3,000 million for each of 1971 and 1972. In proportion to total existing international reserves this is a modest addition. But the important thing is that a beginning has been made in the planned creation of liquidity. Whether SDRs will merely supplement existing reserves or supplant them only the future will show. It has certainly been suggested that SDRs should become the major source of additional liquidity when the United States deficit has disappeared. But whether SDRs will replace existing reserves held in gold is more problematical. The fundamental reason why nations continue to use gold as a reserve asset is the lack of adequate confidence in any alternative; and even SDRs have at present a full gold guarantee. One suggestion which was mooted at the time of the dollar crisis is that there should be composite reserves. In this scheme existing reserve assets of gold, dollars, sterling, and SDRs would all be pooled in a *reserve settlement account* through which central banks would make payments to each other. Payment by a deficit country would be made in a composite of gold, dollars, sterling, and SDRs in the proportions of these assets initially pooled by that country. An increase in the total of reserves in the settlement account would be made solely via the creation of SDRs.

The world is perhaps at a turning-point in matters of international payments, with progress possible in two alternative directions. One direction is that of flexible exchange rates. This would preserve independence of national policies and would leave correction of disturbance basically to the market mechanism. The other direction, while relying on fixed rates of exchange, would be towards an increasing degree of co-ordination of national policies so as to minimize disturbances, and towards an increasing degree of co-operation in matters of mutual assistance, creation of liquidity, and the sharing of the burden of adjustment. The outcome may be, of course, a compromise. The world may become organized in a few large currency areas, within which are fixed rates of exchange and co-ordinated national policies, and between which are flexible rates of exchange.

SUGGESTED READING

B. J. Cohen, *Balance of Payments Policy* (Penguin, 1969).
H. G. Grubel, *The International Monetary System* (Penguin, 1969).
W. M. Scammell, *International Monetary Policy*, 2nd ed. (Macmillan, 1962), chs. ii, iii, iv, v, vi, vii and section v.
L. B. Yeager, *International Monetary Relations* (Harper & Row, 1966).
T. Scitovsky, *Money and the Balance of Payments* (Unwin, 1969), part B.
W. M. Clarke and G. Pulay, *The World's Money: How it Works* (Allen & Unwin, 1970).
Radcliffe Report (H.M.S.O., 1959), ch. viii.
A. B. Cramp, *Monetary Management Principles and Practice* (Allen & Unwin, 1971), ch. iv.
F. Hirsch, *Money International* (Allan Lane, Penguin Press, 1967).
L. B. Yeager, *The International Monetary Mechanism* (Holt, Rinehart & Winston, 1970).

Questions

Each of the questions assembled here has been placed under the heading of the chapter the subject of which appears to be most closely related. But the reader should note that in many cases a satisfactory answer requires knowledge and understanding of other chapters and, indeed, of other books. Questions which are unstarred are intended to represent those which might be asked of a candidate for a professional examination or of, say, a second-year undergraduate. They are generally straightforward. Starred questions are regarded as rather more advanced and more appropriate for an honours candidate in this subject.

Questions marked '(S)' are reproduced with the kind permission of the University of Strathclyde.

CHAPTER 1

1. Examine the ways in which the use of money contributes to the economic well-being of society.
2. Comment on the nature of and the reasons for the evolution of forms of money.
3. Discuss the significance of credit to the functioning of the economic system.
4. Discuss the significance to economic growth and welfare of the development of a wide variety of financial assets. * (S)
5. Comment on the view that 'from the economist's point of view there is no hard and fast dividing line between money, however defined, and less liquid assets'. (T. Scitovsky.) * (S)

CHAPTER 3

6. In what ways can bank deposits be created? What factors limit the creation of such deposits?
7. Examine the considerations which influence the nature and distribution of commercial bank assets.
8. Discuss the concept of liquidity as applied to bankers' assets.

9. Comment on the changes which have occurred in the asset holdings of the London clearing banks since the Second World War.

CHAPTER 4

10. Discuss the use of funding operations as a technique of monetary restraint.
11. Critically examine the theory of the bank deposit multiplier. (S)
12. Examine the contention that a reluctance on the part of the authorities to allow free movement of interest rates will inhibit their ability to control the money supply.
13. 'There is more to the determination of the volume of bank deposits than the arithmetic of reserve supplies and reserve ratios.' (J. Tobin.) Discuss. * (S)
14. 'In a world without reserve requirements the preference of depositors, as well as those of borrowers, would be very relevant in determining the volume of bank deposits.' (J. Tobin.) Explain and discuss. * (S)
15. Discuss the influence of the demand for bank deposits on their supply. *
16. 'The liquidity ratio theory is seriously defective or at best incomplete as an explanation of short-term changes in the level of bank deposits in the U.K.' (A. D. Bain.) Discuss. * (S)

CHAPTER 5

17. Outline the major factors which determine the money supply in practice.
18. Discuss the relationship between budgetary policy and the supply of money.
19. Examine the relationship between 'changes in the money supply' and 'domestic credit expansion'. Which concept do you consider the more important from the point of view of monetary policy? (S)
20. 'At worst it [Domestic Credit Expansion] might involve a harmful gearing of policy to an irrelevant magnitude.' (N.I.E.R.) Discuss. * (S)
21. How far is it (*a*) practicable and (*b*) analytically important to attempt to distinguish a set of assets which can be described as money? *

CHAPTER 6

22. Discuss the contribution made by the development of financial intermediaries to economic growth and productivity. (S)
23. For what purposes should an economist distinguish between deposit banks and other financial intermediaries? (S)
24. Account for the more rapid growth of non-bank financial intermediaries in comparison with deposit banks in the two decades or so after the Second World War.
25. In what ways and to what extent can non-bank financial intermediaries gain deposits from commercial banks?
26. 'It may be said that, because bank deposits are accepted as money, the banks as a group cannot "lose" deposits to other financial institutions.' (P.I.B. Report.) 'Whether deposits are transferred to a public sector non-bank or to a private sector non-bank, the reserves and deposits of the clearing banks suffer in the last analysis a decline.' (P.I.B. Report.) Are these views reconcilable? * (S)
27. 'Not possessing the multiplicative faculty of commercial banks they [non-bank intermediaries] are confined to the brokerage function of simply transmitting to borrowers the funds entrusted to them by lenders.' (B. J. Moore.) How far would you agree with this contention? * (S)
28. Discuss the view that the role of non-bank intermediaries has contributed to the relative decline in the demand for bank deposits and to the frustration of monetary policy. *

CHAPTER 7

29. Discuss the importance of distinguishing 'outside' and 'inside' money.
30. What is meant by the velocity of circulation of money? What are the main causes of change in this velocity? (S)
31. Critically examine the Quantity Theory of Money.
32. Examine the relationship between the supply of money and the level of interest rates in the short run and in the long run.
33. Discuss the effects of an increase in the quantity of money on the rate of interest and on the price level.
34. Examine the contribution to monetary thought of the so-called 'Cambridge Equation'. * (S)
35. 'We cannot find any reason for supposing, or any experience in

monetary history indicating, that there is any limit to the velocity of circulation.' (Radcliffe Report.) Discuss. * (S)

CHAPTER 8

36. 'He [Keynes] regarded changes in the stock of money as of minor importance in times of unemployment, and as exercising a significant influence only in times of full employment.' (M. Friedman.) Discuss.
37. How far would you agree with the assertion that the main characteristic of Keynesian theory is that money does not matter?
38. Explain the role of money in the Keynesian model of income determination.
39. Comment on the view that if expectations were clear and uniform the long-term rate of interest would be what it was expected to be.
40. In what ways do changes in interest rates influence economic activity? (S)
41. What do you understand by the demand for money? What are the major determinants of this demand?
42. Why did Keynes regard liquidity preference as a cornerstone of his theoretical structure? * (S)
43. 'Keynesian economics, while it attributed an important role to the money supply in determining the level of economic activity, destroyed the notion that there was any simple link between the supply of money, the level of output, and the price level.' (A. D. Bain.) Discuss. * (S)
44. Discuss, with particular reference to the role of money and finance, the view that Keynesian economics differs significantly from the economics of Keynes. * (S)

CHAPTER 9

45. Account for the revival of interest in recent years in the importance of the quantity of money. (S)
46. 'The monetarist approach rests on the assumption that velocity rather than the multiplier is the key relationship in the understanding of macro-economic development in the economy.' (H. G. Johnson.) Discuss. (S)

47. Examine the causes of the high level of interest rates in Britain in recent years. (S)
48. Discuss the view that the level of the nominal rate of interest is a poor criterion for monetary policy.
49. Compare the 'transmission mechanism' of the Keynesian and Monetarist schools of thought.
50. 'It is no use trying to control a "flow" (like the expenditure of the public) by operating on a "stock" (like its holding of money or liquid assets).' (J. C. R. Dow.) Discuss this view in relation to the potential effectiveness of monetary policy. * (S)
51. 'What Friedman has actually presented is an elegant exposition of the modern portfolio approach to the demand for money which can only be seen as a continuation of the Keynesian theory of liquidity preference.' (Don Patinkin.) Discuss. * (S)
52. 'The stable demand function is evidence not of the importance of money but only of the impotence of the authorities in controlling it.' (N. Kaldor.) Discuss. * (S)
53. Discuss the view that in the context of U.K. institutions and conventions it is neither desirable nor practicable to increase the money stock at a constant rate per annum. * (S)

CHAPTER 10

54. Examine the significance of 'Bank Rate' as an instrument of policy. (S)
55. Describe the manner in which Bank of England operations can be used to control the volume of bank deposits. To what extent is such control practicable? (S)
56. Discuss the role of special deposits in monetary control in the U.K. (S)
57. Discuss the case for and against the use of quantitative controls on bank lending.
58. Outline the main techniques of monetary policy and compare their relative efficiency.
59. Discuss the case for the establishment of a more competitive banking system.
60. Comment on the effectiveness of monetary policy as a regulator of economic activity.
61. Discuss the compatibility of the major objectives for which monetary policy has been used by the British authorities in the last decade or so.

264   AN INTRODUCTION TO FINANCIAL ECONOMICS

62. 'There can be no doubt, in our judgement, that "bank rate policy" is an absolute necessity for the sound management of a currency and that it is a most delicate and beautiful instrument for the purpose.' (Macmillan Report.) Discuss the applicability of this view to contemporary Britain. * (S)
63. 'To achieve influence over the banks' lending by means of pressure on their cash must involve conscious manipulation of interest rates primarily to that end.' (B.E.Q.B.) Explain this statement and consider the practicability of such policy in the present British setting. * (S)

CHAPTER 11

64. Explain the recent changes in the U.K. presentation of balance of payments statistics and comment upon the difficulty of providing one summary figure for balance of payments surplus or deficit. (S)
65. The analytical distinction between autonomous and accommodating transactions in the balance of payments is useful in theory but is hardly any use in practice. Discuss. (S)
66. Discuss the view that flexible exchange rates are the most appropriate method of adjusting to a balance of payments deficit in modern conditions of full employment. (S)
67. Assess the case for an increase in the price of gold associated with a return to the gold standard as a means of dealing with the financial problems of the international economy. (S)
68. Discuss the view that despite recent crises the International Monetary Fund must be considered a success. (S)
69. The problem facing the international payments system is not one of liquidity but of adjustment. Discuss. (S)
70. To what extent has the introduction of SDRs solved the problem of international liquidity.
71. Consider the advantages and disadvantages of the 'key currency' or 'reserve currency' system both to the reserve country and to the rest of the world.
72. In what ways does the International Monetary Fund system for international payments differ from that of the former gold standard?
73. For what purposes is international liquidity required? What are the main components of this liquidity?
74. With British experience in mind, consider in what ways and in

what circumstances a country can expect to benefit from the devaluation of its currency. (S)
75. Consider the problems faced in trying to reconcile internal and external equilibrium. (S)
76. Consider the problem of adjustment to balance of payments disequilibrium faced by a country if exchange rate variation is excluded from consideration. (S)

Index

Accepting houses, 24–5, 35, 150
  growth rate, 143
  in relation to money supply, 124, 127
  liquidity, 212
Advances, 70, 79, 103
Advertising, 137, 148
Agricultural Mortgage Corporation, 33
Agriculture, 9
Arbitrage, 39
Asset prices, 238
Assets
  bank, 129
  central bank dealings, 99
  effect of purchase on cash, 98
  financial, 167, 194, 195
  liquid, 82, 85, 109
  of deposit banks, 60
  preferences, 136, 137, 142
  relation to money, 15
  tangible, 4, 11, 97, 114
    sale of, 10

Balance of payments, 112, 114, 120, 193, 199, 230–41
  basic balance, 233, 234
  by types of transaction, 122
  controlled by Domestic Credit Expansion, 121–2
  current account, 230
  current balances, 233
  deficits, 121–2
  disturbances, 235
  policies, 240–1
  surplus, 116
  United Kingdom (1970), 232
Bank assets, 129
Bank charges, 57
Bank deposits, 6, 14, 47, 70–104
  as money, 48
  classification, 123
  control through foreign exchange, 101
  conversion into legal tender, 48
  current accounts, 48

Bank deposits—*cont.*
  deposit accounts, 48
  effect of cash base, 89
  effect of decisions of banks and public, 95
  expansion by advances, 95–6
  for debt settlement, 48
  how created, 49
  interest rates, 215–16
  limitations on volume, 70, 71
  multipliers, 89–99, 136, 138
  public preference, 99–100
  See also Deposits
Bank for International Settlements, 242
Bank liabilities, 129
Bank loans, 55, 108, 109
  effect on cash, 141
  in sterling, 130
  to private sector, 114
  See also Credit regulation
Bank notes, 6, 7, 14, 43
  effect of withdrawing from banks, 44–6
  fiduciary issue, 44
  issue regulations, 44
  Northern Ireland, 43–4
  Scotland, 43–4
Bank of England, 22, 25, 35, 43, 50
  Banking Department, 45
  contact with gold market, 40
  Discount Office, 204
  functions, 41–2
  influence on banks' cash holdings, 52
  Issue Department, 44, 45, 210
  last resort lending, 204–5
  loans to discount houses, 59, 204
  overnight loans, 205
  purchase of government securities, 51–2
  Special Deposits, 64, 100–1, 211–12, 215, 216–17, 218
Bank of England Act (1946), 41, 213
Bank of Scotland, 23
Bank rate, 77, 78, 85, 148, 203

Bank rate—*cont.*
 definition, 204
 influence of change on internal activity, 208
 influence on foreign exchange, 207, 208
 influence on gold flow, 207
 interest on deposit accounts, 141, 144
 policy, 204–9
Bankers Balances, 43, 44, 45, 75, 216
 reduction by debt transactions, 51
Banks, 22
 advances, 60
 as financial intermediaries, 12–13, 132
 cash holdings, 57, 58
 cash reserves, 72–4
 classification, 24
 competition for business, 57, 146
 confidence, 57, 147
 current accounts, 124
 deposit accounts, 133
  rates of interest, 147
 in private sector, 92
 inter bank market, 37
 liquid assets, 82, 85
 operating costs, 57
 payments, 56
 profit, 57
 services offered, 24
 statistics, 61
 withdrawals, 56
 See also Clearing banks; Deposit banks; Overseas banks
Barclays Bank Ltd., 23
Baring Brothers, 24
Barter, 3, 170
Bills of Exchange, 24, 25–6, 35, 36, 49, 54, 85, 107, 167, 216
 as money market assets, 58
 discounting, 24
 international, 207
 yield, 80
Bodin, Jean, 152
Bonds, 5, 37–8, 109, 167, 179, 181
 as form of wealth, 187
 effect of sale on interest rates, 180
 new issues, 37–8
 sale to bank customers, 87
 undated, 11
 yield changes, 207
Borrowing
 controls, 203
 See also Financial intermediaries
Bretton Woods system, 247, 252

British Savings Bonds, 32
Budget (1971), 214
Budgetary control, 203
Budgetary policy, 120
Building societies, 27, 29–30, 133, 160
 annual growth rate, 143
 as financial intermediaries, 12–13, 132
 controls on lending, 213
 deposits, 29
 effect of transfer from bank deposits, 137–8
 interest rates, 30, 150
 reductions in lending, 150
 shares, 5
 transfer of bank deposits, 71

Cambridge equation, 164–8
Capital, 172–3
Capital assets
 apparent value, 173
 economic significance to owners, 173
Capital goods, 96
Cash, 79
 bank holdings, 57, 58
 choice of interest rate by Bank of England, 77
 control of cash base, 82, 85–9
 induced changes in holdings, 100
 involuntary losses, 77
 ratio to assets other than deposits, 92
 ratio to deposits, 73, 74, 75
Cash base, 89
Cash ratio, 77, 78, 79, 83
 abondment of requirement, 217
Cash reserves, 72–4
Central Statistical Office, 105
 classification of banks, 24
Certificates of deposit, 36–7
Claims, 7, 10
Clearing banks, 23, 218
 asset distribution, 66, 67
 assets, 61
 'banking assets', 62
 liabilities, 60, 61
 See also Banks; Deposit banks
Clydesdale Bank Ltd., 23
Coins, 6, 7, 14, 43
 supply, 43
Commonwealth Development Corporation, 34
Commonwealth Development Finance Company Ltd., 34

INDEX

Competition between banks, 57, 146
Computer applications, 22
Consumer credit, 34
  advantages of controls, 220
  disadvantages of controls, 220
  statutory control, 219–20
Consumer demand, 172, 175
Consumer expenditure, 46–7, 196
Consumer goods, 11, 32, 97, 184
  as form of wealth, 187
  credit purchases, 219
  financing, 96
Consumption, 9
  influence of long-term interest rates, 183
  reaction to interest rate changes, 181
Consumption function, 172
Co-operation, 256
Co-operative Bank, 23
Coutts and Co., 23
Cramp, A. B., 201, 228
Credit, 10, 34
  availability, 225–8
  basic function, 1
  international, 250
  See also Hire purchase
Credit controls, 214–19
  statutory, 219–20
  summary of arrangements, 215–17
Credit facilities, 160
Credit flow, 214
Credit regulation, 117
  See also Bank loans
Crowther Report on Consumer Credit (Cmnd. 4596, 1971), 34, 35, 219–20
Currencies in relation to gold, 239
Currency, 98
  as proporation of money supply, 94
  effect of public preference, 99–100
  foreign, 230
  holdings by public, 92–3
  in a definition of money, 190
  in active balances, 158
  in circulation, 46–7, 49–50, 110, 124, 129
  International Monetary Fund pool, 246
  public demand, 46
  revaluation, 241
  velocity of circulation, 156
Currency and Bank Notes Act (1954), 44
Currency flow, 235
Currency withdrawals, 72

Current accounts, 48, 96
  as active balances, 158
Current deposits, 15

D.C.E., *see* Domestic Credit Expansion
Dacey, W. M., 82–3
Dept instruments, 11
Debt policy, 209–11
Debt repayment, 96
  by government, 99
Debt transactions, 51
Debts, 7, 10
  settlement, 8, 14, 22
    effect on active balances, 159
    effect on economic activity, 14–15
Deficit spending, 10
Deflation, 21, 184, 239, 245
Deposit accounts, 48, 141, 144
Deposit banks, 23, 25, 35
  absorption of finance houses, 32
  asset structure, 60–8
  call for Special Deposits, 211
  decline, 144, 213
  growth rate, 143
Deposit Multiplier, 89–99, 104, 105
  limitations, 95–9
  non-bank, 140–141
  theory, 89–95
Deposits, 79
  building societies, 29
  ratio to cash, 73, 74, 75
  ratio to liquid assets, 62–3
  See also bank deposits
Devaluation, 241, 243
  effect on gold market, 40
  effect on imports and exports, 243–5
  of sterling (1967), 253
Discount houses, 25–6, 35, 37, 216
  assets, 83
  cash replacement, 78
  loans from Bank of England, 59, 204
  loans from banks, 85
  purchase of securities, 76
Dollars
  inconvertible to gold (1971), 251
  par value, 250
  reserve system, 250
  See also Euro-dollars
Domestic Credit Expansion, 117
  control of balance of payments, 120, 121–2
  definition, 118
  effect of contraction, 120

Domestic Credit Expansion—*cont.*
  equations, 118
  purpose, 118–22
  practical applications, 129–31

E.E.A., *see* Exchange Equalization Account
Employment levels, 155, 166, 238
  See also Unemployment
Equilibrium, 155
Equities, 11, 114
  as form of wealth, 187
  state of market, 133–4
Euro-currencies, 24, 36
Euro dollars, 36, 231
  See also Dollars
Exchange Equalization Account, 41, 44, 53, 106, 227–8, 243
Exchange mediums, 3–4
  other than money, 6
Exchange rates, 7, 39, 239
  devaluation, 241, 243
  flexible, 256
  floating, 254
  related to money growth, 193
  role of International Monetary Fund, 242
Expenditure adjustment, 240
Expenditure controls, 203
Expenditure switching, 240–1
Export credits, 85, 107
Export Credits Guarantee Department, 63
Exports, 130, 229
  competition, 113
  subsidies, 240

F.C.I., *see* Finance Corporation for Industry
Factoring organizations, 34
Finance Act (1965), 31
Finance agencies, 33
Finance companies, 150
  as financial intermediaries, 12–13
  growth rate, 143
  rates of interest, 81
  transfer of bank deposits, 71
Finance Corporation for Industry Ltd., 33–4, 213
Finance costs, 13
Finance houses, 27, 32–3, 133
  absorption by deposit banks, 32
  reserve assets, 217
Finance Houses Association, 32
Financial intermediaries, 12–13, 16–17, 22, 96, 132–51

Financial intermediaries—*cont.*
  advantages to borrowers, 134–5
  advantages to lenders, 135
  building societies, 12–13, 132
  differences between types, 132
  economic significance, 134–6
  effect of control of money supply, 201
  effect on inflation, 136
  expansion rates, 133, 142–7
  functions, 132–4
  multiple claim creation, 137
  non-bank, 26–35
    deposit multiplier, 141
    effect of loans, 141
  to facilitate loan transactions, 132
Financial markets, 22, 35–41
  function, 35
Financial Statistics, 105
Financial system
  basic functions, 22
  British, 22–42
  weaknesses, 18–21
Fisher, Irving, 163
Fisher equation, 163–4, 166
Foreign assets, 234
Foreign banks, 50
  growth in deposits, 143
Foreign exchange, 53, 98, 107, 230
  balances held by commercial banks, 248
  influenced by Bank rate, 207, 208
  private sector transactions, 106, 113
  transactions to control bank deposits, 101
  See also Overseas sector
Foreign exchange market, 35, 39–40
Foreign investment, 113
  See also Investment
Friedman, Milton, 19, 155, 186, 187, 190, 191, 192, 199
Funding, 84, 86–8, 210

G.N.P., *see* Gross National Product
Giro, *see* National Giro
Gold, 6, 189
  flow influenced by Bank rate, 207
  International Monetary Fund stock, 246
  production, 253
  revaluation, 253
  two-tier price, 250
Gold market, 40
Gold standard, 66, 197, 239–40
  collapse, 239

INDEX

Government bonds, 49, 54, 59, 182
  open market sales, 75
Government borrowing, 83, 102
Government control of money supply, 18
Government debt, 168
Government expenditure, 199, 203
Government stock, 25, 26, 30, 31–2
Gross Domestic Product, 46
Gross National Product, 125, 143, 164
  ratio to investment, 135
  ratio to money supply, 125

Hambros, 24
Hire purchase, 32
  See also Credit
Hoare and Co., 23
House purchase, 11, 29, 34

I.C.F.C., *see* Industrial and Commercial Finance Corporation
I.M.F., *see* International Monetary Fund
Imports, 72, 107, 113, 229
  tariffs, 240
Income
  permanent, 187
  relationship with money supply, 199
Income tax, 221
Incomes policies, 203
Industrial and Commercial Finance Corporation Ltd., 33, 213
Industrial Reorganisation Corporation, 34
Inflation, 18, 21, 114, 133–4, 188, 196, 200, 239
  anticipated by wage rates, 192
  influence of financial intermediaries, 136
Inside money, 154
Instalment credit, 32
Insurance, 133, 150
Insurance companies, 27–8
  controls on lending, 213
Inter-bank market, 37
Interest rates, 12, 71, 77–8, 116, 133, 191, 203, 221
  advantages of stabilization, 117
  bank deposits, 215–16
  causes of change, 177–8
  comparison with other sources, 70
  effect of bond sales, 180
  effect of fluctuations, 82, 100, 197
  effect on bank deposits, 81

Interest rates—*cont.*
  effect on idle balances, 159, 162
  effect on liquidity preference, 177
  finance houses, 33
  forced rises, 102
  in relation to money supply, 191
  increases, 144
  influenced by Bank rate, 205, 206
  long term, 180–1, 183, 222
  nominal, 199–200
  real, 199–200
  relation to investment, 177–8
  relation to price levels, 152, 155
  rise affecting building societies, 225
  rise affecting security prices, 224
  short term, 81, 86, 206, 222
Intermediaries, *see* Financial intermediaries
International Bank for Reconstruction and Development, 41, 242
International economic co-operation, 242
International Monetary Fund, 41, 231, 241–7
  currency pool, 246
  drawings by members, 246
  gold stock, 246
  reserve settlement account, 256
  role in exchange rates, 242–3
  stand-by credits, 247
  subscription quotas, 246
  tranches, 246
International payments, 229–57
International trade, 227
International transactions, 53
Investment, 20, 59, 79, 172–4
  expectations, 173
  in housing, 182
  in public utilities, 182
  liquidity, 59
  multiplier, 175–6, 194
  proportion of assets, 64–5
  ratio to Gross National Product, 135
  relation to interest rates, 177–8, 181
  sale to reduce deposit liabilities, 87
  See also Foreign investment
Investment trusts, 27, 30, 133, 150
Invisible trade, 230
Isle of Man Bank, 23
Issuing houses, 37–8

Johnson Matthey, 40
Kaldor, Professor N., 196, 197
Keynes, John Maynard, 155, 156,

Keynes—*cont.*
  163, 169–84, 190, 193, 199–200, 201, 224
  rejection of quantity theory, 183–4
  transmission mechanism, 193–4

Lazard Brothers, 24
Legal tender, 6
Leijonhufvud, Axel, 169, 171, 182
Lending
  controls, 203, 213–14
  See also Financial intermediaries
Lewis's Bank, 23
'Librum', 6
Life assurance companies, 12–13
Liquid assets, 82, 85, 109
  of Scottish banks, 65
  ratio to deposits, 62–3
  types, 83
Liquidity, 4–5, 15–16, 22, 215
  controlled by Special Deposits, 218
  effect of credit controls, 223–5
  function of financial markets, 35
  in regional transactions, 235
  international, 247–57
  of investments, 59
  of money market assets, 59
  of the economy, 17
  preference, 177, 182–3
Liquidity ratio, 29, 30, 62–3, 74, 83
  See also Reserve assets ratio
Lloyds Bank Ltd., 23
Loans
  from non-bank intermediaries, 150
  function of intermediaries, 132
Local authority borrowing, 37
Local authority loans, 34
London Discount Market Association, 25
Long term investment account, 231

M1, M2 and M3, *see* Money supply: official definitions
Macmillan Committee Report (1931), 33, 62
Markets, *see* Financial markets
Marshall, Alfred, 164
  See also Cambridge equation
Mercantile Credit Company, 26
Merchant banks, 50
Midland Bank Ltd., 23, 62
Mocatta and Goldsmid, 40
Monetarists, 155, 156, 163, 186–202
  comparison with Keynes, 193
  statistical testing, 189–90
  transmission mechanism, 195

Monetary Management Principles and Practice, 228
Monetary movements, 231
Monetary policy, 75, 147, 150, 192, 203–28
  after 1958, 144
  definition, 203
  effectiveness, 220–5
  Friedman's analysis, 190
  techniques, 203
  to control interest rates, 194
Money
  as a form of wealth, 187
  as a medium of exchange, 3–4
  as a unit of account, 2
  causative role, 189–90
  circulation velocity, 149–50, 151, 156, 163, 164, 214
  definition, 190
  definition of value of transactions, 156
  emergence of new forms, 201
  financial assets as substitute, 193–4, 195
  forms of, 6–8
  income velocity, 188
  Keynesian definition, 182
  liquidity, 4–5
  purchasing power, 186
  quantity theory, 152, 163–8, 186
  real money balances, 153–4
  role of, 1–6
  substitutes, 195
  value of transactions, 163
Money market, 35–6
Money market assets, 58, 77, 79
  maintaining liquidity, 59
Money supply, 17–18, 176–7, 189, 194, 203
  active balances, 157, 158
  British policy, 116, 117
  changes, 196
  comparison of definitions, 127
  control by Bank rate, 205
  controlled growth, 19
  definitions, 123–7
  effect of controls, 201
  effect of quantity changes, 178–9
  effect on asset distribution, 140
  effect on expenditure, 162
  equations, 106
    practical applications, 127–31
  factors influencing changes, 112
  government control, 18
  idle balances, 157–8
  in relation to interest rates, 191

INDEX

Money supply—*cont.*
  official definitions, 124–7
  ratio to Gross National Product, 125
  ratio to national income, 122
  ratio to national income value, 115
  regulated by expenditure level, 198
  related to demand, 123
  related to income, 199
  related to price levels, 152
  response to changes in demand, 148
  significance in economy, 152
  statistics, 105
  types of change, 178–9
  variability, 18
  velocity of circulation, 156–63
Montague, Samuel, 40
Morgan Grenfell, 24
Mortgages, 29, 132
Multiple claim creation, 136–42
Multiplier, *see* Deposit multiplier; Investment

National debt, 99, 102, 197, 209–11
  finance for two world wars, 210
National Debt Commissioners, 31, 32
National Film Finance Corporation, 34
National Giro, 7, 14, 26, 100, 124
National income, 122
National Income and Expenditure, 113
National Savings, 114
National Savings Bank, 27, 32, 144
  transfer of bank deposits, 72
National Westminster Bank Ltd., 23
Net deposits, 60, 61
Newlyn, W. T., 14, 16, 85
Northern Ireland bank notes, 43–4
Northern Ireland Banks
  assets, 65–6
  See also Deposit banks
Note issue, 196

O.E.C.D., *see* Organization for Economic Co-operation and Development
On Keynesian Economics and the Economics of Keynes, 169
Open market operations, 88, 179, 195, 203, 210
Open market sales of securities, 76–82, 218
Organization for Economic Co-operation and Development, 242

Output
  compared with consumption, 9
  determination of level, 174–5
  stability, 171–2, 175, 176
Outside money, 154
Overdrafts, 15, 55
Overseas banks, 24, 150
  growth in deposits, 143
  in relation to money supply, 124 127
  liquidity, 212
Overseas sector, 107, 110
  See also Foreign exchange

Partnerships, 11
Payments
  imbalance between countries, 237–238
  imbalance between regions, 235–7
Pension funds, 133, 150
  as financial intermediaries, 132
  controls on lending, 213
  See also Superannuation funds
Personal loans, 33
Pigou, A.C., 153, 154, 165, 167
Post Office, 26
Post Office Savings Bank, *see* National Savings Bank
Premium Savings Bonds, 32
Price levels, 2, 184, 191, 196
  absolute, 153
  adjustment, 19
  affecting holdings of money, 188
  as basic information, 2
  controls, 203
  related to interest rates, 152, 155
  related to money supply, 152
  related to production plans, 170
  relative, 153
Private sector
  bank loans, 114
  borrowing requirement, 115
  inside money, 154
  outside money, 154
  transfer of bank deposits, 145
  transfers from public sector, 101–2, 105, 106
  transfers to public sector, 51
Production, 187
  overseas, 229
Production methods, 1, 9
  See also Roundabout production methods.
Production plans, 170
Property unit trusts, 27, 28, 31
Public Deposit Account, 43

Public sector, 98
 borrowing requirement, 106, 108, 110, 112
 changes in expenditure, 116
 debt, 106, 107-8, 114
 external financing, 107, 118
 negative borrowing requirement, 111-12
 repayment of debt to overseas sector, 110
 taxation receipts, 110
 transfers to private sector, 51, 101-2, 105, 106, 110
Public sector intermediaries, 145
Purchases, 156

Radcliffe Report (Cmnd. 827, 1959), 62, 82, 86, 149, 203-4, 214, 220
 consumer credit, 219
 interest-incentive effect, 222
 liquidity effect, 223
Rates of exchange, *see* Exchange rate
Real balance effect, 154
Regional transactions, 235-7
Reserve assets, 74, 109, 216
 categories, 64
 finance houses, 217
Reserve assets ratio, 64
 See also Liquidity ratio
Reserve funds, 250
Reserve ratios, 146
Revaluation, 241
 decisions of 1971, 251
'Roosa' effect, 224
Rothschild, N. M., 40
Rothschilds, 24
Roundabout production methods, 10, 135
 See also Production methods
Royal Bank of Scotland Ltd., 23
Royal Mint, 43

S.D.R.s, *see* Special Drawing Rights
'Save As You Earn' scheme, 30, 32
Savings, 11, 20, 133
 during war-time, 159
 effect of increases on financial intermediaries, 148
 influence of financial intermediaries, 135
 related to increased incomes, 172
Savings banks, 31-2, 133
 as financial intermediaries, 12-13
 deposits, 160
Sayers, R. S., 60
Scottish bank notes, 43-4

Scottish banks
 assets, 65
 Special Deposits, 211
 See also Deposit banks
Securities, 71
 effect of sale on bank deposits, 76, 77
 fall in price, 80
 primary, 12, 13, 132, 135
 purchased by banks, 57
 purchased by banks from customers, 97
 sale on open market, 90
 sale to bank customers, 75-6
 sale to banks, 75, 103
 sale to discount houses, 76
 sale to non-bank private sector, 103
 secondary, 12, 13, 132
Shares, 5
 building societies, 29
 dividend-earning, 11
 new issues, 37
Sharps Pixley, 40
Silver, 6, 189
Sole traders, 11
South African Reserve Bank, 40
Special Deposits, 64, 211-12, 215
 as control on liquidity, 100-1, 218
 calculation of amount, 216-17
 interest rates, 217
Special Drawing Rights, 231, 247, 249, 255-6
Spending, 10
Stamp Plan, 255
Statistics
 changes by banks, 61
 of money supply, 105
Sterling, 54, 123, 124, 130, 253
Stock brokers, 38
Stock Exchange, 38-9
Superannuation funds, 27-8, 31
 See also Pension funds

T.D.R.s, *see* Treasury Deposit Receipts
Tangible assets, 4, 10, 11, 97, 114
Tax payments, 72, 98, 110
Tax rates, 113, 116
Tax revenue, 113
Taxation, 83, 203
 income tax, 221
The Theory of Money, 14, 16
Time deposits, 15
 See also Current accounts; Deposit accounts
Trading, *see* Barter

INDEX

Transmission mechanisms, 193–6
  compared, 196
  Keynesian, 193–4
Treasury bills, 25, 26, 35, 36, 45, 49, 54, 109
  as deposit control, 83
  as money making assets, 58
  in excess of government needs, 206
  in private sector, 83
  mature, 77
  non-bank market, 84–5
  open market sales, 75
  purchase from discount houses, 77
  reduction of issue, 83, 84, 145
Treasury Deposit Receipts, 68
Triffin Plan, 255
Trustee Investment Act (1961), 28
Trustee savings banks, 27, 31–2, 144

Unemployment, 170, 171, 184

Unemployment—*cont.*
  equilibrium level, 191
  See also Employment levels
Unit trusts, 27, 30–1, 133, 150
  as financial intermediaries, 12–13
Units of account, 6

Velocity of circulation of money, 149–50, 151, 156, 163, 164, 214
Visible trade, 230

Wage rates, 184, 191
  anticipating inflation, 192
Williams and Glyn's Bank Ltd., 23

Yields, 222
  effect of open market sales, 80
  from liquid assets, 142
  on forms of wealth, 187
Yorkshire Bank, 23